# THE FORMULA
# FOR HAPPINESS

# THE FORMULA
# FOR HAPPINESS

DOUGLAS R. RAMM, PH.D.

WITH STEVEN N. CZETLI

LIBRARY OF CONGRESS NUMBER: 2003096990
ISBN:   HARDCOVER   1-4134-3208-5
SOFTCOVER   1-4134-3207-7

This book was printed in the United States of America.

To order additional copies of this book, contact:
Xlibris Corporation
1-888-795-4274
www.Xlibris.com
Orders@Xlibris.com
20032

To my wife, Barbara,
for her understanding, patience and support.

## Author's Note

Except for the author, his two daughters, and those acknowledged for their professional, theoretical, technical, or literary contributions, persons described and quoted in this book are fictitious. None of these individuals is an actual human being.

# Notice

The concepts, suggestions, and procedures contained in this book are not intended as an alternative to consulting a mental health professional. This book is not to be used as a substitute for treatment you may be currently receiving. If at any time your answer to any of the following questions is yes, and if you are not already receiving treatment, you should seek an evaluation from a psychologist, psychiatrist, clinical social worker, or licensed mental health professional.

- Do you feel hopeless or suicidal?
- Do you feel so demoralized or overwhelmed that you cannot cope with your job or school?
- Is anxiety or guilt interfering with your ability to enjoy life or to cope with the tasks of daily living?
- Have you been depressed for at least a month without any improvement in your mood despite your own efforts to feel better?
- Do you hear voices which other people do not hear?
- Do you see things, animals, or people other persons cannot see?
- Do other people tell you there is something wrong with your thinking or the way you are making sense of your situation?
- Are you having difficulty controlling your thoughts?
- Do you have difficulty controlling sexual or violent impulses?
- Are you having difficulty developing or maintaining relationships with other people?
- Are you abusing alcohol?
- Are you using illegal drugs?
- Are you misusing prescription medication?

If you are in need of mental health services and you do not know of any good mental health practitioner, the names of qualified psychologists, psychiatrists, and clinical social workers can be obtained from the local chapter of the National Mental Health Association. You can also consult your family physician who should be able to give you a referral. Mental health practitioners are also listed in the Yellow Pages of most phone books under the categories of psychologists, psychiatrists, counselors, and individual and marriage counselors.

# CONTENTS

Foreword ................................................................... XIII

Acknowledgements ............................................. XXXIII

Chapter 1: The Nature of Happiness ........................... 1

Chapter 2: Things .................................................. 18

Chapter 3: Interpersonal Values ............................. 32

Chapter 4: Conditions of Human Existence .............. 54

Chapter 5: The Matrix of Core Values ..................... 81

Chapter 6: Self-defeating Behavior ......................... 107

Chapter 7: Self-defeating Beliefs .......................... 134

Chapter 8: Principles For The Pursuit Of Happiness ........... 150

Chapter 9: Following The Formula For Happiness ............. 166

Chapter 10: Personal Strategic Planning ........................... 184

Chapter 11: Momentous Decision Making ............................. 218

Chapter 12: The General Inventory Of Life Satisfaction .... 241

Index ................................................................. 251

# Foreword

Since the dawn of history, people have yearned for happiness. They sought insight into the basic elements of happiness and how to combine them into a rich and rewarding life. Like you, they understood this knowledge would enable them to make the choices necessary, not only to become, but also to remain content and satisfied with life.

In the beginning people turned to men considered wise. They consulted witch doctors, shamans, and gurus. These sages offered visions of a happy life as well as methods for making it a reality.

Later, religion offered an alternative. People came to believe that God, through his representatives—Moses, Jesus, or Mohammed—provided a basic set of instructions for becoming happy. They studied statements of these holy men and listened to rabbis, priests, or mullahs for guidance in daily life.

Others in the ancient world looked to philosophers to point the way to happiness. Rather than relying on divine revelation, they assumed human intelligence was capable of unraveling the mysteries of life. Socrates, Aristotle, Epicurus, and the Stoic philosophers each offered guidance with respect to achieving contentment and satisfaction in living. Since then, scores of other philosophers have built on their ideas.

With the advent of science, people began to believe the scientific method could reveal the structure and dynamics of a high-quality life. They assumed that just as the human condition had otherwise improved when research replaced folk wisdom, religion, and philosophy, the scientific study of happiness would yield insights superior to prescientific thought. They hoped those scientists who study human nature—psychologists, psychiatrists, sociologists, and anthropologists—would disclose the elements of happiness and how those elements could be combined into a rich and rewarding life.

My interest in learning what science could reveal about happiness began when I decided to become a clinical psychologist. Since William James, the father of American psychology, maintained that all human motivation and behavior could be understood in terms of the pursuit of happiness, I expected a major portion of my education would involve learning about the nature of happiness. Believing happiness is to mental illness what wellness is to physical disease, I assumed becoming a clinical psychologist would begin with an in-depth study of optimum quality of life just like training to become a physician involves a detailed study of healthy human anatomy and physiology.

I was surprised to discover this was not the case. Rather than studying happiness, training in clinical psychology involved learning about unhappiness. Rooted in the work of Sigmund Freud, Karl Jung, Harry Stack Sullivan, Karen Horney, and Carl Rogers, clinical psychology is the scientific study of those who developed some type of abnormal mental or emotional condition which renders them unhappy, discontent, or dissatisfied with life. Becoming a clinical psychology consists of learning how to diagnose these conditions and mastering psychotherapeutic techniques with which they can be treated.

As I became a clinical psychologist, I acquired the ability to apply these methods to a wide variety of unhappy children, adolescents, and adults. I was trained in psychiatric hospitals and outpatient services. I learned how to treat virtually every type of mental and emotional disorder ranging from chronic mental illness to relatively simple difficulties adjusting to a new phase in life.

As my career developed, I was able to help most of those who came to me for care. My clients were satisfied, and I enjoyed my work. However, I also found myself repeatedly reminded that William James was onto something when he said we can make sense of human nature by observing how people go about the personal pursuit of happiness.

Gradually I became aware that several of the people I worked with became miserable as a result of some ill-fated effort at achieving happiness. Believing a lover would make them happier than simply living within a marriage which had become empty and flat, some got into extramarital affairs only to suffer significant losses as a result. Others remained in romantic relationships with a partner they thought would make them happy but eventually ended up with a broken heart. Believing that having a child would improve a troubled marriage, some couples decided to make a baby. Conflict over childcare led to a divorce. Still others chose careers or took jobs, anticipating vocational satisfaction, but instead found their occupation rendered them significantly discontent.

Cases such as these led me to believe that much of the unhappiness of people who came to me for help could have been avoided if they had a clear understanding of the basic elements of happiness and a reliable set of guidelines for acquiring and maintaining them. I imagined these guidelines could be developed something like the way in which people in the medical community had come up with principles for achieving and maintaining physical well-being. Having identified the basic features of a healthy body and how behavior affects health, physicians, physiologists, and nutritionists were able to formulate a set of instructions for making choices which enhance the potential for becoming and remaining healthy. Based on this research, we know that when we consistently get adequate amounts of rest and exercise, eat a low-fat, high-fiber diet, and avoid the use of tobacco and excessive amounts of alcohol, we are doing what we can to maximize the likelihood we will live a healthy life.

I thought psychologists could accomplish something similar with respect to emotional well-being. This process would consist of determining the nature of happiness and then identifying the relationship between happiness and human behavior. Once research revealed the causal connections between behavior and quality of life, instructions could be developed which would enable people to find contentment and satisfaction in living. Like wellness principles, these guidelines could be easily remembered and readily applied in the course of daily living. If followed consistently, they would maximize the potential of becoming and remaining happy.

As I envisioned it, this formula for happiness would have great value, not only to mental health practitioners but to the rest of society as well. It could be presented to the public much the way we were already promoting wellness principles. The formula for happiness could be the subject of public service announcements on radio and television, and it could be incorporated into the curriculum of public schools.

Since the formula for happiness seemed so basic and so important, I found myself expecting some prominent psychologist or research center to come up with it virtually any day. I thought surely there would be an announcement from the National Institute of Mental Health, some major university, or maybe even the American Psychological Association indicating that the formula had finally been found. When it failed to materialize, my expectations began to fade. Finally, after nearly twenty years of practicing clinical psychology, I became tired of waiting. I decided to apply my training in the scientific method to see if I could find the formula on my own.

After several years and a lot of work I eventually discovered the formula for happiness. I introduced it to the scientific community in 1996 in a technical article published in *New Ideas in Psychology: An International Journal of Innovative Theory in Psychology.* This is a forum for psychologists to present what the editors judge to be seminal and heuristic theory. Printed by the world's largest publisher of scientific research, it is peer reviewed and overseen by an editorial board made up of faculty from psychology departments at several of the world's major universities. Since the publication of this article, I have received requests for reprints from numerous universities in the United States and Canada as well as Europe, North Africa, Australia, and Japan.

The book you are holding is the result of my effort to share the formula with the greatest number of people possible. In it, I describe the formula in a way which requires no formal training in the social sciences. In addition to presenting the basic theory, this book contains several examples intended to bring the theory to life. If you are interested in how I arrived at the formula, the rest of this foreword describes that process. If not, you can skip to the first chapter and find out what the formula will do for you.

## SEARCH FOR THE FORMULA

My search for the formula started with a review of what other scientists had already detected about the nature of happiness. I learned there were several different approaches to the study of happiness within the scientific community. The totality of what had been discovered could be organized into five basic schools of thought.

The *biochemical* theory maintains emotional well-being is a matter of brain chemistry. It is based on research which reveals that when people get depressed changes occur in the chemical composition of the fluids between nerve cells in the human brain. Since antidepressant medication restores levels of neurotransmitters such as dopamine and serotonin to approximate normality, this school of thought hypothesizes that happiness is a matter of balancing brain chemistry.

The *genetic* approach is based on studies showing depression tends to run in families. A correlation has been discovered between levels of discontent and dissatisfaction in parents with those in their natural children. A high correlation between levels of depression observed in identical twins separated at birth and raised in different adopted families has also been observed. These findings have led to the notion that happiness is a matter of inborn disposition ultimately determined by a person's genes.

For other psychologists, this tendency for depression to run in families reflects patterns of conditioning. According to the *behavioral* approach, behavior patterns associated with contentment and satisfaction in living are reinforced by parents and other family members during a child's formative years. Within this school of thought, happiness is determined by the degree to which people acquire specific patterns of behavior.

*Cognitive* psychologists base their understanding of happiness on research revealing that specific mental processes influence how a person feels. Several studies show that unhappy people tend to have negative attitudes and unrealistic expectations as well as certain types of self-defeating thought processes which render them dissatisfied with life. People who have positive attitudes, realistic expectations, and different patterns of thinking tend to report higher levels of happiness.

The fifth school of thought is currently referred to as *positive psychology*. It is based on the notion that several factors correlate with subjective well-being, a sense of contentment, and satisfaction in living. The findings of positive psychology tend to fall into three basic groups.

The first includes specific patterns of behavior, some of which have also been identified by psychologists within the behavioral approach. The second is made up of a number of mental factors which includes those referred to by cognitive psychologists as well as a sense of mastery, self-confidence, and positive self-esteem. The third consists of circumstances such as quality of housing, amounts of available money, and interpersonal relationships providing opportunities for love, intimacy, and companionship.

When I finished reviewing what other scientists had discovered about happiness, it was evident brain chemistry, genetics, behavior, mental processes, and circumstances all play some part in our ability to become and remain happy. At the same time, it was also clear that these studies did not reveal which factor has the most influential role in our overall contentment and satisfaction in living. It seemed a formula for happiness would have to be based on the factor which most influences a person's overall quality of life.

In order to sort this out, I began looking at how brain chemistry, genetics, behavior, mental processes, and circumstances affected the happiness of those people I was working with in psychotherapy. The factor which most often played the most critical role in determining their overall level of happiness quickly became apparent to me. What happened to one of my clients will show you what I mean.

Malina was a happily married attorney and mother of two. She loved her husband, enjoyed her work, and relished the time she spent with her children. When asked whether she was happy, Malina would instantly respond, "Absolutely, my life is everything I hoped it would be."

One day her husband was taking their children for ice cream when a drunk driver lost control of his car. All three were killed in the ensuing crash. Suddenly Malina became clinically depressed; her happiness disappeared.

Of course there were changes in Malina's brain chemistry, but rather than being the *cause* of her unhappiness these changes were the *effect* of her losses. It makes no sense to attribute the discontent brought on by this tragic accident to the genetic coding of her DNA. Since she wasn't at the accident, it is hard to imagine how her behavior could be considered a causal factor in her depression. Despite the fact that the patterns of thought which she routinely employed, her attitudes and expectations, and her level of self-esteem probably will play a role in how she recovers from these loses, there is little logic in explaining Malina's current unhappiness by reference to any of these mental processes which heretofore had served her quite well. Clearly, what most influenced her level of happiness was the change in circumstances brought about by this heartbreaking event.

As I came to a similar conclusion in several other cases, I began to see the role circumstances occupy in determining our quality of life is reflected in the way clinical psychologists and psychiatrists conceptualize the development of symptoms which characterize less-than-optimal mental health. Clinicians frequently use the term *precipitating cause* to refer to changes in a person's circumstances which have the effect of generating anxiety, depression, or some other emotional or mental difficulty. Given the fact that these changes generate unhappiness it is reasonable to infer that preexisting circumstances somehow supported a sense of satisfaction and contentment in life.

Since my experience in clinical practice suggested that circumstances are the most critical factor with respect to whether people are happy, I decided the formula for happiness should be based on a sound understanding of the relationship between circumstances and quality of life. This meant temporarily putting aside considerations of how biochemical, genetic, behavioral, and mental processes contribute to contentment and satisfaction in living. I reasoned once the relationship between circumstances and happiness was clarified I would be able to understand the role these other factors play in becoming and remaining happy.

## HAPPINESS AND CIRCUMSTANCES

In adopting this approach, I realized the notion that happiness is a matter of circumstance has long been a source of controversy and confusion.

The ancient Israelites believed it was important to remain on good terms with God because He would then bless them with peace and prosperity. On the other hand, over the centuries, many Christians have advanced the notion that it is possible to be happy regardless of the circumstances within which a person is situated. Some Eastern mystics maintain spiritual development consists of arriving at a state of consciousness characterized by complete detachment from circumstances. Others take the position that it is to become one with the totality of reality.

A similar debate has occurred within Western philosophy. In ancient Greece the Epicureans insisted happiness is a matter of circumstance while the Stoics of the Roman Empire maintained it could be achieved by developing the ability to be unaffected by the things, people, and events of life. Even today, many philosophers recommend an approach to living which is consistent with one of these two schools of thought.

Similar differences have also emerged within the scientific community. Some psychologists agree with Mihaly Csikszentmihalyi, who has taken the position that happiness is determined by a state of consciousness more than the circumstances within which a person is situated. At the same time, those who conduct studies designed to find a correlation between happiness and factors such as housing, income, and marriage presume circumstances are a central factor in whether and to what degree people become and remain happy.

Although the practice of psychotherapy led to my position that circumstances are the most significant factor in determining whether and to what degree people find contentment and satisfaction in living, I also began to note other reasons to support this way of trying to get a handle on what determines whether and to what degree we become and remain happy.

First, I observed people spontaneously referring to circumstances when talking about happiness in everyday life. A restaurant owner attempts to have happy customers by making sure meals are tasty and cooked to order. Loving parents try to find a stuffed animal, a toy, or a game which delights their child in order to provide a happy birthday. Wedding guests wish the bride happiness because they recognize she marries with the expectation her life will be more satisfying with her new spouse than it would be without having him as a partner in living.

Second, the significance of circumstances in determining whether and to what degree we are happy became even more evident when I recognized that happiness is essentially an emotion or an emotional state. Psychologists define emotion as complex changes in nervous, visceral, and skeletal muscular tissue in response to a stimulus. The stimuli for emotions are those things, people, and events which make up the reality of daily living. This complex response expresses how these circumstances affect what a person considers to be essential to his or her quality of life. Assuming that happiness is an emotion and that emotions are determined by how circumstances affect a person's life, it would follow that happiness consists of being situated within a set of circumstances which bring about a sense of contentment and satisfaction in living. Or, to put it more succinctly, *happiness occurs when people have more or less continuous access to those circumstances which enhance or enrich the quality of human life.*

## UNIVERSAL VALUES

Having come to the conclusion that the basic elements of happiness could be found in those circumstances which enhance quality of life, I realized the next step would involve identifying precisely *which* circumstances actually contribute to contentment and satisfaction in living.

The circumstances I was looking for would have to be, in one way or another, universal. This meant that they would have to contribute to the quality of life for any human being, anywhere, and at any time. They would have to be circumstances which affect happiness across the lines of gender, race, religion, and nationality. What's more, they would have to be circumstances which not only make a difference in quality of life today but which made a difference in levels of happiness for people in the past, as well as those yet to be born. Since these circumstances would have natural, inherent, and intrinsic worth, I decided to refer to them as *values.*

In an effort to identify universal values, I reviewed the results of the research done within positive psychology as well as what I had learned from studying the other social sciences— anthropology, sociology, economics, and political science. I also considered what I knew from my study of history and philosophy because each of these bodies of knowledge provides insight into what people in the past viewed as important with respect to the quality of their lives.

As I proceeded, I discovered many of the circumstances identified by positive psychology also showed up in the other social sciences as well as in historical writings and the works of major philosophers. These values could be grouped into three basic categories.

- The first consists of *things* such as food, clothing, shelter, and money.
- The second consists of *interpersonal interactions* including institutions such as marriage and interpersonal processes such as companionship and intimacy.
- The third consists of *conditions of human existence* such as health, equality, freedom, security, and justice.

I was compiling a list of these universal values when I realized simply identifying the things, interpersonal interactions, and conditions of existence which enhance the quality of life does not reveal which ones are actually needed in order for people to be happy. I considered the correlation between contentment and adequate housing and the fact that people are even more content when they have access to running water and electricity. Clearly, life is further enhanced when those who have electricity are able to get a refrigerator, a stove, a radio, a television set, and even the latest video recording device. Yet, simply because quality of life improves when people obtain these things does not necessarily mean they are unhappy when they don't.

In attempting to develop a means of determining which universal values are *essential* to happiness, I found myself reasoning as biologists do when they determine which substances certain living organisms need in order to survive. The biological notion of need is rooted in the observation that living entities can only survive when they obtain certain substances—for example, oxygen, water, and food. If an organism dies when it is deprived of one of these substances, that substance is identified as essential to the organism's life. Likewise, if I wanted to identify those things, interpersonal interactions, and conditions of human existence people actually need in order to be happy, I would have to determine which universal values are threatened or lost when people became unhappy, discontent, or dissatisfied with life.

## CORE VALUES

At this point I began to research how a threat to, or loss of, universal values contribute to the unhappiness of people who enter psychotherapy. I reviewed the work of significant clinical psychologists including Sigmund Freud, Harry Stack Sullivan, Karen Horney, Carl Rogers, Eric Erickson, Nathaniel Brandon, Aaron Beck, and David Burns as well as several family therapy theoreticians. I eventually identified ten universal values which, when threatened or lost, resulted in a person becoming unhappy. I began to refer to these as *core values* because they appeared to be those things, interpersonal interactions, and conditions of human existence which actually make a difference in terms of whether and to what degree people are happy.

While I was working all of this out at a theoretical level, I was also engaged in the day-to-day practice of psychotherapy. This meant that as I was thinking about the whole business of core values, I had an opportunity to observe how they affected people in everyday life. In doing so I realized what it must have been like when the pioneering psychologists, whose theories I was reviewing, began formulating their insights about human nature based on daily encounters with actual human beings. At some point I realized I could follow in their footsteps and view the psychotherapeutic relationship, not only as a place to help people, but also as a sort of laboratory where important observations and generalizations could be made.

Once I came to this conclusion, I designed a study, part of which was aimed at determining whether people who enter psychotherapy had experienced a threat to, or loss of, one of the ten core values. I approached a number of my clients to see if they were willing to let me analyze their case histories. One hundred, who represent a cross section of my practice, agreed. There were equal numbers of males and females ranging in age, from eleven to seventy-eight. Their overall level of intelligence ranged from "average" to "superior" and their level of education from third grade to doctor's degrees. The result of the study confirmed that the discontent and dissatisfaction which motivates people to seek psychotherapy could be directly linked to a threat to, or loss of, one or more of the ten core values which had already been identified.

Confident I was onto something, I began describing core values to many of the people I was treating in my practice of psychotherapy. Once they became aware of how these values play a part in their lives, many were able not only to make sense out of how they had become unhappy, but they also began to see a direction for improving the quality of their lives. They frequently described a sense of optimism and hope they had never experienced before.

At the same time, I began to talk about core values with people who had immigrated to the United States as well as others who were here on student visas. They came from countries including Brazil, Egypt, Israel, Syria, India, Ethiopia, Pakistan, China, and Japan. Once they became aware of these values and were asked where and how they thought they contributed to quality of life in each of their homelands, they all reported that the ten core values played a critical role.

I also talked about core values with other professionals within psychology, medicine, and law. I started to give seminars to groups of people who were interested in this approach to enhancing quality of life. The feedback I received from all of these sources was similar to what I was hearing from my clients. In addition, several questions emerged about the role each value plays in a person's value system, how the values relate to one another, and whether it is possible to measure a person's overall level of happiness.

My attempts to answer these questions led to the development of a questionnaire—the *General Inventory of Life Satisfaction* (GILS)—which can be used to evaluate a person's access to each of the ten core values. It also includes a means of determining a respondent's overall satisfaction in living. This measurement—the *Global Estimate of Life Satisfaction* (GELS)—is a score which ranges from 0 to 100 and which reflects the degree to which a person is satisfied with life.

To establish how well the GILS and the GELS actually measure happiness, I conducted a validity study. This involved fifty people of both genders. Eighty percent of the participants were Americans, 10 percent were African-Americans. Twenty percent were of other nationalities, including people from Latin America, Asia, Africa, and the Middle East.

Immediately before starting the GILS, each participant was asked to estimate his or her overall level of satisfaction on a scale of 0 to 10. Once the GILS was completed, a GELS score was calculated. Dr. Deborah Evans-Rhodes, a professor of psychology specializing in measurements and statistics at Pennsylvania State University, then conducted a statistical analysis designed to determine the degree to which subjective ratings of overall satisfaction in living correlated with the GELS scores.

The result was an extremely high overall correlation coefficient ($r = .88$). This level of correlation means that the GELS is an accurate means of measuring a person's overall satisfaction in living. Furthermore, there were no statistically significant differences between the correlation coefficient obtained by men and women, Caucasians and African Americans, and Americans and people of other nationalities. The power of the overall correlation coefficient was $p = <.0005$, which means that the likelihood of obtaining these results by chance is less than one in two thousand. This also indicates that the number of participants in this study was statistically significant enough to conclude the GELS is a legitimate means of measuring overall satisfaction in living regardless of gender, race, or nationality.

Beyond establishing the validity of the GILS, the results of this study are significant in two other ways. First, they provide scientific evidence that the degree to which people are happy *is primarily* a matter of the circumstances within which they are situated at any given point in time. Second, the results provide statistical confirmation that the ten core values it measures *are* those circumstances which actually make a difference in terms of whether and to what degree people become and remain happy.

Once I was confident circumstances are the most significant contributing factor, I was also able to understand how biochemical, genetic, behavioral, and mental processes fit into a cohesive theory for quality of life. The behaviors which contribute to happiness are those which enable people to obtain and maintain the ten core values. Some mental processes—such as attitudes, expectations, and beliefs—contribute to happiness by supporting these behaviors while others—such as confidence, a sense of mastery, competence, and self-esteem—are consequences of these patterns of behavior. Biochemical factors can interfere with a person's ability to get and keep core values, and they can also be affected by the degree to which a person already has been able to obtain and maintain them. Genetic factors seem to influence the degree to which a person is motivated to acquire core values as well as a person's ability to appreciate them once they have been obtained.

## CORE PRINCIPLES

While identifying the ten core values as the essential ingredients for happiness, I was also attempting to figure out which behaviors enable us to acquire and maintain them.

Once I determined that the one hundred people in my study had become unhappy as a result of a threat to, or loss of, one or more of the ten core values, I began reviewing each person's history in terms of any behavior on his or her part which contributed to that threat or loss. After identifying behaviors which contributed to their unhappiness, I began looking for similarities between the cases. By the time I got to the thirty-eighth case, seven basic behavior patterns emerged. Thereafter, all of the behaviors resulting in a threat to, or loss of, one or more of the core values in each of the other cases could be identified as one of these seven types of behavior. This redundancy led me to conclude that reviewing one hundred cases was sufficient to determine there are only seven basic patterns of behavior which tend to bring about a threat to, or loss of, one or more of the ten core values. I began to refer to these as *self-defeating* patterns of behavior.

The study also examined whether there was a correlation between a person's tendency to engage in one or more of these seven self-defeating behaviors and their overall level of intelligence, education, and family income. The results did not reveal a strong correlation with respect to any of these variables. This finding suggests people generally have about the same tendency to engage in self-defeating behaviors regardless of overall level of intelligence, education, or socioeconomic status.

Since my vision of the formula for happiness had always

included guidelines for making choices which have happiness as their effect, I next developed alternatives to the self-defeating behaviors. This involved the formulation of a set of principles—ideas about what's right—which people can use to avoid the seven self-defeating patterns of behavior when making choices in daily living. When people consistently act on this set of principles they maximize their potential to find happiness in their lives. Since these principles are essential to the effective pursuit of happiness, I decided to refer to them as *core principles*.

As I began sharing these insights with my clients, many disclosed their reasoning for engaging in self-defeating behaviors. Analyzing the similarities in these motivations, I discovered that they seemed to have something to do with a set of basic ideas about life and how to live. I eventually began to refer to these as *self-defeating beliefs*. As time went on I discovered the core principles of the formula for happiness served not only as a means of avoiding self-defeating behaviors but also as a means of identifying and correcting self-defeating beliefs.

## APPLYING THE FORMULA FOR HAPPINESS

Since discovering the formula for happiness I have shared it with hundreds of people I have worked with in psychotherapy as well as with other professionals in human services and with people in the business and religious communities. The result has been a fascination with the ideas and repeated requests for some sort of self-help material which could be used as a means of applying this approach in daily living. Utilizing the General Inventory of Life Satisfaction as a starting point, I went on to develop two workbooks containing self-administered, self-scoring programs enabling an individual to utilize the formula for happiness in two specific ways.

The first is a method of personal strategic planning based

on goals emerging from a person's responses to the GILS. It enables a respondent to develop courses of action which render greater access to one or more of the ten core values when a deficiency is identified on the GILS. It also contains an evaluation process ensuring a potential course of action is not some sort of self-defeating behavior and that achieving the goal is actually likely to raise a person's level of happiness. Those who have used this workbook have found it an extremely useful approach to enhancing quality of life.

The second workbook contains a program for making momentous decisions. It is designed to help people deal with critical moments in life when they are confronted with choices which will clearly have a long-term impact on future quality of life. This workbook enables people to effectively deal with decisions such as whether to get married, get divorced, have a child, take a job, select a career, retire, or relocate to another part of the country. This program provides a means of determining whether any of the alternatives available constitute some type of self-defeating behavior. It also uses a modified version of the GILS to forecast how the various alternatives available in the decision-making process are likely to impact on overall quality of life at some future point in time. Like the workbook for personal strategic planning, many of those who have used this program report that it has been an extremely useful method of managing quality of life.

As more and more people learned about these workbooks, I was repeatedly asked if I could write a comprehensive self-help book which they could take home and read to get greater insight into the formula for happiness. A number of folks requested a book which would give a more detailed presentation of the core concepts of the formula and which would contain the General Inventory of Life Satisfaction as well as the workbooks for Personal Strategic Planning and Momentous Decision Making. The book you are now holding is my response to those requests.

# Acknowledgements

Putting this book together was a long and arduous process. It involved not only doing the research and developing the formula for happiness, but also the painstaking task of figuring out how to make this paradigm for living accessible to as many people as possible, irrespective of differences in levels of intelligence and education. This task required several trials with numerous groups of people as well as countless revisions in conceptualizations and terminology. Along the way a number of people played a significant role in bringing this mission to fruition.

First and foremost I want to acknowledge the contributions of my coauthor, Steve Czetli, and my office manager, Carol Boyd. Steve brought to the table an uncanny ability to show me how to communicate esoteric and highly abstract concepts in a simple, yet powerful way. Carol's tireless work on countless drafts of the manuscript kept me going even when I was tempted to walk away.

Of equal importance was the support of my family. This work would not have been completed were it not for the understanding, patience, and support of my wife, Barbara, and the encouragement of my daughters, Jennifer and Jessica. My mother, Dr. Gladys Darling, a retired school psychologist, also made significant contributions by reading over the manuscript and providing conceptual and editorial feedback. Tom and Denise Stephens, my brother-in-law and sister-in-law, also have my gratitude for painstakingly going over early drafts of these ideas while we were all on vacation at Indian Lake.

Several professionals also contributed to my efforts at developing the formula for happiness. Early on, my thinking about happiness was influenced by Dr. Richard Creel, a professor of philosophy at Ithaca College. Dr. Ulric Neisser, professor of psychology at Cornell University, not only suggested that I go into psychology to pursue my interest in quality of life, but he also opened some of the doors to this field. And then there was my mentor, Dr. Anthony Barton, professor of psychology and director of clinical training at Duquesne, who taught me to be an effective psychotherapist and showed me how to learn about human nature by observing what was going on in the lives of people I was attempting to help.

Dr. Constance Fischer, professor of psychology at Duquesne University, and Dr. Diane Marsh, professor of psychology at the University of Pittsburgh, helped with the development of the article about my clinical case study which presented the formula for happiness to the scientific community when it was published in *New Ideas in Psychology* in 1996. I also wish to express my appreciation to Dr. Richard Kitchener of Colorado State University for his decision to accept that article for publication. Dr. Deborah Evans-Rhodes of Pennsylvania State University and Sue Brownfield from the University of Pittsburgh each helped with the statistical aspects of my study of the connection between behavior and quality of life. Elaine Masters-Eddins provided editorial assistance and stylistic feedback which moved the process of writing this book forward. Pam Leonard proofread many drafts of this and other manuscripts.

In part, the formula for happiness is based on a distillation and synthesis of the results of research and theoretical insights of hundreds of other psychologists who have made an effort to determine what contributes to happiness, subjective well-being, contentment, and satisfaction in living over the past century. Since this is a self-help book, rather than an academic text, I am acknowledging their contribution to the development of the formula here, rather than in a reference section.

William James, the so-called father of American psychology, opened my eyes to the central role happiness plays in human motivation and human behavior. The ability to view happiness as a matter of intentionality came from Martin Heidegger's *Being and Time*. The ability to appreciate the significance of embodiment in understanding happiness, subjective well-being, contentment, and satisfaction in living is rooted in Maurice Merleau-Ponty's *Phenomenology of Perception*.

Insights into the basic elements of happiness emerged from three publications, each of which is a collection of summarizations of hundreds of studies on happiness, subjective well-being, contentment, and satisfaction in living. The first is *Subjective Well-Being: An Interdisciplinary Perspective* which is edited by Fritz Strack, Michael Argyle, and Norbert Schwartz and which was published in 1991. The second is *The Pursuit of Happiness* written by David Myers in 1992. The third is a special edition of *American Psychologist* devoted to happiness, excellence, and optimal human functioning which was edited by Martin Seligman and Mihaly Csikszentmihalyi and which was produced in January 2000.

I also want to recognize the contribution of a number of scientist-practitioners who provided insight into the nature of happiness through their study of unhappy people who came to them for help. The importance of learning about happiness by listening to persons I was working with in psychotherapy emerged from Carl Rogers's *On Becoming a Person* which was published in 1964. The realization that happiness, contentment, and satisfaction in living is a matter of obtaining and maintaining certain requirements came from Abraham Mazlow's hierarchy of basic needs which is described in *Motivation and Personality*, published in 1970. A sense that the pursuit of happiness is a lifelong process arose from Eric Erickson's *Identity, Youth and Crisis* published in 1968. My appreciation for the role freedom and security play in our overall contentment and satisfaction in living and my recognition of the potential value of scientifically formulated principles of morality is rooted in Sigmund Freud's *Introductory Lectures on Psychoanalysis* written between 1915 and 1917. My ability to grasp the relationship between choices we make in daily life and our ability to become and remain happy emerged from *Man's Search for Himself* written by Rollo May in 1953. The insight that interpersonal interaction and reflected appraisals are significant contributing factors to subjective well-being, contentment, and satisfaction in living came from Harry Stack Sullivan's *The Interpersonal Theory of Psychiatry* published in 1953. Appreciation for the relationship between interpersonal style and subsequent quality of human life emerged from Karen Horney's *Neuroses and Human Growth* published in 1950. An awareness of the importance of reciprocity and an appropriate sense of obligation arose from *Invisible Loyalties, Reciprocity, and Intergenerational Family Therapy* written by Ivan Broszormenyi-Nagy and Geraldine Spark in 1973. Insight into the role attitudes, expectations, and thought processes play in our ability to become and remain happy is rooted in *Cognitive Therapy and Emotional Disorders*, written by Aaron Beck and published in 1976 and *Feeling Good: The New Mood Therapy*, written by David Burns and published in 1980.

Finally, I want to acknowledge two psychologists whose in-depth study of principled reasoning and action contributed to my ability to discover the connection between volitional behavior and quality of life. The first is Lawrence Kohlburg who, in *Moral Stages and Moralization*, published in 1975, provided evidence that the majority of people who act on principle do so when they believe they will receive some benefit as a result of doing what they did. The second is Nathaniel Brandon who clarified the role principled reasoning and action play in the ability to become and remain happy in *The Psychology of Self-Esteem* which was published in 1969.

DRR
July 2003

# Chapter 1

## THE NATURE OF HAPPINESS

Happiness. What is it? How do we get it? How do we keep it? You probably opened this book with one or more of these questions in mind. You are not alone. These questions have been asked, and answers have been offered since the dawn of time. Yet, you may find yourself wondering if you will ever be able to find this desirable but elusive quality of life.

Consider Sarah. Her husband, Tom, recently filed for divorce. Thirty years old and coping with chronic colitis, she wakes up each morning at six to get her two older children off to elementary school. Having taken him back twice before, she was shocked to discover Tom was still having afternoon trysts with Dianne, even while he was attending counseling sessions with her. Now, constantly fatigued and completely demoralized, Sarah finds herself trying to keep her house in some semblance of order while spending her days with three-year-old Susie, discussing ongoing support hearings with her attorney and worrying where and how she and the kids will be living a year from now. "Happiness, that's a childhood dream. I expected I'd be happy at this stage in life. But now I don't have time to think about happiness. What's important to me is simply making it through the day."

Right now you may be in similar circumstances. You might have suffered a significant disappointment or loss. It may have been a separation or divorce. It could have been the death of a loved one or the loss of a job, a career, or a house. Maybe you are wondering what you can do to pick up the pieces and go on to regain contentment and satisfaction in a world which has become empty, meaningless, and flat.

Or you might be someone who has been living day-to-day and recently found life surprisingly unfulfilling. Pete and Nicholas have been best friends since college. Now middle-aged, these two have approached life differently. After four years of carefree living at the university, Pete chose a fast-track career in computers. His townhouse is the ultimate bachelor's pad providing a comfortable staging area for his frequent domestic and international trips, both business and personal. The studious and reserved Nicholas, on the other hand, married his college sweetheart and has worked at the same accounting firm since graduation. Twenty years, two kids, and five homes later, Nicholas celebrates his latest promotion with Pete.

"I love women, and women love me!" Pete quips, pulling out a picture of himself and his latest girlfriend. Nicholas proudly shows off photos of his family. Yet, while successful in his own right, each man feels as if something is missing in his life. "I love my work, Nick. Sensational things are happening in the computer industry. I've been to amazing places, met fascinating people, but when I see the way Ida still looks at you after all these years, it makes me realize how alone I really am."

Nicholas admits his life must appear fulfilling from Pete's point of view. "When I think about all I have—a beautiful wife and kids, a great house, a challenging job, and good money—I feel greedy wishing for more. I don't even know what it is I want. But every day I wake up resenting the same old grind."

Peter and Nicholas talk late into the evening about how turning forty affected them. Both have anxiety and restlessness stemming from their growing realization that life is short. They consider colleagues who seem more content and who seem to experience a joy in living neither of them has yet found. Perhaps you, too, envy happy people and wonder what it is that enables them to deal with life so comfortably and so successfully.

On the other hand, you may be satisfied with your life now, but you are confronting a decision likely to have a profound effect on your future quality of life. Maybe you are deciding whether to get romantically involved with someone you just met or whether to marry someone you have been with for some time. You might be contemplating a divorce or breaking off a long-term relationship. You may even be thinking about having an extramarital affair. In any case, you realize you are facing a momentous decision, but you may not be sure which of your alternatives will bring you more or less satisfaction over time.

Maybe you are considering taking a new job or leaving the one you have and going back for training in a new career. Perhaps you are wondering if relocating to another part of the country will make your life more rewarding than it is today. Maybe you have reached a stage in life where retirement has become a possibility. You would like to pack it in, but you're not sure if it's really the right move for you.

Irene has worked in banking for twenty-five years. While she finds her work fulfilling, she would like to call it quits and enjoy more time with her family. This would allow her to get to know her grandchildren better and take those long camping trips she and her husband, Willy, have dreamed about for years.

Despite the temptations, Irene isn't sure what impact the financial consequences of retiring before she qualifies for full pension benefits and social security will have on her golden years.

Or, you could be on the other end of life. Noah is a senior in high school. Because neither of his parents completed college, they are determined that their eldest son, a gifted mathematician, pursue an accounting degree from the local university. But Noah wants to work with underprivileged youth. For the past three years, he worked at a summer camp for disadvantaged kids and found it quite fulfilling. "My friends are all out enjoying senior activities and making plans for graduation, but I just sit around trying to decide what to do. I feel caught between pleasing my parents and wanting to make a difference in the world."

Like Noah, you may have just finished high school and are wondering whether to join the military, get a job, go to college, or enter a technical program. Perhaps you are on the verge of selecting a major or picking a career. Maybe you are considering whether to have a child. You could be wondering if buying your dream house will enrich your life, or whether it will render you less happy than you are today.

Maybe you were happier in the past. You may be wondering how a rich and rewarding life somehow slipped away. You could be asking yourself, "If I had made different choices, would I still be as happy as I used to be?"

Whatever your motivation for reading this far, I promise to deliver something you can use. Whether you are currently unhappy, live a humdrum monotonous existence, find yourself on a treadmill of emergencies and disasters, or are facing a momentous decision, this book will help you manage your life more effectively. You will come to understand the nature of happiness with a new clarity and discover what you can do to become and remain happy.

## THE PROMISE

A United States Supreme Court justice once stated that although he could not define pornography, he knew it when he saw it. Something like this may be true for you when it comes to the nature of happiness.

Armando Sancho wakes each morning full of energy. He takes a morning jog in the park across from his home. With a smile and a wave, he greets Mrs. Cortez each day as she walks her cocker spaniel. When Armando finally walks into the real estate office where he works, everybody turns and smiles. Javier looks up from his desk, "Armando, I don't know how you do it! No matter what happens, you're always smiling. I've never seen anyone else lose a sale and look so happy about it. Now you got all of us smiling all day—it must be contagious." After twenty years at Dominges Realty, Armando has a reputation for sales leadership. His clients find him thoughtful, reliable, and a pleasure to work with. It's no wonder most of his business comes from referrals.

While he enjoys work, Armando loves spending time with his family. Every Sunday, his four children and ten grandchildren visit Armando and his wife, Manuela. They gather for dinner and spend the day together. When they lost their house to a fire five years ago, everybody joined in to rebuild it. Armando and Manuela lived with their eldest daughter until their home was finished. She could always hear Armando singing over the hammers and circular saws. Now they all reminisce about how much closer that experience brought the family. Manuela pulls him close, "It's that smile of yours that keeps us going, no matter what."

You may know someone like Armando. The zest for living is hard to miss. You also may have realized that happy people are actually alike in a number of different ways.

Happy people tend to wake up fresh and rested most mornings. They greet the day with a sense of joy in being alive. They look forward to meaningful tasks and satisfying interpersonal interaction. Happy people like their work, but they also take time to play.

Happy people are generally satisfied with where they live. They enjoy the company of their family as well as those they encounter in the community and on the job. They are liked by members of their families, by neighbors, and those they encounter at work and in their leisure time. Happy people have a reputation for being thoughtful, reliable, and responsible. Other people want to have them in their lives.

Happy people spend the majority of their day engaged in some sort of work they enjoy. They are good at what they do, whether it involves operating a piece of machinery, writing technical reports, delivering mail, performing surgery, or keeping house. Happy people generally feel they are appropriately compensated, even if they do not receive a paycheck for doing what they do.

When the workday is done, happy people have ways of having fun. They may enjoy playing golf, building furniture, reading books, or throwing pots. Whatever the activity, these leisure moments render happy people renewed and refreshed when they return to the tasks of life.

Happy people have a relatively high level of optimism. They see the glass half full. They appreciate what they have and seldom complain about what they don't. They view other people as basically good, and they are willing to lend a helping hand.

They don't envy, and they rarely become jealous. Although they experience success in a variety of ways, they rarely boast or brag.

Occasionally, happy people experience significant frustration, disappointment, and loss. They can become angry, anxious, and depressed. But happy people are durable. Even when they encounter setbacks, these troubling emotions never last. Happy people have the ability to recover relatively efficiently from the crises, disasters, and indignities of life. They pick themselves up, dust themselves off, and get on with their lives.

Happy people go to bed with a sense of accomplishment and contentment with the day. They are unburdened with regrets about what they did or anxieties over what they failed to do. Happy people slip into sleep with an abiding sense of joy in being alive and excited by their anticipation about what will greet them when they arise.

If you continue to read this book, you will discover how happy people become and remain happy. You will learn the secrets for making happiness a tangible reality. You will have an understanding of the basic structure and dynamics of happiness which will enable you to develop and sustain a rich and rewarding quality of life.

## THE VALUE OF THE FORMULA

I first met John when I was working as a clinical psychologist in a community hospital. I was asked to evaluate his suicide potential the morning after he was involuntarily committed to the psychiatric ward. He came in through the emergency room where he had been treated for minor injuries suffered when he intentionally drove his car into a utility pole. John had become so unhappy life no longer seemed worth living.

In our first conversation, John revealed that his problems actually began two years earlier. This was when his wife, Vicky, told him to leave home because he was still involved with Mona, his chair-side assistant. After catching him twice before, Vicky had reached the end of her patience when she walked in on John and Mona making love in his office after work.

Bitter over the betrayal, Vicky vigorously pursued a campaign of parental alienation. Soon, John's two kids were unwilling to spend time with him. When he did manage to get them for a visit, things did not go well. They would berate him about his relationship with Mona and press him to explain why he was not sending their mom all of the money he was supposed to provide.

Part of what made these encounters dissatisfying was John's guilt about not keeping up with child support. Vicky had hired the most aggressive divorce attorney in the county. Her lawyer had managed to get a substantial settlement which obligated John to continue paying the mortgage on the dream house he and Vicky had purchased about six months before he started his affair.

Once separated, John lived in a small apartment, but he spent most of his time at Mona's place. Although things went fairly well between them early on, John's distress over the loss of the relationships with his children eventually took its toll. He started drinking more heavily, and Mona began complaining about his use of alcohol. Lost hours of sleep and too much Jack Daniels resulted in John showing up for work tired and hung over.

The fact that he was becoming impaired became apparent to his patients. As time passed, the office manager began receiving letters from other dentists requesting transfer of records for reasons never fully explained. Faced with a declining caseload, John decided to deal with the increasing difficulty of paying child support by billing Medicaid for services he had not actually performed.

The day before we met, Mona had ended both her romantic and professional relationships with John. The same day, a certified letter arrived at the office informing John that the Commonwealth of Pennsylvania was initiating an investigation for suspected Medicaid fraud. Adding to the loss of his marriage, the loss of his children, the loss of many of his patients, and the loss of his lover, John was now confronted with the likelihood of losing his license to practice and the possibility of doing some time in jail.

Although John's story is more dramatic than most, it illustrates aspects of what I encounter almost every day. Many of the people who come to see me are unhappy as a result of something they did or failed to do. Often their unhappiness is the result of pursuing a course of action they believed would make them more content and satisfied with life.

Although Samantha thought she would be happy if she organized her life around those things and activities important to her husband, after eighteen years of marriage she became depressed when she realized she was generally discontent. Joel accepted a promotion because he thought the increased pay and prestige would make him happier. The new job turned out to be dissatisfying, and he was miserable as a result. Joanna assumed she and Frank would be happier by relocating to Florida once he retired, but she ended up regretting the move because the distance they lived from the children meant limited opportunities to participate in the lives of her grandchildren.

Each of these people became dissatisfied and discontent because he or she did not have a clear understanding of happiness nor did he or she realize what needed to be done in order to become and remain happy. If they had known what happiness required, they might have decided to do things differently. Very likely they could have avoided undermining their contentment and satisfaction with life.

The formula for happiness is a sort of manual or blueprint for building a life which creates and sustains happiness. It identifies the basic elements of happiness and provides a set of guidelines for becoming and remaining happy. With the formula, you will be able to proceed with your pursuit of happiness confident that what you are doing is maximizing your potential for finding and holding on to a rich and rewarding quality of life.

## HAPPINESS AND EMOTIONS

The formula for happiness is rooted in the reality that happiness is an emotion or, more precisely, an emotional state. Emotions are complex bodily changes which occur in response to the things, people, and events we encounter in daily living. Emotions express how these things, people, and events affect what we consider to be essential to our contentment and satisfaction with life.

Victor is walking down a street on a bright spring morning. He has just kissed his loving wife goodbye, and he is on his way to work at a job he enjoys. As he strolls along, he is aware of how the sunlight attaches to the leaves of the trees and marvels at the beauty of the flowers and shrubs he passes along the way. Suddenly he hears the squeal of brakes and observes an out-of-control large dump truck rapidly bearing down on him. Filled with fear, Victor's contentment instantaneously vanishes as he suddenly finds himself running to get out of its way. His fear expresses the reality that his circumstances now constitute a threat to his physical well-being.

Sometimes, as in this situation, the relationship between emotions and the things, people, and events which cause them is crystal clear. At other times, the relationship is more difficult to discern. Stan appears to be depressed, Veronica seems to be angry, and Clark is noticeably anxious. The circumstances giving rise to their emotions are anything but obvious.

Yet, the cause of their emotions becomes apparent when each of these people discloses the circumstances within which they are situated. In talking to Stan, we learn that he has been working extended hours for the past month and just had a greatly anticipated day of golf cancelled due to rain. Veronica recently discovered one of her best friends made a disparaging remark about her to a mutual acquaintance. Clark tells us the organization he works for is about to be sold to a competitor. As a mid-level executive, he is faced with the possibility of losing his job.

While all emotions are caused by the way in which things, people, and events affect what we consider to be essential to our contentment and satisfaction in living, different emotions express something unique about the way in which these things, people, and events impact on our quality of life. In other words, each emotion is defined by the specific way in which the things, people, and events encountered in daily living affect what we consider to be essential to our contentment and satisfaction with life.

Like fear, *anxiety* involves a threat. Unlike fear, where the threat is clear and present, anxiety occurs when the threat is ill-defined and not yet here. Although nobody has told him that he will be terminated, Clark is anxious because he is faced with the possibility he will lose a job he very much enjoys. Jim, a combat soldier on patrol in hostile territory, is constantly anxious because a sniper could be hiding behind any tree. Joan, a single mother living in a high-crime neighborhood, is anxious over the possibility of being assaulted when she leaves her home as well as the possibility that, even if she isn't, she might return to her apartment to discover it has been burgled while she was out buying groceries.

*Depression* occurs when we lose someone or something we view as essential to our contentment and satisfaction in living. Ten-year-old Rocco is depressed over the death of his dog. When the boy of her dream ditches her for another girl, Gayle finds herself becoming depressed. Richard is depressed when he is laid off from a job he expected to have until he reached retirement.

*Anger* is a felt sense of injustice. We become angry when we believe someone's unfair behavior has resulted in a threat to, or loss of, something or someone we consider essential to our quality of life. Three-year-old Tatiana gets angry when an older playmate takes away her doll. Troy becomes angry when a drunk driver runs into his recently refurbished roadster. Heather was angered when she discovered that her husband, Fred, was involved in an extramarital affair.

*Envy* occurs when we encounter another person who has what we believe is essential to our contentment and satisfaction in living and which we do not ourselves possess. Heather envies her sister's relationship with her husband. Whenever she and Fred go out with Theresa and Chris, Heather finds herself becoming upset over the attention and affection Chris shows Theresa while her husband is basically non-affectionate and appears to be disinterested in her.

We experience *jealousy* when we believe someone is going to take away who or what we consider essential to our quality of life. Vicky became jealous of John when she discovered he was spending many hours after work alone in his office with

Mona. She continued to be jealous as she discovered more and more evidence the two of them were romantically involved. Her jealousy eventually subsided when she decided she no longer wanted to be married to a man she couldn't trust.

We feel *guilt* when we have done something which results in a threat to, or loss of, that which is essential to our contentment and satisfaction in living. Guilt involves a wish that we could somehow undo what we did. John felt guilty about filing false Medicare claims when he was confronted with the possible loss of his license to practice dentistry. He found himself wishing he could somehow go back in time and pursue a different course of action than the one he chose.

Fear, anxiety, depression, anger, envy, jealousy, and guilt are all negative emotions. Negative emotions occur when we experience a threat to, or loss of, what we consider essential to the quality of our lives. Positive emotions occur in response to those things, people, and events which enrich or enhance the quality of our lives.

*Pride* is a positive emotion we experience when what we have done has enabled us to get or keep something we consider essential to our overall contentment and satisfaction in living. Lucinda is proud of her bachelor's degree. It was the product of a tremendous amount of work and self-control. Her degree not only represents the promise of good job opportunities, but it also enhances her self-esteem.

*Love* occurs when we have relationships with those things, people, and events which bring us a sense of contentment and satisfaction. Five-year-old Sheila loves her teddy bear because when she hugs it in the darkness of her bedroom it makes her feel more secure. Theresa loves Chris because she has someone with whom to share her passion for classical music, rock climbing, and traveling. When Stan says he loves golf, he is expressing the reality that this activity offers an opportunity for physical exercise as well as a break from a stressful job.

We experience *joy* when we are in direct contact with those things, people, and events which we, in some sense, love. Married for fifteen years, Theresa still feels joy when she spends an evening with Chris. Stan is joyful when his tee shot goes long and lands in the center of the fairway. June loves the beach, and she experiences joy watching the sunrise over the horizon of the Atlantic.

*Excitement* occurs when we anticipate we will have an opportunity to enjoy those things, people, and events, which contribute to our contentment and satisfaction in living. Sheila becomes excited on Christmas Eve as she anticipates what she will find under the tree the next morning. Theresa becomes excited when she thinks about spending an evening with Chris. June becomes excited as the week of a seaside vacation draws near.

*Happiness* is a positive emotional state, which is more complex and multifaceted than any single positive emotion reviewed so far. While it involves pride, love, joy, and excitement, happiness is more a matter of how we are simultaneously situated with respect to the totality of those things, people, and events which constitute the circumstances of our lives. In other words, *happiness occurs when we have more or less continuous access to what is essential to our contentment and satisfaction with life.*

## CORE ELEMENTS OF THE FORMULA

The combination of things, people, and events which make a difference in whether and to what degree we are happy are the basic ingredients of the formula for happiness. Since they have natural, inherent, or intrinsic worth they are referred to as *core values.*

Core values determine the quality of life for anyone, anywhere, at any time. This means they impact a person's quality of life irrespective of gender, race, or nationality. These core values also enhanced the quality of life of people in the past, and they will contribute to the happiness of people yet to be born.

In the next three chapters, I will describe ten core values. I will show you where and how they are encountered in daily living. You will see what happens when we do not have sufficient access to each of these values as well as how placing excessive priority on any one of them can have a negative effect on our overall quality of life. As you go through these core values I will also give you an opportunity to measure your personal level of satisfaction with respect to each of them.

In chapter 5 I will show you how the core values relate to one another. You will have an opportunity to measure your overall level of happiness. You will also learn about the role that priorities, attitudes, expectations, and thought processes play in our ability to experience contentment and satisfaction with life.

In chapter 6 I will show you what research has revealed about the relationship between behavior and our ability to get and keep core values. I will describe seven patterns of behavior which tend to result in a threat to, or loss of, one or more of our core values. These are referred to as *self-defeating behaviors,* because they are courses of action which *appear* to enhance overall happiness but often *actually* have the opposite effect.

Chapter 7 describes nine *self-defeating beliefs.* These are ways of thinking about life and how to live which tend to support self-defeating patterns of behavior. When we operate on any of these beliefs, we are likely to pursue courses of action which result in a threat to our contentment and satisfaction in living because we see nothing wrong with doing what we do.

Once you have a full understanding of self-defeating behaviors and beliefs, chapter 8 will introduce you to four *core principles*—ideas about what's right—for the effective pursuit of happiness. These are guidelines for making choices which were formulated as alternatives to the seven self-defeating behaviors. You will see how acting on these principles enhances our ability to avoid courses of action which, in one way or another, pose a threat to our contentment and satisfaction in living.

In chapter 9 I will show you how acting on the combination of the four core principles maximizes your potential for becoming and remaining happy. You will see how regularly utilizing these principles for making choices in daily living generates emotional well-being and enhances your self-confidence, optimism, and self-esteem. I will show you how others benefit when you follow the formula and how you can reconcile following the formula with your religious beliefs.

The core concepts of the formula will provide you with the ability to effectively deal with things, people, and events you encounter in daily life. You will have a roadmap for navigating in a way which makes happiness a genuinely achievable reality. But beyond providing you with a solid set of concepts for putting together a high-quality life, I will also give you a set of tools which will enhance your personal pursuit of happiness. Each of these tools is a self-administered program for evaluating where you stand with respect to core values and how what you do will impact your future quality of life.

In chapter 10 you will be given a workbook you can use to develop a plan of action for enhancing your overall happiness. Once you have identified deficiencies in your access to one or more of the ten core values, you will be shown how to develop potential courses of action which will raise your overall contentment and satisfaction in living. You will be given a decision tree which ensures that your potential course of action is not some sort of self-defeating behavior. I will provide you with a method of forecasting how your potential course of action is likely to impact your future quality of life. Once you determine a potential course of action is likely to make you happier, you will be provided with a set of instructions for developing an action plan with which that goal can actually be achieved.

In chapter 11 I will give you a program for making momentous decisions. It will assist you in making choices such as what to major in at college, which career to pursue, whether to take a particular job, whether to remain in a romantic relationship, whether to get married, whether to have a child, whether to get a divorce, whether and when to retire, or any other major life decision. You will be provided with a means of forecasting how the consequences of each of your alternatives are likely to affect your level of happiness. This will enable you to determine which alternative is more likely to enhance your overall happiness at some future point in time.

You may have read other books about happiness only to end up feeling disappointed by the time you have finished. You may have gotten encouragement, commonsense, or advice for handling specific problems such as low self-esteem, self-defeating thinking, poor communication skills, getting along with a spouse, handling difficult people, improving mood, defeating anxiety, losing weight, or even dying more happily. But resolving a single source of dissatisfaction does not ensure a happy life.

This time your experience will be different. You are now holding the formula for happiness. When you finish reading this book you will have finally learned what you need to know, and what you need to do in order to become and remain happy.

# Chapter 2

## THINGS

In this chapter we will look at the first two elements of the formula. They are tangible entities which we can see, touch, and feel. They are the things we need to get and hold on to in order to become and remain happy.

### MEANINGFUL MATERIAL OBJECTS

The day had been hectic. Getting up early, Jen helped her mother prepare for the party scheduled to follow the commencement ceremony. After a trip to the salon to work on her tan and get her hair styled, she returned home just in time to eat, dress, and get to the high school on schedule. Suddenly the phone rang. It was her grandfather calling from Florida. He told her to look out the kitchen window so she could see her graduation present. Sitting in the driveway was a brand-new cinnamon red convertible. "Pops says that car's for me," she exclaimed to her mom and dad. "I can't believe it—this is the happiest day of my life!"

Hector grabbed Louisa as they walked down the steps in front of the Clark Building after finalizing the purchase of their new home. Having spent the last two years working overtime twenty hours a week, Hector had just become the first man in his family to buy a house. Filled with pride in his accomplishment and his ability to provide for his wife and kids, he looked into Louisa's eyes saying, "I never thought I could be as happy as I am right now."

Sometimes after making love, Theresa finds herself gazing at her engagement ring and remembering the evening Chris proposed. He took her to an expensive restaurant down by the waterfront. The sun was setting and they had just ordered when he took the little box out of his pocket, placing it on the table in front of her. As she opened it, her hopes for their relationship were realized. There it was, the thing that expressed what she meant to him. She now remembers this as one of the happiest moments of her life.

Like Jen, Hector, and Theresa, I am sure you have had at least one situation in which you were clearly aware that some *thing* played an important role in your overall contentment and satisfaction in living. Research reveals that we tend to be happier when we are able to get and keep certain types of material objects. These things are referred as *meaningful material objects.*

At an elementary level, meaningful material objects are those things which satisfy basic needs. Recall the last time you saw pictures of people forced to flee their homes by war or some sort of natural disaster, and who were arriving at refugee camps with less-than-adequate supplies of food and clothing. Their crestfallen faces vividly express how much contentment and satisfaction in living is a matter of having those material objects which satisfy basic human needs.

Yet, for most of us a satisfying life involves more than simply getting food, clothing, and shelter. In America, survival is possible by rummaging for food in restaurant trash bins, getting clothing from the Salvation Army, and sleeping under an interstate overpass. But, if you are reading this book, you would probably not be very happy if you had to live this way.

Happiness depends not only on our ability to meet basic needs but also on whether and to what degree we are able to get the type of food, clothing, and shelter which are consistent with our personal set of expectations. When we get those things which reflect the standard of living we expect, we are generally satisfied with what we have. Never anticipating more lavish digs, Hans is happy with a one-bedroom apartment. Juanita is happy when she and her husband are able to purchase a house in the suburbs because this is the type of housing she expected to live in when the two of them were raising kids. Believing he could someday live a life of luxury, Raymond is not satisfied until he is able to acquire a house in an upscale gated community.

Other material objects which contribute to our happiness include the furnishings in our home. Heather rarely invites people to her house because she is embarrassed by the frayed couch and the indelible stains on her living room rug. She wishes she and Fred could replace them, but they can't afford to spend money on furniture and carpeting. Marianne enjoys her home, in part, because she likes guests to see the antiques she and Cliff have collected and refurbished over the past ten years.

For most of us a reliable vehicle is essential to contentment and satisfaction in living. Lance is frequently distressed because his twelve-year-old car is repeatedly in the shop needing one repair after another. Ursula is content with her automobile in part because it is always running well. George is happy because he knows he can catch the train every morning and arrive at work on time.

Electrical devices also play a significant role in our overall contentment and satisfaction in living. Telephones, refrigerators, electric stoves, microwave ovens, furnaces, air conditioners, and water heaters all add comfort and convenience to our lives. Vacuum cleaners, washing machines, and electric clothes dryers are just some of the appliances enabling us to save tremendous amounts of time and effort in going about the tasks of daily living. You probably use radios, television sets, and video recording devices for entertainment as well as to get the news and information you feel you need. You may also be one of those for whom life would be unbearable without a personal computer.

In addition, toilet paper, toothbrushes, toothpaste, mouthwash, and deodorant are probably essential to your contentment and satisfaction in living. Your meaningful material objects may also include tubes of lipstick, curling irons, bars of soap, razors, shaving cream, pots and pans, a bicycle, a motorcycle, a speedboat, a tennis racket, a set of golf clubs, and scores of other things you make use of every day. Dental drills, x-ray machines, surgical instruments, and pharmaceuticals are clearly meaningful material objects when we need certain types of healthcare. For persons with clinical depression, antidepressant tablets can play an extremely important role in overall satisfaction and contentment with life.

The value of a material object is always determined by how it contributes to our quality of life. As far as Nick is concerned, a carburetor for a 1962 Corvette is simply a piece of junk. For Pete, it is an extremely meaningful object because it is the part he needs to keep his car on the road.

Most meaningful material objects can be replaced by other objects as long as they occupy a similar role in our value system. You may consider a cell phone to be one of your meaningful material objects. If you lose the one you have and replace it with another, the second phone will have the same value as the first as long as it has a similar or better set of functions.

On the other hand, not all meaningful objects can be replaced. Some photographs, furniture, jewelry, or other objects which have significance because they remind us of former times and places may play a very meaningful role in our overall quality of life. Since the meaning of these objects is rooted in the memories or emotions they evoke, they are referred to as having sentimental value.

At the same time, the meaning of a particular object may not always be identical over the course of a lifetime. You may have had a stuffed animal, a doll, or an action figure which was essential to your contentment and satisfaction as a child, but the object now plays no role in your overall quality of life. There may be material objects essential to your happiness today which will be much less meaningful twenty years from now.

Even though the value of any given material object may vary from person to person or over the course of a lifetime, there are always a set of material objects each of us requires in order to be content and satisfied with life at any given time. This group of things is your unique set of meaningful material objects. The ability to get and keep these things is an essential ingredient in the formula for happiness.

Some people believe happiness can be achieved simply by acquiring as many material objects as possible. This approach to happiness is referred to as *materialism*. The notion that material objects are the key to satisfaction and contentment in living is rooted in the reality that material objects are our most important source of pleasure. *Hedonism* is the belief that happiness is a matter of achieving a maximum amount of pleasure in living.

You probably already realize that neither materialism nor hedonism is an effective means of becoming and remaining happy. The reason for this is rooted in what research has revealed about our capacity to experience pleasure. Studies have shown pleasure is not simply a matter of sensation but that it also involves complicated neuropsychological processes which are influenced by the circumstances within which we are situated.

This reality is exemplified by the fact that even though two people have an identical material object, there may be wide differences in terms of the degree to which they obtain pleasure from the sensual experience it provides. Dining with friends in a comfortable restaurant and looking forward to a weekend filled with rest and recreation, Elton experiences more pleasure from his entree than a man who is eating an identical dish as his last meal on death row. What determines our capacity to experience pleasure is not simply our ability to get and keep meaningful material objects but also how we are situated with respect to other aspects of life which are essential to our contentment and satisfaction in living.

This means that the pursuit of happiness requires obtaining and maintaining our meaningful material objects while we also get and keep the other nine core values which we are going to review.

As we go through each of the core values, you will be given an opportunity to measure the degree to which it is contributing to your overall happiness. What follows is a questionnaire dealing with your level of satisfaction with respect to meaningful material objects. This is the first section of the General Inventory of Life Satisfaction (GILS). The GILS is a means of measuring your overall level of contentment and satisfaction with life.

Once you have completed the items in this section of the GILS, you will have instructions for scoring your responses and a way of making sense of your score. Once we go through the remainder of the nine core values, you will learn how to combine your scores on each section of the GILS into a Global Estimate of Life Satisfaction (GELS). The GELS is a score which ranges from 0 to 100 reflecting your overall contentment and satisfaction with life.

*Please respond to the following statements in terms of your level of agreement:*

A = Agree / SA = Somewhat Agree / SD = Somewhat Disagree / D = Disagree / NA = Not Applicable

| A | SA | SD | D | NA | | |
|---|----|----|---|----|---|---|
| O | O | O | O | O | 1. | I am satisfied with my current housing situation. |
| O | O | O | O | O | 2. | I am satisfied with the furnishings in my home. |
| O | O | O | O | O | 3. | I am satisfied with my wardrobe. |
| O | O | O | O | O | 4. | I am satisfied with my access to reliable transportation. |
| O | O | O | O | O | 5. | I am satisfied with the electronic devices which provide entertainment or save time and effort. |
| O | O | O | O | O | 6. | I am satisfied with my access to stores where I can find an adequate variety of reasonably priced products which I consider essential to my quality of life. |

*Once this portion of the GILS is complete, score your responses by going through the following procedure:*

1. *Count the number of items marked "A" then multiply that number by 10 and fill in this blank* → _____

2. *Count the number of items marked "SA" then multiply that number by 7.5 and fill in this blank* → _____

3. *Count the number of items marked "SD" then multiply that number by 2.5 and fill in this blank* → _____

4. *Count the number of items marked "D" then multiply that number by zero and fill in this blank* → _____

5. *Add all of these numbers together and fill in this blank . . .* → _____

6. *Subtract the number of items marked "NA" from 6 to fill in this blank . . . .* → _____

7. *Divide the number on line 5 by the number on line 6 to get your* **Meaningful Material Objects** *score* → _____

*Once you have finished scoring your responses, you can interpret your score as follows:*

7.6 -10    *You are satisfied with respect to meaningful material objects.*
5.1-7.5    *You are somewhat satisfied with respect to meaningful material objects.*
2.6-5.0    *You are somewhat dissatisfied with respect to meaningful material objects.*
0-2.5     *You are generally dissatisfied with respect to meaningful material objects.*

If you are a little confused, the example below shows how to calculate your score.

| A | SA | SD | D | NA | |
|---|----|----|---|-----|--|
| ● | O | O | O | O | 1. I am satisfied with my current housing situation. |
| O | ● | O | O | O | 2. I am satisfied with the furnishings in my home. |
| ● | O | O | O | O | 3. I am satisfied with my wardrobe. |
| O | O | O | ● | O | 4. I am satisfied with my access to reliable transportation. |
| O | O | ● | O | O | 5. I am satisfied with the electronic devices which provide entertainment or save time and effort. |
| O | O | O | O | ● | 6. I am satisfied with my access to stores where I can find an adequate variety of reasonably priced products which I consider essential to my quality of life. |

1. *Since the number of items marked "A" is 2, 2 is multiplied by 10, so the result is. . . . . . . . . . . . . . .*     20
2. *Since the number of items marked "SA" is 1, 1 is multiplied by 7.5, so the result is . . . . . . . . . . . . . .*     7.5
3. *Since the number of items marked "SD" is 1, 1 is multiplied by 2.5, so the result is . . . . . . . . . . . . . .*     2.5
4. *Since the number of items marked "D" is 1, 1 is multiplied by zero . . . . . . . . . . . . .*     0
5. *The total for these scores is . . . . . . . . . . . . . . . . . . . . . . . . . . . . . . . . . . . . . . . . . . . . . . .*     30
6. *Since the number of items marked "NA" is 1, 6 minus 1 equals . . . .*     5
7. *When 30 is divided by 5, you get a **Meaningful Material Objects** score of . . .*     6

# MONEY

Numerous studies have shown that when asked what would make them happier, most people say it would be having more money. Yet, research also reveals that when people suddenly acquire significant amounts of money, they report an immediate increase in their overall happiness, but that, as time goes on, this burst of happiness subsides. These results make sense when we realize what money is and recognize the role it plays in daily life.

If you think back to what you learned in elementary school, you will remember that in prehistoric times, human beings spent virtually all of their waking hours searching for food. The species continued to exist as hunters and gatherers until someone figured out how to plant and harvest. With the discovery of agriculture one person was able to produce more food than he needed, which meant others were able spend their time and energy in some other way. Eventually, some of these people learned how to make tools and shoes.

You will recall that early on, a farmer who needed a shovel traded some of his potatoes with a toolmaker who needed something to eat. He would also trade some of his potatoes with a shoemaker who was looking for some food. In simple transactions like this everybody was happy because each person was able to get what he wanted from the person with whom he traded.

But when a farmer in search of a shovel approached a toolmaker with enough to eat, things got complicated. One way of dealing with this situation would have been for the toolmaker to tell the farmer he was not interested in his potatoes, but he actually needed a pair of shoes. The farmer could trade his potatoes with the shoemaker and then take the shoes to the toolmaker where he would exchange them for a shovel. Although in this arrangement everybody still got what he wanted, the process was complicated and time consuming. It became even more cumbersome when the shoemaker was not interested in trading his shoes for potatoes but instead was eager to get a bottle of wine.

Recall that as time went on barter economies were eventually replaced when everybody in a community agreed to trade with something they all agreed to accept. This medium of exchange had to meet certain requirements. It had to be relatively scarce, it had to be easy to carry, and it had to be something which would not spoil.

In the early days, seashells, stones, and crude pieces of metal served as money. As time went on, wampum was replaced with minted coins. When they became too cumbersome or the supply of metal from which they were made was exhausted, printed pieces of paper replaced coins. Eventually, bank checks became more common than cash. Recently paper money has given way to plastic credit cards and configurations of electrons floating in cyberspace as a means of recording our monetary transactions. But, whatever its form, money is and always has been what we trade with one another as a means of getting what we want and need.

Although we typically think of money as currency it also includes bank checks, lines of credit, stocks, bonds, insurance benefits, vouchers, and coupons. Since we obtain most of our meaningful material objects with money and since we have already seen that meaningful material objects contribute to our overall contentment and satisfaction in living, it is easy to see how money enhances happiness with respect to our ability to get those things. But, money also contributes to our happiness because it has an effect on many other aspects of human life.

The amount of money we have influences what goes on in our interpersonal interactions. Marianne feels she has the respect and admiration of her friends and neighbors in part because she and her husband have enough money to maintain their home and drive two relatively late-model cars. Heather is hounded by a sense of shame whenever she drives her rusted sports utility vehicle to her daughter's soccer games. The fact that she and Fred cannot purchase a nicer automobile renders her feeling inadequate in relation to her peers.

Milt and Fred are members of the local chapter of the VFW. Milt enjoys spending evenings swapping war stories with the boys as they buy one another rounds of drinks. Proud of his performance as a combat marine, Fred would like to join in, but he feels uncomfortable not being able to afford to pay when it is his turn to buy a round.

Marianne and Cliff frequently talk about their fantasies. They have enough money to pay their basic costs of living and enough leftover to take a yearly vacation. They spend hours talking about their alternatives, mulling over where they want to go and what they want to do. Heather and Fred work hard at their jobs, but after paying their monthly bills, there's never much leftover. They used to talk about taking a trip to Hawaii, but it has become obvious they will never be able to afford it. Sometimes Heather lays awake at night, wishing her life had been more exciting and resenting Fred for not finishing his degree. Not wanting him to think he has somehow failed her, she never reveals how she feels. Yet, she realizes her resentment has somehow diminished the sense of openness she used to find in their relationship.

The amount of money we have also has an effect on our health and physical well-being. When we can afford to purchase healthy foods and engage in activities which promote health, we are less likely to experience obesity, cancer, and heart disease. When we can afford to get timely healthcare, we are generally happier than when we lack the resources to see a physician, a dentist, or a psychotherapist.

The amount of money we obtain for the work we do also contributes to our self-esteem. Stan finds his work to be extremely rewarding, partly because his salary indicates his employer views him as a valuable resource. Warren is almost always angry because he feels he is grossly underpaid. He is earning much less than most of the fellows he went to high school with, and he sees himself as a failure. He wonders if his employer doesn't appreciate his value or whether he simply isn't worth any more than what he earns.

The amount of money we have also influences what we do for fun. Stan can afford to go golfing once a week, and in the winter he gets out to ski. When he was a student, Fred used to golf and ski, but now he can't afford the greens fees or the lift tickets.

In a larger sense, the amount of money we have makes a difference in terms of our ability to do what we want when we want to do it. Yvonne lives in New York City and wants to visit her mother in Florida. She would like to fly, but she only has enough money to take the bus. Her sister, Irma, who also lives in the city, has a greater number of options. Irma can afford to take the bus, rent a car, or fly to see her mom.

Money impacts our overall level of security. Marianne and Cliff have had the ability to bank enough money to be able to pay their bills for approximately six months should either one of them become disabled or lose a job. Heather and Fred have nothing in savings, and they have maxed out their credit cards. Heather finds she is frequently distressed by the thought that if either of them is laid off they will probably lose at least one of their cars and maybe even their house.

Because the amount of money we possess has such a profound effect on so many aspects of our life, it is easy to understand why many people equate the pursuit of happiness with the accumulation of wealth. The problem with this approach to living has been evident for a long time. For centuries the notion that happiness does not result from a preoccupation with money has been expressed in folklore and literature.

You are probably familiar with the story of King Midas. He was a mythical fellow who got his wish that everything he touched would turn to gold. While he was initially delighted with his newfound means of amassing wealth, he became extremely unhappy when he kissed his daughter and she turned into an inert mass of metal.

Moliere's *The Miser* is a classic French play depicting a relatively wealthy man who spends most of his time counting his money while failing to engage in any recreational activities or to invest time and energy cultivating relationships with his wife and children. Far from being happy, he has become obsessed with his wealth, and he is paranoid someone is somehow going to take it away. When watching this play, we realize this fear is rooted in the miser's sense that money is the only thing which matters to him and that the possibility of losing it would render him with nothing of value in life.

Studies of persons who experience sudden wealth provide new insight into the relationship between money and happiness. When Adam hit the state lottery, he was working as a grinder in a foundry. He lived in a lower-middle-class neighborhood, he was married, and he had two kids. Soon after his good fortune, Adam quit his job, and he and his wife began looking for a new house in an upscale part of town. Once they found their dream home, he joined a country club where he spent countless hours honing his game of golf. He believed he would be living the life he had always wanted to live.

As all of this was going on, several other things were happening which eventually led to Adam becoming depressed. Shortly after his winnings were announced in a local newspaper almost everyone he knew began positioning themselves for a piece of the pie. After giving away hundreds of thousands of dollars, Adam realized he had to cut back on his largesse or he was going to eventually give away all of his newfound wealth. He also learned most of his family members and friends actually resented him because he had not given them more, and because they also envied what he now had. They stopped spending time with Adam, and he found he was no longer invited to their homes or get-togethers.

Before becoming rich, Adam enjoyed spending time with neighbors and playing golf with fellows from the foundry where he worked. Moving into an upper-middle-class neighborhood, he had little in common with the other residents. The people he now lived with were doctors, lawyers, and successful businessmen. They were friendly, but they never visited, and he was never invited to their homes. When Adam went to the clubhouse he had difficulty finding other members of the country club interested in including him in a round of golf. It was apparent they had little in common with a fellow who never finished high school and who had spent the past twenty years sitting in front of a grinding wheel.

The story of King Midas, Moliere's *The Miser*, and what happened to Adam all point to the fundamental relationship between money and quality of life. Although money contributes to our contentment and satisfaction in living, it is only one of several values which we require in order to become and remain happy.

Now, take a few minutes to rate your level of satisfaction with respect to money on the next section of the General Inventory of Life Satisfaction.

*Please respond to the following statements in terms of your level of agreement:*

A = Agree / SA = Somewhat Agree / SD = Somewhat Disagree / D = Disagree / NA = Not Applicable

| A | SA | SD | D | NA | | |
|---|----|----|---|----|---|---|
| O | O | O | O | O | 1 | I have sufficient money to acquire and maintain those material objects that make my life satisfying. |
| O | O | O | O | O | 2 | My level of income and/or assets is sufficient to secure the respect and perhaps admiration of those people who are important to me. |
| O | O | O | O | O | 3 | I have enough money to engage in the interpersonal activities that interest me. |
| O | O | O | O | O | 4 | Money does not block me from participating in close and revealing interpersonal interactions. |
| O | O | O | O | O | 5 | I can afford to participate in activities that enhance my health and prevent illness. |
| O | O | O | O | O | 6 | I have sufficient money to obtain quality healthcare when I need it. |
| O | O | O | O | O | 7 | My level of compensation is fair and reasonable for the work I do. |
| O | O | O | O | O | 8 | I can afford to participate in a sufficient variety of renewing recreational activities. |
| O | O | O | O | O | 9 | My income and/or assets are sufficient to provide me with an adequate number of options in everyday living. |
| O | O | O | O | O | 10 | My income or assets are sufficiently reliable to make me feel safe. |

*Once this portion of the GILS is complete, score your responses by going through the following procedure:*

1. *Count the number of items marked "A" then multiply that number by 10 and fill in this blank*  →  _____
2. *Count the number of items marked "SA" then multiply that number by 7.5 and fill in this blank*  →  _____
3. *Count the number of items marked "SD" then multiply that number by 2.5 and fill in this blank*  →  _____
4. *Count the number of items marked "D" then multiply that number by zero and fill in this blank*  →  _____
5. *Add all of these numbers together and fill in this blank . . . . . . . . . . .*  →  _____
6. *Subtract the number of items marked "NA" from 10 to fill in this blank . . . .*  →  _____
7. *Divide the number on line 5 by the number on line 6 to get your **Money** score . . .*  →  _____

*Once you have finished scoring your responses, you can interpret your score as follows:*

*7.6-10   You are satisfied with respect to money.*
*5.1-7.5   You are somewhat satisfied with respect to money.*
*2.6-5.0   You are somewhat dissatisfied with respect to money.*
*0-2.5   You are generally dissatisfied with respect to money.*

# Chapter 3

# INTERPERSONAL VALUES

The reality that others play a role in our contentment and satisfaction in living is evident to anyone who has observed what goes on between a mother and her infant child. The cries and screams, the facial contortions, and the flailing arms and legs of a hungry baby vividly display human discontent. The baby's expression of satisfaction is equally evident when mom provides a breast or a bottle of formula.

Yet, contentment and satisfaction is not simply determined by those meaningful material objects other people provide. It is also a matter of how we get what is given. Research reveals that the baby being held by a loving mother who cradles and talks to her infant while nursing is much happier than one who is given a bottle by an insensitive caregiver simply providing nourishment.

Other studies indicate human beings have an inborn interest in other people. Newborns automatically focus attention on drawings resembling a human face. Very young children spontaneously react to adult facial expressions of emotions. Toddlers tend to become distressed when confronted with criticism or disappointment on the part of mom or dad. They express positive reactions when their parents offer praise and encouragement.

Still, other research documents that as childhood unfolds our relationships with parents and siblings impact our overall contentment and satisfaction in life. Subsequently our happiness is affected by interactions with peers, teachers, and other figures of authority encountered in the community. Finding satisfaction in relationships with members of the other gender is a central task of adolescence. In adulthood, whether and to what degree we are happy, is in many ways a matter of our interactions with romantic partners, members of our family, people in our community, and those we have to deal with at work. Clearly understanding the connection between happiness and interpersonal interaction is an important aspect of the study of contentment and satisfaction in living.

Some of this research has revealed a correlation between happiness and certain types of relationships. Married people tend to be happier than do persons who are not married. Adults who have been raised in intact families more frequently report being happy than persons whose parents divorced while they were children. These findings suggest that being involved in certain types of relationships contributes to our overall level of contentment and satisfaction in living.

Yet, this way of understanding the role other people play in the quality of our lives fails to explain why many people who are in these types of relationships are less happy than those who are not. Studies show a large number of people who are clinically depressed maintain their greatest source of discontent is their relationship with their spouse. Other research reveals that children who grow up in significantly dysfunctional families are frequently less satisfied and content with life than those whose parents divorced when they were young. These findings suggest happiness is not simply a matter of being in certain types of relationships, but that it is also a matter of entering into and maintaining relationships with certain individuals.

This way of understanding the connection between happiness and other people does not explain why one person can have an entirely different effect on two different individuals with whom that person has the same type of relationship. Don finds a degree of satisfaction in spending time with his father while his brother, Jay, can't stand being in the same room with the man. Maryanne finds her husband, Cliff, significantly contributing to her happiness while his ex-wife, Lisa, considers time spent with him to have been a period of profound discontent. These exceptions, along with the results of other studies which show a high correlation between happiness and certain types of interpersonal interactions such as love, companionship, and intimacy, suggest happiness is better understood in terms of our ability to experience these interpersonal interactions.

Accounting for happiness in terms of certain types of interpersonal interactions fails to account for the fact that many people are unhappy because they are having these interpersonal interactions in relationships which do not enhance the quality of their lives. Carla and Judith are both experiencing a high level of intimacy in the context of their romantic relationships. Carla, however, is much happier than Judith because she finds her intimacy with her husband while Judith is intimately involved with a married man who continues to tell her he wants to share her life while making no effort to leave his wife.

All of these research findings have led to the observation that happiness is not simply a matter of being involved in certain types of relationships, being involved with a particular individual, or experiencing specific types of interpersonal interactions. Rather, it is a combination of all three. In other words, we now know happiness depends on having certain types of relationships with particular individuals who provide specific interpersonal interactions. In this chapter I will show you where and how we encounter these interpersonal values in everyday life.

## TYPES OF RELATIONSHIPS

There are five basic types of relationships within which we are able to find the interpersonal interactions which enrich and enhance the quality of our lives.

*Community relationships* include those we have with people who live in our neighborhood. They also include the relationships we have with the postal carrier, the police officers, and the firemen who work where we live. Other community relationships are those we have with people we interact with at the PTA, the American Legion, the church or temple, or any other noncommercial organization within which we participate.

*Commercial relationships* involve some sort of monetary exchange. They include a relationship with the cashier at the convenience store, and the relationships we have with our hairdresser, dentist, physician, accountant, attorney, and psychotherapist. Commercial relationships also encompass all of the relationships we have at work. They include relationships with coworkers, supervisors, subordinates, clients, customers, and anyone else we encounter on the job. When we have a commercial relationship with a person who is also a part of our community, the connection we have is both a commercial and a community relationship. Anytime we have more than one type of relationship with another individual we are involved in some sort of dual relationship.

We form *friendships* based on mutual interest and a desire to share certain types of experiences. Friendships may be lifelong or relatively short lived. We may be friends with a person who lives nearby and whom we encounter every day, or we may have a friendship with someone who lives hundreds or even thousands of miles away and whom we only see infrequently.

*Family relationships* are those based on blood, marriage, and adoption. They consist of parent-child, spousal, and avuncular relationships. They also include affiliations we have with those people who live in our household for an extended period of time even though we are not legally related.

*Romantic relationships* are based on erotic attraction and exchanges of affection. When we marry we typically have a romantic relationship with the person who becomes our spouse. Once married, maintaining a romantic relationship depends upon the degree to which a husband and a wife continue to experience erotic attraction and to express affection toward one another.

Now that you are familiar with this way of conceptualizing your network of interpersonal relationships we will look at how happiness is a matter of being involved with people who provide certain types of interactions within one or more of these types of relationships.

## AFFIRMATION

*Affirmation* occurs when other people indicate that we are in some sense acceptable, competent, adequate, and/or desirable human beings.

There are a number of ways we get affirmation in community relationships. Roberto is affirmed by his third-grade teacher when she says he is a good reader after he reads aloud in front of the rest of the class. Libby is affirmed when the basketball coach tells her she has made the team. The leadership of the congregation affirms Richard when they invite him to take a seat on church council.

Affirmation can also occur in a variety of ways in commercial relationships. Ursula is affirmed when she is offered a job at the corporation where she hoped she would be hired. Receiving a positive performance appraisal, Pete is affirmed by his supervisor. Marianne is affirmed when she is given a promotion. For Jay, who recently started practicing chiropractics, affirmation occurs when his patients return for further care.

Affirmation also occurs in relationships with friends. Ten-year-old Rocco is affirmed when his classmate, Kent, invites him to come over to play video games after school. Wendy affirms Gayle when she tells her she likes the way Gayle plays the guitar. Javier affirms Armando by telling him he couldn't have a better friend. Todd is affirmed by Cliff when Cliff spends Sunday afternoon helping Todd repair his roof after it was damaged in a thunderstorm.

Within family relations, affirmation usually involves some sort of feedback with respect to how well we fill a family role. Rocco is affirmed by his father when his dad tells him he's proud to have him as a son. Joanne is affirmed when she gets cards and calls on Mother's Day from her adult children who live hundreds of miles away. Marianne affirms Cliff when she tells him she could not imagine having a better husband.

Within romantic relationships affirmation has to do with positive feedback concerning gender. Theresa is affirmed by Chris when he tells her she is beautiful. Juan is affirmed by Vencenza when she tells him she thinks the two of them make an attractive couple. Juan is also affirmed when she tells him he's a wonderful lover.

While affirmation typically occurs in interactions with people, we can also find it in two other types of relationships.

Pet owners often experience affirmation from their animals. You are affirmed by the excitement your dog displays when you come into a room or when your cat curls up on your lap and purrs. Several studies have demonstrated that persons living in nursing homes and prisons tend to be happier when they are permitted to have pets. This is due, in part, to the reality that residents of these institutions receive little affirmation from persons they encounter in the course of daily life.

Several other studies have also found a correlation between happiness and strong religious faith. Persons of faith typically report having a personal relationship with God. When we experience God as a loving presence, a powerful form of affirmation occurs.

While affirmation contributes to our happiness, any feedback indicating we are in some sense unacceptable, incompetent, inadequate, or undesirable tends to have a negative effect on our contentment and satisfaction in life. *Disaffirmation* can occur in any type of relationship. Seven-year-old Logan is disaffirmed when his classmates refer to him as a "jerk" and a "geek." Gretchen is disaffirmed when she is unable to obtain a job after applying for numerous positions. Giles is disaffirmed when Wendell tells him he no longer wants him as a friend. Sophia is disaffirmed when her mother exclaims she is ashamed to have her as a daughter. Maureen is disaffirmed when her fiancé suddenly and unexpectedly calls off their engagement.

Sometimes failure to get affirmation in the context of a relationship where we expect to be affirmed contributes to our sense of discontent. Sarah is upset with her friend, Beatrice, once she realizes Beatrice has not returned her last few phone messages and that she is the person in the friendship who is always making an attempt to talk. Eleven-year-old Zelda is very upset because her parents never praise her for getting good grades while they are overjoyed when her older sister brings home mediocre marks. John was unhappy with Vickie because she paid less attention to him than he thought she should once their kids came along.

Some people equate happiness with obtaining and maintaining affirmation. As long as Ted could remember, he had always wanted his father to think well of him. When he was a child, his dad would come to his baseball games. Although he never offered praise, he would yell at Ted if he struck out or if he failed to make a play. In high school, this pattern of behavior continued as Ted played wide receiver for the football team where, twenty-five years earlier, his father had been an outstanding athlete.

Ted attended the university where his father had studied mechanical engineering. He majored in business administration, because his dad wanted him to learn how to manage the family wholesale plumbing business. Ted was expected to work for him once he finished school and eventually to take over the business when his dad was ready to retire.

In his sophomore year, Ted informed his father he discovered a subject which was much more interesting than business administration. He wanted to change his major to sociology, go on to get a PhD, and pursue a teaching career at a university. Once his father told him how disappointed he would be if Ted didn't come back to Morgantown once he finished his degree, Ted abandoned these ideas.

In his junior year, Ted fell in love with Esther. Also a junior, she was majoring in drama and literature. Ted could not believe how being with her made him feel. For the first time in his life he really felt he was alive. They would see one another nearly every day, but he most enjoyed the weekends. After sleeping together Saturday nights, they would lounge around Sunday afternoons, talking about books she was reading. Sometimes he would help her memorize her lines. As graduation approached they began to talk about what they were going to do once they finished school.

They both realized that if Esther was going to make it in acting, she would have to relocate to New York or Los Angeles. One of her professors had some connections in California, and he told her she had a good shot at a professional career. Eventually, they decided they could get jobs waiting tables while Esther went through auditions and tryouts for a couple of years. Esther told Ted that if by then she couldn't make it in acting, she would be willing to come back with him to West Virginia where he could make a living working for his dad and she could find a teaching job.

Learning about their plans, Ted's father became enraged. He told Ted that only a fool would follow an actress to Los Angeles. He let Ted know he would never approve of him if he went ahead with what he and Esther wanted to do.

Upon graduation Ted returned to his family home while Esther headed for the coast. At first she called him every week, but eventually the calls became much less frequent. One day a letter arrived announcing she had fallen in love with a fellow she met while working as a waitress. Ted was devastated by the news.

After working a couple of years for his father, Ted found his job boring and monotonous. He began dating one of the women who worked in accounts receivable. After about six months they got married. Looking back on that decision, he realized his feelings for her were never as intense as they had been for Esther, but his father was pushing him to marry because his mother wanted grandchildren.

By thirty-five Ted had two children. He and his wife had just moved into a larger house. He still hated his job, he had nothing in common with his wife, and he was drinking close to a fifth of Captain Morgan every day, when he got the news his father had suffered a heart attack. Once his dad was moved to intensive care, Ted spent hours at his father's bedside. For the first time in his life his dad told him he was proud to have him as a son. The next day he died from a massive stroke.

Faced with his father's death, Ted realized his whole life had been based on attempting to get and keep this man's affirmation. Now he finally had it. But, he also realized that although he had been able to get his father's affirmation, he had little else to make him happy.

In Ted's story we can see that although affirmation is a significant factor in determining whether and to what degree we are happy, it only contributes to our overall contentment and satisfaction in living when we are able to acquire and maintain affirmation along with the other nine values which are essential to becoming and remaining happy.

Now, take a few minutes to rate your own level of satisfaction with respect to affirmation by filling out the next portion of the GILS.

Please respond to the following statements in terms of your level of agreement:

A = Agree / SA = Somewhat Agree / SD = Somewhat Disagree / D = Disagree / NA = Not Applicable

| A | SA | SD | D | NA | | |
|---|----|----|---|----|---|---|
| O | O | O | O | O | 1. | I am satisfied with the affirmation I get from people in my community. |
| O | O | O | O | O | 2. | I am satisfied with the affirmation I get from coworkers. |
| O | O | O | O | O | 3. | I am satisfied with the affirmation I get from my supervisors. |
| O | O | O | O | O | 4. | I am satisfied with the affirmation I get from friends. |
| O | O | O | O | O | 5. | I am satisfied with the affirmation I get from my children. |
| O | O | O | O | O | 6. | I am satisfied with the affirmation I get from my parents. |
| O | O | O | O | O | 7. | I am satisfied with the affirmation I get from my extended family. |
| O | O | O | O | O | 8. | I am satisfied with the affirmation I get from my spouse or romantic partner. |
| O | O | O | O | O | 9. | I am satisfied with the affirmation I receive from my pet. |
| O | O | O | O | O | 10. | I am satisfied with the affirmation I get from God. |

*Once this portion of the GILS is complete, score your responses by going through the following procedure:*

1. *Count the number of items marked "A" then multiply that number by 10 and fill in this blank*        → _____
2. *Count the number of items marked "SA" then multiply that number by 7.5 and fill in this blank*      → _____
3. *Count the number of items marked "SD" then multiply that number by 2.5 and fill in this blank*      → _____
4. *Count the number of items marked "D" then multiply that number by zero and fill in this blank*      → _____
5. *Add all of these numbers together and fill in this blank . . . . . . . .*      → _____
6. *Subtract the number of items marked "NA" from 10 to fill in this blank*      → _____
7. *Divide the number on line 5 by the number on line 6 to get your* **Affirmation** *score . . . . .*      → _____

*Once you have finished scoring your responses, you can interpret your score as follows:*

7.6-10    *You are satisfied with respect to affirmation.*
5.1-7.5    *You are somewhat satisfied with respect to affirmation.*
2.6-5.0    *You are somewhat dissatisfied with respect to affirmation.*
0-2.5      *You are generally dissatisfied with respect to affirmation.*

## COMPANIONSHIP

*Companionship* occurs when we share what we experience with others. Companionship gives rise to our sense of togetherness. Also referred to as fellowship, fraternity, and camaraderie, companionship is the basis for our sense of belonging.

Companionship can be found in one-to-one encounters as well as in a group. Sharing what we experience may consist of facial expressions, certain types of eye contact, or some other form of body language. But, for the most part, companionship occurs when we share what we experience with words.

Curt and Mike are sitting next to each other at the airport. Even though they are in the same situation, companionship does not occur until Curt begins to complain to Mike about his frustration over not being able to make an important meeting later that morning because his flight has just been cancelled. Companionship continues when Mike expresses a similar complaint.

In addition to sharing what we think or how we feel about our current situation, companionship can also include sharing experiences from the past as well as expectations about the future. Mike discloses how he was similarly frustrated a few weeks earlier and reminisces about how much easier it was to fly prior to 9/11. Curt shares his ideas about promoting the software he sells and his hopes for doubling his annual income next year.

We often find companionship in community relationships. Seventeen-year-old Tyrone spends several hours a week playing pick-up basketball with kids who live nearby. After getting her youngest son off to school, Ida sits down with her next-door neighbor for a cup of coffee and a conversation about what's going on with their husbands and children. Milt spends at least three nights a week at the VFW where he and other vets talk about their years in Vietnam.

We can also find companionship in commercial relationships. Carlotta and Olive have worked side by side, boxing crackers at Nabisco for almost twenty years. On breaks they talk about how much they despise their supervisor and gossip about some of the other women they work with at the bakery. Each tells the other what they would rather be doing and how they can't wait until they have enough time in to retire. Eating together at mid-shift in the lunchroom, they talk about what they did last weekend and about what they are going to do when the next one rolls around.

Companionship is an important aspect of any friendship. In fact, whether and to what degree people are friends in many ways depends on how much they share with one another. Toni and Alisha shop and go to the movies together once or twice a month. They are in daily contact over the phone. Even though Pete and Nicholas have lived thousands of miles away from one another after college, they continue to keep in touch and manage to get together just about once a year. Their companionship continues as they talk about what has happened since their last reunion and what they plan to do.

Companionship can occur in the context of day-to-day family interaction. Sixteen-year-old Mercedes and her fifteen-year-old sister, Carlotta, share many of their thoughts and feelings about what is going on at home as well as what they are doing at school. Bob and his dad enjoy time spent fishing and hunting together each year. Colleen and her daughter, Hope, share the joy of victory and the heartbreak of defeat as they spend weekends with Hope's traveling soccer team.

Romantic relationships contribute to our happiness, in part, because of the companionship they provide. Tavia looks forward to the weekends she spends with Pavel. She enjoys going to parties and to the movies, but she also savors simply spending the evening with Pavel at her apartment. She finds that she is quite content when they make some popcorn and lay on the couch watching a rented movie.

Pets can also be a source of companionship. Living alone, Juanita obtains a fair amount of companionship from her cat, Roxie. She frequently finds herself talking to Roxie, and she has the sense that Roxie enjoys sitting on her lap and being petted as much as Juanita enjoys petting her.

Ruth obtains a fair amount of satisfaction from companionship with God. She spends the first part of each day in prayer and meditation, sharing her interests, desires, and whatever else is on her mind. As the day unfolds, she has an abiding sense that she is sharing her experiences with Him.

The absence of companionship, *loneliness*, is a significant source of unhappiness. Seven-year-old Ross has been depressed since shortly after moving from Florida to a high-rise in Manhattan. His dad is almost never home, and his mother is continuously on the phone or the computer. He finds himself thinking about what his friends are doing back home and resenting his father for making the decision to move. His mother has reassured him he will make new friends when he starts school. But, September seems a long way off and, in the meantime, he is unhappier than he ever was before.

As with the other core values, some people equate companionship with happiness. After being depressed for a couple of years, Loretta sought treatment. She experienced no pleasure in living and found she was crying frequently. In addition, she felt worthless and hopeless, and occasionally she thought about taking her own life.

Conceived out of wedlock, Loretta never knew her father and her mother rarely spent time with her. Loretta always felt her mother never wanted her around because her mom rarely talked or showed any interest in what she had to say. Instead, her mother focused her attention on a parade of men she entertained in the bedroom of their apartment. When Loretta was twelve, her mother married and subsequently spent most of her time drinking with her new husband.

For reasons Loretta couldn't figure out, the other kids at school never wanted to be her friend. She didn't fit in with any of the groups of girls even when she got into high school. Occasionally, she would think one of them was interested in being her friend, but it soon became apparent she had been mistaken.

As an adolescent, Loretta never seemed to be able to get into a solid romantic relationship. Boys rarely showed an interest in her, and when they did, it never seemed to go anywhere. On a few occasions, she thought she could get a boyfriend by having sex, only to discover that, after a few dates, the boy stopped calling and started avoiding her when he would see her in the halls at school.

A couple of years after graduation Loretta met Ross when she took a job in housewares at a department store where he was selling washing machines. He was the first fellow who didn't drift away after a few sexual encounters, and he was also the first to take her out and introduce her to his circle of friends. For the first time in her life, Loretta had a sense of belonging.

Ross was unwilling to marry Loretta because, having been burned in his divorce, he did not want to take a second chance.

He would spend a couple of nights a week with her, they would go out to eat, and they would do things with other couples on the weekends when Ross wanted to socialize. At the same time, Ross prohibited Loretta from spending time with any potential girlfriends, he insisted she remain in her apartment when she was not with him, and he expected her to be available anytime he wanted sex. When they made love, he never seemed interested in whether Loretta was satisfied.

Hoping to move the relationship to a deeper level, Loretta would occasionally try to talk to Ross about his lack of commitment to her, and she would express an interest in spending more time with him. In response, he usually became angry and defensive. He repeatedly told her she should appreciate the time they had together, because nobody else would do as much with her as he did. On several occasions, he went so far as to assert that she should stop whining, because no other man would be willing to have any type of relationship with her.

When her psychologist pointed out that Loretta was paying a high price for remaining in this relationship, she responded by stating she had to put up with whatever Ross doled out. "If I left him or if he left me, I would be alone. I can't imagine that. I might as well be dead." For Loretta, life without companionship was worse than having to live with the loss of autonomy, the lack of security, and the frustrations she experienced by remaining in relationship with Ross.

Loretta's unhappiness illustrates the reality that although companionship is an essential ingredient in overall contentment and satisfaction in living, it only contributes to our happiness when we are able to get it along with the other requirements for a happy life.

Now, take a few minutes to rate your own level of satisfaction with respect to companionship by filling out the next portion of the GILS.

Please respond to the following statements in terms of your level of agreement:

A = Agree / SA = Somewhat Agree / SD = Somewhat Disagree / D = Disagree / NA = Not Applicable

| A | SA | SD | D | NA | | |
|---|----|----|---|----|---|---|
| O | O | O | O | O | 1. | I am satisfied with the level of companionship I receive from the people in my community. |
| O | O | O | O | O | 2. | I am satisfied with the level of companionship I receive from coworkers. |
| O | O | O | O | O | 3. | I am satisfied with the level of companionship I receive from my friends. |
| O | O | O | O | O | 4. | I am satisfied with the level of companionship I receive from my children. |
| O | O | O | O | O | 5. | I am satisfied with the level of companionship I receive from my parents. |
| O | O | O | O | O | 6. | I am satisfied with the level of companionship I receive from my spouse or romantic partner. |
| O | O | O | O | O | 7. | I am satisfied with the level of companionship I receive from my extended family. |
| O | O | O | O | O | 8. | I am satisfied with the level of companionship I receive from my pet. |
| O | O | O | O | O | 9. | I am satisfied with the level of companionship I receive from God. |

*Once this portion of the GILS is complete, score your responses by going through the following procedure:*

1. *Count the number of items marked "A" then multiply that number by 10 and fill in this blank* → _____

2. *Count the number of items marked "SA" then multiply that number by 7.5 and fill in this blank* → _____

3. *Count the number of items marked "SD" then multiply that number by 2.5 and fill in this blank* → _____

4. *Count the number of items marked "D" then multiply that number by zero and fill in this blank* → _____

5. *Add all of these numbers together and fill in this blank . . . . . . . .* → _____

6. *Subtract the number of items marked "NA" from 9 to fill in this blank . .* → _____

7. *Divide the number on line 5 by the number on line 6 to get your* **Companionship** *score . . . . .* → _____

*Once you have finished scoring your responses, you can interpret your score as follows:*

*7.6-10   You are satisfied with respect to companionship.*
*5.1-7.5   You are somewhat satisfied with respect to companionship.*
*2.6-5.0   You are somewhat dissatisfied with respect to companionship.*
*0-2.5     You are generally dissatisfied with respect to companionship.*

## INTIMACY

*Intimacy* is an interpersonal interaction which involves both affirmation and companionship. In an intimate encounter, we share personal aspects of ourselves and we experience a profound sense of being affirmed. Intimacy occurs when we share experiences, thoughts, or feelings which could be a source of shame or embarrassment while, at the same time, we receive feedback that we are adequate, competent, acceptable, or desirable despite what's been shared.

Because what we share in an intimate encounter may become a topic of gossip or possible public ridicule, we rarely find intimacy in the context of community relationships. One exception is what goes on with a priest, a minister, or a rabbi. These relationships provide opportunities to share personal thoughts and feelings because we have the assurance that whatever is revealed will be kept in confidence.

Intimacy also rarely occurs in commercial relationships. Sharing personal information with coworkers or a supervisor could have disastrous consequences if what has been revealed is disclosed to those we interact with on the job. We may also become embarrassed by personal revelations made to a hairdresser, a bartender, or any other person who provides some type of personal service and who is not bound to be confidential. On the other hand, we are able to express personal thoughts and feelings with our psychotherapist, physician, or attorney, confident in knowing there are laws governing what these professionals can reveal about what has been disclosed.

Some friendships have a value precisely because they offer opportunities for intimacy. Tina looks forward to spending Thursday afternoons with Alice. They usually get together for lunch at one another's apartment, and they spend the next few hours talking about what is going on in one another's romantic relationships.

Since family life typically involves many personal disclosures, opportunities for intimacy are frequently available in the context of family interactions. Hope tells her mother she's feeling fat, and her mother helps her stay on her diet. She would be mortified if her friends knew how she felt about her shape.

Even when family members do not live together they may be a primary source of intimacy. Angela spends at least an hour on the phone with her mother every day. She shares thoughts and feelings with her mother she would never disclose to her husband, her children, or even her best friend.

For many people, romantic relationships are their primary source of intimacy. A profound sense of intimacy can occur in sexual encounters. In a vital romantic relationship, this ability to share at a physical level is also lived out in revealing thoughts and feelings with reference to other aspects of life.

Although intimacy is not available in our relationship with pets, it can be an important part of a relationship with God. Mark delights in the intimacy he experiences in his faith. He feels free to share his thoughts and feelings with his Heavenly Father, confident he will be affirmed no matter how embarrassed he is over what he shares.

The absence of intimacy is isolation. *Isolation* is a profound sense of loneliness. This is the experience that nobody knows what we really think and how we really feel.

The absence of intimacy often motivates people to seek professional help. Joyce was admitted to the psychiatric ward after being found in her garage with the engine running. She felt she had no reason to live because no one actually cared about her. She was living with a marriage in which her husband never listened to her or seemed concerned about what she thought or felt. Her son was away at college. He never wrote or called. She couldn't stand her parents, in part, because whenever she contacted them, all they were interested in doing was complaining. The day she tried to end her life she realized she didn't even have a friend.

Equating happiness with intimacy can be just as problematic as living life without it. Although he had been married to Kristen for fourteen years, Marshall never felt as close to her as he felt to Ursula upon their first sexual encounter. Eventually, Marshall began believing the intimacy he had with Ursula was more important than anything else.

Telling Kristen he had fallen in love with another woman, Marshall moved out of their home and into his own apartment so he could spend more time with Ursula. Although he recognized he would suffer several losses from the divorce, he accepted the reality that he would no longer be living in the house he built, and he was unconcerned with the financial losses which he expected to suffer as part of a settlement. He knew he would have to pay child support and probably experience alienation from his kids. He also knew his parents would be dismayed with his decision, that they would probably side with Kristen in order to maintain their relationships with his children, and that he would probably have much less contact with them as a result. But none of these prospects deterred him from pursuing his relationship with Ursula.

Roughly two years after moving in with Ursula, Marshall entered psychotherapy. He had become fairly depressed. He felt he and Ursula still had a deeply intimate relationship. The sex was good, and he could talk to her about what he thought and felt. But lately Marshall found himself much less interested in talking or in listening to what she had to say.

Marshall couldn't quite put his finger on why living with Ursula wasn't as satisfying as it had been during their first year together. He thought it might have something to do with the stress he was under from working two jobs to keep up his child support and maintain the apartment where the two of them lived. He also considered the possibility that he was depressed over not being able to spend weekends at the lake since his boat had been sold as part of the divorce settlement. But, most of all, Marshall suspected his doleful mood had something to do with his inability to take his son along on fishing trips with his dad, the way Marshall and his father used to go with his grandfather when Marshall was a little boy.

What happened to Marshall is a good example of how intimacy only contributes to our overall contentment and satisfaction in living as long as we are able to find it while obtaining and maintaining the other core values which are essential to a rich and rewarding quality of life.

Now, take a few minutes to rate your own level of satisfaction with respect to intimacy by filling out the next portion of the GILS.

Please respond to the following statements in terms of your level of agreement:

A = Agree / SA = Somewhat Agree / SD = Somewhat Disagree / D = Disagree / NA = Not Applicable

| A | SA | SD | D | NA | | |
|---|----|----|---|----|---|---|
| O | O | O | O | O | 1. | I am satisfied with the intimacy I have with my friends. |
| O | O | O | O | O | 2. | I am satisfied with the intimacy I have with my children. |
| O | O | O | O | O | 3. | I am satisfied with the intimacy I have with my parents. |
| O | O | O | O | O | 4. | I am satisfied with the intimacy I have with my extended family. |
| O | O | O | O | O | 5. | I am satisfied with the intimacy I have with my spouse or romantic partner. |
| O | O | O | O | O | 6. | I am satisfied with the intimacy I have within a professional relationship, such as with a pastor, rabbi, or mental health practitioner. |
| O | O | O | O | O | 7. | I am satisfied with the intimacy I have with God. |

*Once this portion of the GILS is complete, score your responses by going through the following procedure:*

1. Count the number of items marked "A" then multiply that number by 10 and fill in this blank       → _____
2. Count the number of items marked "SA" then multiply that number by 7.5 and fill in this blank       → _____
3. Count the number of items marked "SD" then multiply that number by 2.5 and fill in this blank       → _____
4. Count the number of items marked "D" then multiply that number by zero and fill in this blank       → _____
5. Add all of these numbers together and fill in this blank . . . . . . . .  → _____
6. Subtract the number of items marked "NA" from 7 to fill in this blank . .  → _____
7. Divide the number on line 5 by the number on line 6 to get your **Intimacy** score . . . . .       → _____

*Once you have finished scoring your responses, you can interpret your score as follows:*

| | |
|---|---|
| *7.6-10* | *You are satisfied with respect to intimacy.* |
| *5.1-7.5* | *You are somewhat satisfied with respect to intimacy.* |
| *2.6-5.0* | *You are somewhat dissatisfied with respect to intimacy.* |
| *0-2.5* | *You are generally dissatisfied with respect to intimacy.* |

# Chapter 4

# CONDITIONS OF HUMAN EXISTENCE

The remaining core values are more complex than the ones we've reviewed so far. They consist of combinations of things, people, and events which we regularly encounter in the course of daily life. They are specific circumstances which contribute to our contentment and satisfaction in living.

## HEALTH

Physicians define health as a condition of the human body in which the organ systems function in harmony with one another to perpetuate life. Psychologists refer to health as the sense of physical and emotional well-being. In daily living *health* is the absence of pain, disease, and acquired disability.

When we enjoy good health, the human body is a source of comfort and pleasure. A healthy body enables us to do what we want to do when we want to do it. When we are healthy, we experience ease of movement and a presence to our surroundings which we tend to take for granted as we go about the activities of everyday life.

One way to appreciate how health contributes to happiness involves reflecting on what happens when you recover from an illness. Remember how good it felt when the pounding headache, sore throat, and aching muscles of the flu began to go away. The sense of joy found in simply going about the tasks of daily living with renewed vigor reveals how much health contributes to our overall quality of life.

The value of health becomes most evident when we encounter those who are not well. Florence suffers from chronic migraines. "Looking back on my life, I didn't know how happy I was before these headaches began. I was never a very active person, but I used to enjoy reading novels and watching TV. Now I get no pleasure from these simple things. I try to read, and I keep getting distracted; I try to focus on the book or the TV, but the pain just seems to get in the way. Some days I don't even pick up a book or turn on the tube because all I am aware of is the pain. These days it seems that my whole world is pain, pain, and more pain."

Like chronic pain, acquired physical disability is a condition which can continuously undermine our ability to experience contentment and satisfaction in living. While working as a painter Seth fell from scaffolding and suffered a severe back injury. He is no longer able to work, he walks with a cane, and he cannot stand for extended periods of time. "I hate my life," he exclaimed in his first session of psychotherapy. "I used to like my job, and I enjoyed cutting my grass, working on my house, and playing softball in the spring. But now I can't do any of that. I just look around and see other people who are enjoying life. I find myself wishing this never happened to me and wondering what reason I have for being alive these days."

Even in the absence of pain or disability, the presence of disease can undermine our quality of life. April considered herself lucky. A lump had been discovered in her breast. The surgeon assured her he was able to remove the entire tumor. But, she continues to be haunted by the realization that her mother lost both breasts to cancer and it also killed her aunt. "You know, I'm happy to be alive, but I have to admit, since the surgery I have never been as happy as I was before. It is like I've been handed a death sentence. I find myself thinking about dying at the strangest times. Like when I am doing things I used to enjoy, you know, walking in the park or playing with my kids. These days I wonder if I will be around when they go to the prom, graduate high school, or get married."

In addition to physical well-being, this core value includes mental health. Quinton was diagnosed with schizophrenia during his freshman year in college. He had been hearing voices, and he developed the belief his roommate was trying to murder him. Although he now takes medication which keeps him from hallucinating, he still has a hard time thinking things through. He was not able to stay in school, and he cannot hold a job. Since he was hospitalized, his buddies from high school stopped spending time with him, and he has been unable to make new friends. These days he spends most of his time sleeping and watching television. Occasionally, he considers ending it all by downing his bottle of pills.

Beyond the capacity to think clearly and to distinguish fantasy from reality, mental health also involves the ability to have appropriate emotional reactions to the events of daily life. Ginger was anxious most of the time. When she initially entered therapy, she attributed her apprehension to what she referred to "screwing things up" at work and in her romantic relationships. She was never confident she could go through the day without something blowing up in her face. "I'm not sure what the problem is, but people always tell me I'm overreacting when things don't go the way I think they should. Lots of people tell me I'm irrational and that my emotions have nothing to do with reality."

It is hard to imagine how we can put an excessive priority on health, but this can happen when we become obsessed with obtaining and maintaining physical well-being. Some people spend excessive amounts of time exercising and managing their diets while neglecting work and their interpersonal relationships. Others become continuously focused on attempting to determine whether they are ill. The time and money hypochondriacal people invest in seeking a proper diagnoses and worrying about their health often interferes with their ability to obtain and maintain core values they might otherwise experience with friends and family.

And then there are those whose lives have become extremely constricted as a result of a preoccupation with the possibility of becoming sick. Roseanne showed up for psychotherapy at the insistence of her supervisor. Over the course of the previous year she had become increasingly concerned with the possibility of becoming ill. She was convinced she was going to touch something with germs on it and that these microorganisms would be transferred from her fingers to the food she put in her mouth. She stopped going to grocery stores, and she spent most of her time, when she was not at work, cleaning her kitchen counters and food containers with antibacterial soap.

At first her husband had some sympathy. He would shop for food, and he was willing to run to the bank and do a few of the errands she used to do. But, as time went on and Roseanne refused to go to restaurants or to pump gas at the convenience store, he began to lose patience with her. He became constantly resentful, and his frustration developed to the point he rarely spoke to her.

At the same time, Roseanne's fifteen-year-old son and fourteen-year-old daughter avoided her whenever they could. When they found her cleaning, they would make fun of her. They referred to her as "a wacko" and "a nut case" when talking to their friends.

At work, Roseanne became distressed over handling the mail. Once she opened the envelopes she would spend fifteen minutes washing her hands in the restroom. She also felt she needed to wash them after she used the copy machine or the postage meter or when her boss handed her correspondence. Given her decreased efficiency, he finally told Roseanne he would have to let her go if she did not get help.

Although Roseanne was able to maintain her physical well-being, she was far from content and satisfied with life. By the time she entered psychotherapy, she had lost the affirmation of her husband, her children, her supervisor, and her coworkers. The companionship and intimacy she used to obtain from her marriage had also disappeared. Finally, she was also faced with the possibility of losing a job she used to enjoy and the money it provided.

Through Roseanne's experience we can see that health only contributes to our happiness when we are able to obtain and maintain it along with the other values which are essential to becoming and remaining happy.

Now take a few minutes to evaluate where you stand with respect to the value of health.

Please respond to the following statements in terms of your level of agreement:

A = Agree / SA = Somewhat Agree / SD = Somewhat Disagree / D = Disagree / NA = Not Applicable

| A | SA | SD | D | NA | | |
|---|----|----|----|----|---|---|
| O | O | O | O | O | 1. | I have a general sense of physical well-being. |
| O | O | O | O | O | 2. | I rarely feel physical pain or discomfort. |
| O | O | O | O | O | 3. | I rarely feel depressed. |
| O | O | O | O | O | 4. | I rarely feel anxious or worried. |
| O | O | O | O | O | 5. | I am confident that I will continue to experience physical and emotional well-being. |

*Once this portion of the GILS is complete, score your responses by going through the following procedure:*

1. *Count the number of items marked "A" then multiply that number by 10 and fill in this blank* → _____
2. *Count the number of items marked "SA" then multiply that number by 7.5 and fill in this blank* → _____
3. *Count the number of items marked "SD" then multiply that number by 2.5 and fill in this blank* → _____
4. *Count the number of items marked "D" then multiply that number by zero and fill in this blank* → _____
5. *Add all of these numbers together and fill in this blank . . . . . . . .* → _____
6. *Subtract the number of items marked "NA" from 5 to fill in this blank . . .* → _____
7. *Divide the number on line 5 by the number on line 6 to get your **Health** score . . . .* → _____

*Once you have finished scoring your responses, you can interpret your score as*

7.6-10    *You are satisfied with respect to health.*
5.1-7.5    *You are somewhat satisfied with respect to health.*
2.6-5.0    *You are somewhat dissatisfied with respect to health.*
0-2.5    *You are generally dissatisfied with respect to health.*

## REWARDING OCCUPATION

Human life requires work. Anthropologists tell us that for hundreds of thousands of years our distant ancestors spent most of their waking hours trying to satisfy basic needs. Foraging for edible vegetation and hunting animals was essentially a full-time job. The rest of the day was invested in fabricating clothing and securing shelter from the elements, wild animals, and other hostile human beings.

Once people figured out how to grow and harvest food it was possible for one man to produce more than he needed to survive. This permitted others to spend their days making tools, shoes, and other material objects which enhanced and enriched the quality of life. As time went on, more occupations developed as fewer farmers were required to supply food for greater numbers of people. Today, although few of us farm, we still need to spend our days doing some sort of work to get the money necessary to meet our basic needs and to obtain whatever else we require for contentment and satisfaction in living.

Most of us are occupied with a job or the practice of a profession. But, not all occupations generate an income. Homemakers, students, and priests have occupations even though they do not receive a paycheck for doing what they do.

Research reveals that one way work contributes to our contentment and satisfaction in living involves the degree to which we enjoy the tasks of our occupation. Anton works as a police officer. He likes going to morning report and spending the day in his patrol car. He finds helping people who are in trouble to be very fulfilling, and he relishes the adrenaline rush he experiences when he pursues those who have committed crimes. Anton even finds some gratification writing up his reports and making occasional appearances in court.

Kendra enjoys the tasks of homemaking. She looks forward to getting up early, preparing breakfast, and getting the kids off to school. She takes some pleasure in cleaning her kitchen, doing the wash, and vacuuming her living room. Although she hates to admit it, Kendra even takes some delight in ironing her husband's shirts.

While some people find the tasks of homemaking relatively rewarding, Molly can't stand washing dishes, dusting, or running the sweeper. She hates doing the wash, and she loathes ironing. As far as she is concerned, these activities are demeaning drudgery. She feels dissatisfied with her life and bristles when she is referred to as a housewife or a homemaker.

The second aspect of a rewarding occupation involves whether we have the aptitudes, abilities, education, training, and know-how necessary to successfully complete the tasks involved in doing what we do.

In addition to enjoying the process of selling real estate, Armando is also able to frequently make a sale. He has an engaging interpersonal style, and he can quickly discern the interests of prospective buyers and match them with available properties. In addition to this intuitive savvy, Armando has a good grasp of real estate law and the ability to explain complicated technical concepts to his clients in a way which they can easily understand.

Earl took over his father's electrical contracting business when his father decided to retire and relocated to Florida. Although Earl always enjoyed the tasks of an electrician, he now finds himself in situations requiring a different type of conceptual competence and an entirely new set of interpersonal skills. He is frequently anxious in negotiating contracts, dealing with customers, and supervising employees because he has no education in business administration and he has never been a people-person. Recognizing his own ineptitude, Earl is never happy when he is at work.

A third aspect of an occupation which makes a difference in our overall quality of life has to do with whether what we do results in a sense of accomplishment. When we can see we have accomplished something, we experience satisfaction with a job well done. A sense of accomplishment also provides positive reinforcement, engenders feelings of competence, and enhances self-esteem.

In addition to enjoying the tasks of homemaking and having the ability to do them well, Kendra also experiences a sense of accomplishment when she is finished with her daily routine. After dusting and vacuuming, she frequently takes a break in the early afternoon to appreciate the beauty and peace her home affords. Looking at her living room, Kendra finds a sense of fulfillment as she drinks a cup of tea.

Although Heather has the ability to handle the tasks of her job, she hates working as a cashier in a grocery store. It's not so much that she dislikes the tasks involved, as it is a feeling of futility. "All day long its scanning one item after another for an endless parade of people," she bemoans. "At the end of the shift I don't have anything but a paycheck to show for what I've done."

When we enjoy and are competent at the tasks of our occupation, and when we experience a sense of accomplishment in a job well done, there is a profound sense of contentment and satisfaction. Given the degree to which rewarding occupation contributes to our quality of life, it is easy to equate this value with happiness. As a result, some people spend the majority of their time and energy in tasks somehow connected with their work.

Winston was a very successful physician who practiced in a group with three other neurosurgeons. Following his residency, he continued to spend between sixty and seventy hours a week at the hospital while passing up opportunities to go to his children's birthday parties, ball games, and school functions. He rarely saw his wife, and when he did, he had no energy to invest in family activities. The day his youngest daughter was handed her bachelor's degree, Winston suddenly realized he barely knew her. He was overwhelmed with a profound sense of loss. He found himself regretting the reality that he had missed out on countless opportunities for companionship and intimacy with his wife and their children before the kids became adults.

As with other core values, rewarding occupation only contributes to happiness when we are able to obtain and maintain this value along with the rest of those essential to contentment and satisfaction in living.

Now take a few minutes to evaluate where you stand with respect to rewarding occupation by filling out the next portion of the GILS.

Please respond to the following statements in terms of your level of agreement:

A = Agree / SA = Somewhat Agree / SD = Somewhat Disagree / D = Disagree / NA = Not Applicable

| A | SA | SD | D | NA | | |
|---|----|----|----|----|----|----|
| O | O | O | O | O | 1. | I have mastered the skills required to successfully complete the tasks of my occupation. |
| O | O | O | O | O | 2. | I enjoy performing the tasks required by my occupation. |
| O | O | O | O | O | 3. | Completing the tasks required by my occupation gives me a sense of accomplishment. |

*Once this portion of the GILS is complete, score your responses by going through the following procedure:*

1. *Count the number of items marked "A" then multiply that number by 10 and fill in this blank*  → _____
2. *Count the number of items marked "SA" then multiply that number by 7.5 and fill in this blank*  → _____
3. *Count the number of items marked "SD" then multiply that number by 2.5 and fill in this blank*  → _____
4. *Count the number of items marked "D" then multiply that number by zero and fill in this blank*  → _____
5. *Add all of these numbers together and fill in this blank . . . . . . . .*  → _____
6. *Subtract the number of items marked "NA" from 3 to fill in this blank . .*  → _____
7. *Divide the number on line 5 by the number on line 6 to get your **Rewarding Occupation** score . . . . .*  → _____

*Once you have finished scoring your responses, you can interpret your score as follows:*

7.6-10    *You are satisfied with respect to rewarding occupation.*
5.1-7.5   *You are somewhat satisfied with respect to rewarding occupation.*

2.6-5.0   *You are somewhat dissatisfied with respect to rewarding occupation.*

0-2.5     *You are generally dissatisfied with respect to rewarding occupation.*

## RENEWING RECREATION

In many ancient cultures, people were required to rest their animals and slaves at least one day out of seven. This practice was based on the observation that when continuously worked, beasts of burden and human beings would eventually collapse and die. Today, scientific evidence supports the ancient realization that people need to have some sort of break from the labor of their lives.

Several studies show a connection between excessive work and a variety of stress-related illnesses. These conditions include heart disease, gastrointestinal disorders, and a number of psychophysiological maladies. Other studies connect continuous work with deterioration in emotional well-being. Burnout is frequently the result of overwork. In addition to a sense of exhaustion, those with burnout experience a pervasive sense of discontent and dissatisfaction with life.

While most animals rest by lying around and sleeping, human beings tend to engage in some sort of recreational activity once the need for sleep is satisfied. Anthropologists and historians tell us that in virtually every culture there has always been some socially sanctioned behavior people engage in for the mere pleasure it provides. Today there are countless forms of recreation including participant and spectator sports, playing various types of games, attending movies and plays, boating, biking, skiing, hiking, reading books and magazines, drawing, painting, listening to music, playing musical instruments, watching television, and simply taking walks to name only a few. Whether and to what degree recreation contributes to our overall contentment and satisfaction in living is determined by three aspects of what we do for fun.

First, to be truly renewing, recreation has to provide some sort of regular escape from the stresses of daily living. Nancy joined a golf league as a means of forcing herself to spend each Monday afternoon on the golf course, a place where she rarely thinks about work. Scott goes boating with his family almost every weekend in the summer. He finds floating down the river an effective way of removing himself from the heat and noise of the steel mill where he works. Taylor watches television every night as a means of decompressing from a twelve-hour workday as a retail clerk.

Renewing recreation is also an activity we look forward to while we are at work. As her week at the office unfolds, Nancy frequently imagines how she is going to approach some of the holes she bogeyed the week before when she plays next Monday's round of golf. Encumbered by heavy clothing and swimming in his own sweat while working around massive ladles of molten steel, Scott frequently finds himself visualizing the green trees lining the riverbank and his children swimming off the back of his boat on a sunny summer afternoon. Throughout the workday Taylor anticipates being able to push back in his recliner and watching one of his favorite television shows while eating some pretzels and sipping on a beer.

Finally, recreation is genuinely renewing if it renders us refreshed when we return to the tasks of living. Tuesday morning Jane finds she is reenergized as she returns to her secretarial duties. Having spent the weekend on the river, Scott goes back to work near the blast furnace with a renewed appreciation for life. When he watches television before going to bed, Taylor feels a lot less stressed at work the next day.

Not all recreational activities render us renewed when we return to our occupations. Loretta started using marijuana and binge drinking as a freshman in college. Relatively quickly she began spending weekends getting high. As time went on, she found herself waking up hung over Monday mornings. She had to drag herself to class, she experienced difficulty following the lectures, and she had a hard time making sense of her required reading.

Anton got into gambling as a means of having fun. Although initially his monthly trips to Atlantic City were very exciting, as time went on he found himself losing money and getting into debt. After each weekend he returned to work with a knot in his stomach, worrying about how to pay off maxed-out credit cards, trying to figure out how to conceal his losses from his wife, and wondering whether he should be attending Gambler's Anonymous.

Some people equate the pursuit of happiness with maximizing time spent in recreational activities. When we play too much, we typically don't have the time and energy to do what we need to do in order to get and keep other core values. As with each of the core values we have already reviewed, renewing recreation only contributes to our overall contentment and satisfaction in living when we are able to obtain this value along with the rest of what we need in order to become and remain happy.

Now, take an opportunity to evaluate the degree to which rewarding recreation is contributing to your overall contentment and satisfaction in living.

Please respond to the following statements in terms of your level of agreement:

A = Agree / SA = Somewhat Agree / SD = Somewhat Disagree / D = Disagree / NA = Not Applicable

| A | SA | SD | D | NA | | |
|---|----|----|----|----|----|----|
| O | O | O | O | O | 1. | I have sufficient opportunity to engage in activities which have the primary purpose of pleasing me in some way. |
| O | O | O | O | O | 2. | The recreational activities I choose send me back to the tasks of living with a sense of being refreshed and renewed. |
| O | O | O | O | O | 3. | I look forward to my recreational activities when I am involved in the tasks of living. |

*Once this portion of the GILS is complete, score your responses by going through the following procedure:*

1.  *Count the number of items marked "A" then multiply that number by 10 and fill in this blank* → _____
2.  *Count the number of items marked "SA" then multiply that number by 7.5 and fill in this blank* → _____
3.  *Count the number of items marked "SD" then multiply that number by 2.5 and fill in this blank* → _____
4.  *Count the number of items marked "D" then multiply that number by zero and fill in this blank* → _____
5.  *Add all of these numbers together and fill in this blank . . . . . . . .* → _____
6.  *Subtract the number of items marked "NA" from 3 to fill in this blank . . .* → _____
7.  *Divide the number on line 5 by the number on line 6 to get your **Renewing Recreation** score . . . . .* → _____

*Once you have finished scoring your responses, you can interpret your score as follows:*

7.6-10   *You are satisfied with respect to renewing recreation.*
5.1-7.5   *You are somewhat satisfied with respect to renewing recreation.*
2.6-5.0   *You are somewhat dissatisfied with respect to renewing recreation.*
0-2.5   *You are generally dissatisfied with respect to renewing recreation.*

## FREEDOM

The reality that freedom contributes to our quality of life is evident to anyone who has spent time around a young child. The smiles and giggles of a little boy doing what he wants to do when he wants to do it are an unmistakable expression of contentment and satisfaction with life. When mom stops him from acting on spontaneous mobilizations, his disappointment and tears dramatically express unhappiness and discontent.

As we grow up we realize freedom is not absolute. We learn that our right to the pursuit of happiness is protected by reasonable constraints on our ability to do what we want to do when we want do it. Part of maturing means coming to understand *freedom* in terms of self-chosen courses of action which do not interfere with the efforts of others to become and remain happy.

The connection between freedom and happiness is fairly obvious when we look at how living under different types of governments affects quality of life. Research reveals a correlation between reports of contentment and satisfaction and the levels of freedom a nation enjoys. People who live in countries where there are reasonable and appropriate constraints on their behavior tend to be happier than those living in settings where unreasonable restrictions on freedom are imposed.

Anna was born and raised in totalitarian East Germany. Shortly after the fall of the Berlin Wall, she reminisced about how she felt at the time that momentous event occurred. "You know," she said, "up until then I thought I had a pretty good life. I was happy the day I got married. I was even happier the day I gave birth to my son. But, looking back on everything, I have to admit the day they knocked down the wall was the best day of all. I mean, for the first time in my life, I knew I was going to have a taste of freedom. Nothing I experienced before could compare with how happy I felt that day."

While a free society is a significant contributing factor in our quality of life, the ability to express our thoughts and feelings without fear of being ridiculed, criticized, or rejected by others within our network of interpersonal relationships also makes a difference in terms of our overall contentment and satisfaction in living.

Rudy is a volunteer fireman. In addition to being available to respond to emergencies, he is also required to attend monthly meetings at the fire hall. During these get-togethers new policies and procedures are reviewed and members of the fire company are encouraged to participate in discussions about operations. In addition to the satisfaction he finds in the camaraderie, Rudy enjoys these meetings because he is able to share whatever's on his mind.

Melissa lives in a conservative small town. The center of her social life is the Antioch Baptist Church. After serious reflection, she has come to the conclusion she is going to vote for a candidate for Congress who holds the position that a woman impregnated by rape or incest should be allowed to obtain an abortion. Although she has strong feelings about this issue, Melissa does not feel free to express her opinion. She is convinced she would be ostracized by members of the church if she were to verbalize her views.

The degree of freedom available at work also contributes to our contentment and satisfaction with life. One thing Dwight enjoyed about his job is the flexibility he has in organizing his week. As a financial advisor, he has the freedom to schedule his meetings with clients at his convenience, and he enjoys the option of doing some of his paperwork in the evenings at home. This flexibility gives him an opportunity to coach his oldest son's softball team as well as to participate in some of the parent-teacher conferences and afternoon programs put on by the elementary school.

Sybil dreads going to work each morning. She spends the day entering insurance claim data into a computer terminal. Although she enjoys her work, is good at it, and obtains a sense of accomplishment, her supervisor is very rigid about the time Sybil is required to sit at her workstation. Sybil is told when to take her break and when she can have her half-hour lunch. She is particularly unhappy about being required to request permission to go to the restroom and being reprimanded when she spends more time there than her supervisor deems necessary.

Freedom is also a matter of the degree to which we are able to express ourselves in relationships with friends. One of the reasons Tina enjoys the times she and Alice get together is her ability to simply be herself. Tina always feels free to make suggestions about things they can do together even though other people would probably find many of her ideas immature, irresponsible, or just plain foolish. She also feels she can ask Alice questions about a wide variety of subjects without Alice looking at her like she is stupid or dumb.

After having suffered for years with chronic headaches, Cecelia found herself attending a faith-healing service. Although skeptical about whether prayer could accomplish anything, she let the minister pray over her while placing his hands on her head. To her astonishment the headache instantaneously disappeared. Remaining pain-free for a month, Cecelia came to the conclusion she had been cured by the Holy Spirit. She began going to church, reading the Bible, and studying Christianity. When she shared her enthusiasm with her best friend, Bonnie, Bonnie began to make fun of her. After repeatedly being called a Jesus freak and a church lady, Cecelia no longer felt free to share her thoughts and feelings with her friend.

The degree of freedom we are able to enjoy is also determined by how family members react to our self-initiated courses of action and how they respond to the thoughts and feelings we express. Christine enjoys her relationship with her mom. When she was a child, and even when she was an adolescent, her mother almost always supported Christine in her decisions as long as what she wanted to do was safe. Now that she is an adult, Christine feels that she can talk to her mother about absolutely everything without worrying that what she says could cause a rift in their relationship.

Upon entering his senior year of college Byron sought counseling on what to do about his career. Up till then he had assumed he would follow in his father's footsteps, becoming an optometrist and eventually taking over his father's successful practice. But, as time went on, he became disillusioned with the prospect of making a living as an eye doctor. He came to view optometry as a boring occupation with little to offer beyond the financial rewards. At the same time he was afraid to share his thoughts and feelings with his father because he expected his dad to become angry and reject him if his real feelings were revealed.

Our overall contentment and satisfaction is also a matter of the amount of freedom we experience in the context of romantic relationships. Laura is entering her senior year in college. She is on the verge of realizing a dream she has had for several years. At the age of forty she will finally have a bachelor's degree and looks forward to becoming a CPA. Laura also recognizes she would not have been able to achieve these goals without the support of her husband who actively encouraged her to return to college and to pursue a professional career.

Angelo finds he is frequently angry with Vivian. Although he thought she was neat and clean before the wedding, she stopped doing much housework after they started living together. Coming home to a sink full of dishes and clothes strewn all over the bedroom floor, Angelo has now become very resentful. He can't understand why Vivian is unable to take care of some of these homemaking tasks given the fact she only works a couple hours a day at a convenience store while he puts in a ten-hour workday. Angelo wants to tell Vivian how angry and frustrated he is, but he fears sharing his thoughts and feelings with her would result in her shunning him or refusing to have sex.

Some people equate happiness with freedom. They are typically unwilling to enter into any relationship which imposes restrictions on their ability to do what they want to do when they want to do it.

Arlo sought counseling in his mid-fifties. He had never been married and described a series of romantic relationships which had been fairly exciting but none of which lasted more than a couple of years. Looking back on his love life, Arlo realized he would always find some reason to get away from each of his girlfriends when she began talking about marriage.

"You know, up till now I never wanted to be married, have kids, and buy a house. It always seemed doing these things would lock me in. I mean, I wouldn't be able to go fishing and hunting if I had to answer to a wife. You know, I saw all those guys who couldn't take off for the weekend or go out drinking all night because the old lady would kill them if they did. I mean, I didn't want what they put up with all those years. But now, when I look at these guys and their grown kids, I think I've missed out on something important in life. I mean, now I feel kind of lonely and lost."

Like each of the other core values, freedom only contributes to our overall contentment and satisfaction when we are able to obtain and maintain it along with the rest of what we require in order to become and remain happy.

Now, take some time to evaluate where you stand with respect to the value of freedom by taking the next portion of the GILS which deals with it.

Please respond to the following statements in terms of your level of agreement:

A = Agree / SA = Somewhat Agree / SD = Somewhat Disagree / D = Disagree / NA = Not Applicable

| A | SA | SD | D | NA | | |
|---|----|----|---|----|---|---|
| O | O | O | O | O | 1. | 1. Any constraints that restrict my actions are reasonable, appropriate, and acceptable. |
| O | O | O | O | O | 2. | I can express my thoughts and feelings without fearing I will be rejected, ridiculed, or punished in some way by people in my community. |
| O | O | O | O | O | 3. | At work, constraints on my actions and the expression of my thoughts and feelings are reasonable, appropriate, and acceptable. |
| O | O | O | O | O | 4. | Among friends, I can express my thoughts and feelings without fear I will jeopardize the relationship in some way. |
| O | O | O | O | O | 5. | With my parents, I can express my thoughts and feelings without fear I will jeopardize the relationship in some way. |
| O | O | O | O | O | 6. | With my spouse or romantic partner, I can express my thoughts and feelings without fear I will jeopardize the relationship in some way. |

*Once this portion of the GILS is complete, score your responses by going through the following procedure:*

1. *Count the number of items marked "A" then multiply that number by 10 and fill in this blank*    → _____
2. *Count the number of items marked "SA" then multiply that number by 7.5 and fill in this blank*    → _____
3. *Count the number of items marked "SD" then multiply that number by 2.5 and fill in this blank*    → _____
4. *Count the number of items marked "D" then multiply that number by zero and fill in this blank*    → _____
5. *Add all of these numbers together and fill in this blank . . . . . . . .*    → _____
6. *Subtract the number of items marked "NA" from 6 to fill in this blank . . .*    → _____
7. *Divide the number on line 5 by the number on line 6 to get your **Freedom** score . . . . .*    → _____

*Once you have finished scoring your responses, you can interpret your score as follows:*

*7.6-10    You are satisfied with respect to freedom.*
*5.1-7.5    You are somewhat satisfied with respect to freedom.*
*2.6-5.0    You are somewhat dissatisfied with respect to freedom.*
*0-2.5    You are generally dissatisfied with respect to freedom.*

## SECURITY

At the most basic level, security consists of physical safety. It is the ability to walk down the street without being robbed, raped, or killed. It is being able to sit or sleep at home without being exposed to illness, injury, or death.

Research reveals that, like freedom, the degree to which we have security is, in many ways, determined by the society within which we are situated. People who live where government protects them from those who would threaten their safety and property report higher levels of subjective well-being than those who live where law enforcement does not provide adequate protection. People also experience a better quality of life when they live where government is effective in providing some safeguards against disease, natural disasters, and terrorist or military attacks.

In addition to safety, security includes confidence we will be able to get and keep what is essential to our quality of life. This means the level of *security* we enjoy is a matter of the degree to which we believe we can hold on to the core values we already have. It also involves confidence we will be able to get and keep core values we have yet to obtain.

Armando enjoys a high level of security. Having become the top salesperson at Dominges Realty, he is sure he will have a job as long as Mr. Dominges continues to run the agency. If for some reason it goes belly up, he is confident he will be able to find a similar position with another broker. His current employment also gives him reason to believe he will be able to hold on to his savings as well as the meaningful material objects which he and Manuela currently enjoy.

In addition, Armando has a good deal of security at home. He is sure Manuela will continue to love him, and he is confident he will always have the affirmation, companionship, and intimacy his marriage has so far provided. He assumes he will continue to enjoy the interpersonal values he finds in his relationships with his children, his extended family, and the network of friendships he has developed over the years. He presumes he will always be able to watch the Yankees, the Rangers, and the Jets, and he will be able to continue playing poker with his pals on Friday nights. He is reasonably confident he will also remain healthy.

Clark is a mid-level executive who has spent most of his work life in a major corporation from which he expected to retire. At fifty-five he learned it was going to be sold to a competitor. Since getting the news, Clark has felt uneasy and generally discontent. Faced with possible termination, he wonders where he will be able to find another job as rewarding as the one he already has. He also finds himself mulling over the lifestyle changes he would be faced with if he had to take a lesser-paying job. He frequently awakens sick to his stomach after dreaming about the possibility he may have to sell his house, give up his membership at the country club, and lose his current circle of friends.

Regina sought treatment for depression about six weeks after she discovered that her husband had been communicating with another woman on the Internet. After repeatedly denying anything was going on, Dino eventually admitted to making plans to get together with her. Stating he still loved Regina, he agreed to no longer communicate with the other woman. Despite this reassurance, Regina finds herself continuing to wonder how far Dino would have gone had she not intervened. No longer confident in her husband's fidelity, Regina finds she has lost interest in redecorating her home, an activity which previously brought her a great deal of joy. She is also haunted by a nagging awareness of how a divorce would impact her social life, her recreational opportunities, and the freedom she currently enjoys. For the first time since her wedding, Regina is generally dissatisfied with life.

As with the other core values, some people tend to equate happiness with security. By the time Dixie sought counseling she had been married to Ben for fifteen years. He was rarely home, and he almost never took her out. When he was around the house he spent little time with her, and he was frequently critical. Ben often told Dixie she was stupid and lazy, and he never affirmed her in any way.

Ben required Dixie to turn over her pay from the part-time job she had, working at a clothing store in a nearby mall. He controlled the checkbook. When Dixie needed money, she would have to ask him for it. She had to account for every nickel she spent.

Dixie rarely socialized with her girlfriends or members of her family of origin. Ben would give her a hard time if she did anything other than work outside the home. He finally consented to Dixie seeing a psychologist after the internist, who was treating her for irritable bowel syndrome, told her he would not continue providing care if she did not make an appointment.

In the course of the initial interview, Dixie was questioned concerning whether she ever thought about leaving Ben. "I think about it almost every day," she sighed. "But, those thoughts actually make me feel even worse. It's not so much that I would miss him; it's I don't want to lose my home and all the stuff I have. I can't imagine where I'd live or how I'd get by on the support I'd get from Ben. And, then again, what would I do for medical insurance? If I left he might quit his job. Without Blue Cross I couldn't get treatment for my IBS."

Dixie's story reveals how security only contributes to our overall contentment and satisfaction in living when we are able to obtain this value along with the rest of what we require in order to become and remain happy.

Now take a few minutes to evaluate your current level of security by completing the final portion of the GILS.

Please respond to the following statements in terms of your level of agreement:

A = Agree / SA = Somewhat Agree / SD = Somewhat Disagree / D = Disagree / NA = Not Applicable

| A | SA | SD | D | NA | | |
|---|----|----|---|----|---|---|
| O | O | O | O | O | 1. | In the future I will be able to maintain possession of or access to those material objects which I currently enjoy. |
| O | O | O | O | O | 2. | In the future I will have enough money to maintain a reasonably satisfying quality of life. |
| O | O | O | O | O | 3. | I will be able to maintain those interpersonal relationships which provide affirmation. |
| O | O | O | O | O | 4. | I will be able to maintain those interpersonal relationships which provide companionship. |
| O | O | O | O | O | 5. | I will be able to maintain those interpersonal relationships which provide intimacy. |
| O | O | O | O | O | 6. | I am confident I will continue to have the degree of health and emotional well-being I currently enjoy. |
| O | O | O | O | O | 7. | In the future I will continue to experience at least the degree of occupational satisfaction I currently enjoy. |
| O | O | O | O | O | 8. | In the future I will be able to continue at least the degree of enjoyment that my recreational activities currently provide. |
| O | O | O | O | O | 9. | I am confident future constraints on my actions will be reasonable and appropriate, and I will be able to express my thoughts and feelings with members of my community, workplace, and family as well as with friends and my romantic partner without fear of jeopardizing those relationships as a result. |

*Once this portion of the GILS is complete, score your responses by going through the following procedure:*

1. *Count the number of items marked "A" then multiply that number by 10 and fill in this blank*  →  _____
2. *Count the number of items marked "SA" then multiply that number by 7.5 and fill in this blank*  →  _____
3. *Count the number of items marked "SD" then multiply that number by 2.5 and fill in this blank*  →  _____
4. *Count the number of items marked "D" then multiply that number by zero and fill in this blank*  →  _____
5. *Add all of these numbers together and fill in this blank . . . . . . . .*  →  _____
6. *Subtract the number of items marked "NA" from 9 to fill in this blank . . .*  →  _____
7. *Divide the number on line 5 by the number on line 6 to get your* **Security** *score . . . .*  →  _____

*Once you have finished scoring your responses, you can interpret your score as follows:*

*7.6-10   You are satisfied with respect to security.*
*5.1-7.5   You are somewhat satisfied with respect to security.*
*2.6-5.0   You are somewhat dissatisfied with respect to security.*
*0-2.5   You are generally dissatisfied with respect to security.*

# Chapter 5

# THE MATRIX OF CORE VALUES

So far we have looked at how core values contribute to our quality of life. We have seen how failing to get or keep each of the core values contributes to discontent and dissatisfaction. We have also observed how equating the pursuit of happiness with attempting to obtain any core values without acquiring and maintaining the others results in a less-than-satisfactory quality of life. Now we will look at how happiness actually depends on all of the ten core values.

A *matrix* is that within which something else develops or endures. Since the ten core values are the set of circumstances within which happiness occurs, we can refer to all of them together as a matrix. Within the *matrix of core values*, quality of life is a matter of the degree to which we are able to obtain and maintain all, or almost all, of the ten core values more or less simultaneously.

Armando is happy because he is satisfied with the house he lives in, the car he drives, and the other material objects he considers essential to a satisfying life. He finds his work highly rewarding, and it provides him with enough income to support his lifestyle and render him feeling financially secure. He gets affirmation from the people he encounters in the course of the workday, and he obtains companionship from some of his coworkers, several friends, family members, and Coco, his Labrador retriever. His relationship with Manuela is his primary source of intimacy. He is in good health, and he has several opportunities for rewarding recreation. He is free to express his thoughts and feelings in virtually all of his day-to-day interpersonal relationships. He lives in a low-crime neighborhood and in a nation which respects basic human rights.

The relationship between happiness and the matrix of core values becomes evident when we observe what happens to those who experience a threat to, or loss of, one or more of their core values. Clint was rendered paraplegic at the age of thirty-seven when he suffered a spinal cord injury while working as a roofer. Although confined to a wheelchair, his wife continues to provide him with a fair amount of affirmation, companionship, and intimacy. He was retrained to become a computer specialist, and he is able to work from home. With the money provided by insurance he was able to get a car with hand controls and can now drive to the movies and professional baseball games which he has always enjoyed. Even though he readily acknowledges he would be happier if he had not been injured, he continues to experience a fairly high level of contentment and satisfaction with life.

Despite the deterioration in his health, Clint continues to be fairly happy because he was able to hold on to most of the other nine core values. The stability of his relationships with friends and family has enabled him to continue to enjoy all of the interpersonal values he had before he was injured. The insurance benefits and rehabilitation funding have helped Clint to return to the workforce, to hold on to his meaningful materials objects, and to have enough money to meet ongoing expenses.

His new career provides him with a rewarding occupation, and he is able to maintain a fairly high level of freedom despite his physical limitations. His ability to hold on to what he requires in order to be content and satisfied with life has provided Clint with an abiding sense of security.

Like Clint, Hugh sustained an injury which rendered him paraplegic at just about the same age. Six months after he was hurt his wife announced she couldn't go on living with him. She took the children and moved in with her parents who lived five hundred miles away.

The divorce settlement required Hugh to move out of the house he once built for his wife and family. He found himself living in a high-rise apartment with a number of elderly residents. He had little in common with his new neighbors, and most of the friends he had before he ended up living in a wheelchair gradually drifted away. Hugh became increasingly lonely and isolated.

Since Hugh was no longer able to work as a carpenter, the state office of vocation rehabilitation provided funding for him to enroll in a course to be trained as a jeweler. His counselor put together a plan which would allow him to finish the program and start his own business, selling merchandise over the Internet from his apartment. Too depressed to pay attention while in class, Hugh dropped out of school after the first three weeks. Thereafter he spent his days sitting in his apartment and watching television.

In his suicide note, Hugh wrote about how lost, useless, and hopeless his life had become. He reminisced about how happy he had been before he got hurt. He wrote about good times he had with his wife and fond memories of playing ball with his kids. He recalled how much he used to like working with wood and how he enjoyed playing pool and having a few beers with his buddies after work. At the end he talked about how he couldn't imagine ever being happy again. In what happened to Hugh we can see how the loss of a number of core values can lead to a profound sense of discontent and dissatisfaction with life.

If you've taken an introductory psychology course, you probably learned about the work of Abraham Mazlow. After studying what Abraham Lincoln, Eleanore Roosevelt, Albert Einstein, and a number of other outstanding and high-achieving individuals had in common, he put together a model for conceptualizing the way we obtain satisfaction in living. There are a number of similarities and differences between the matrix of core values and his hierarchy of basic needs.

In the broadest sense both of these quality-of-life theories are based on a set of requirements for contentment and satisfaction in living. Both theories maintain these requirements are universal—they are what all of us need in order to find contentment and satisfaction with life. In each, our level of satisfaction increases as we are able to acquire and maintain a greater number of these requirements.

Several of the same requirements appear in both theories. Those things which satisfy basic biological needs in the hierarchy are included in the matrix as some of our meaningful material objects. Mazlow's reference to reputation and self-esteem are aspects of the core value of affirmation. A sense of belonging and a need to be loved are contained in the core values of companionship and intimacy. Both theories recognize security as essential to contentment and satisfaction with life.

On the other hand, some of the requirements contained in the matrix are not included in Mazlow's hierarchy. The hierarchy makes no mention of meaningful material objects, other than those which satisfy basic biological needs. It does not explicitly refer to money. Also missing are the core values of health, rewarding occupation, renewing recreation, and a full appreciation for the role freedom plays in determining overall contentment and satisfaction with life.

Another difference between the hierarchy and the matrix is the significance placed on actualizing our potentials for self-development. Within the hierarchy self-actualization is required for complete satisfaction in living. Self-actualization is not one of the core values in the matrix. This means that within this theory it is possible to become and remain happy without necessarily becoming self-actualized.

Finally, each of these quality-of-life theories has a different way of conceptualizing how we go about obtaining and maintaining the requirements for contentment and satisfaction in living. Within Mazlow's hierarchy, a need for some of the requirements only emerges after others have been obtained. Within the matrix, contentment and satisfaction with life is a matter of the degree to which we are able to acquire and maintain all, or almost all, of the requirements for happiness, more or less, simultaneously.

## LIFE SATISFACTION

Since you now see how the ten core values form the matrix within which happiness occurs, you are ready to calculate a score reflecting the degree to which you are already happy. This is accomplished by combining the scores on each of the section of the GILS into a Global Estimate of Life Satisfaction (GELS) score. You can do this by going back to the scores you got on each of the core value scales in the last three chapters and writing them on the appropriate line in the list of core value scores on the next page.

*Core Values*                                         *Core*
                                                                           *Value*
                                                                            *Score*

*1. Meaningful Material Objects* ................................. _____

*2. Money* .................................................................. _____

*3. Affirmation* .......................................................... _____

*4. Companionship* ..................................................... _____

*5. Intimacy* ............................................................... _____

*6. Health* ................................................................. _____

*7. Rewarding Occupation* ........................................... _____

*8. Renewing Recreation* ............................................. _____

*9. Freedom* ............................................................... _____

*10. Security* .............................................................. _____

*Global Estimate of Life Satisfaction (GELS) Score* ... _____

Once you have filled in your core value scores add them together to get your GELS score. If one of your scores is zero because all items were market NA, multiply the sum of the other nine by 1.1 in order to obtain a prorated GELS score. If for any reason more than one score is zero because all items were market NA an accurate GELS score cannot be calculated.

Your GELS score ranges from 0 to 100. It reflects your current level of happiness. You can make a mark on the next page to see where you stand on the Range of Life Satisfaction.

*Range of Life Satisfaction Scale*

| 0 | 25 | 50 | 75 | 100 |
|---|----|----|----|-----|
| Dissatisfied | Somewhat Dissatisfied | Somewhat Satisfied | Satisfied | |

You can interpret your score according to the following classifications:

A score in the *satisfied* range indicates you are generally a happy person. Although there may be some areas in your life in which you are less than fully content, the degree of satisfaction you are currently experiencing means you are enjoying a rich and rewarding quality of life.

A score in the *somewhat satisfied* range indicates you are less happy than you would probably like to be. You have good access to several core values, but you are less than fully satisfied with your access to others. Your quality of life could probably be better than it is today.

A score in the *somewhat dissatisfied* range indicates you are currently unhappy. You have limited access to a number of core values, and you are probably less than satisfied with the degree to which you have been able to obtain and maintain most of the others. Your quality of life could probably be much better than it is today. If you are not already in treatment you could probably benefit from consulting a mental health professional.

A score in the *dissatisfied* range indicates you are currently extremely unhappy. In all likelihood your access to virtually all of the ten core values is limited. In addition to being terribly unhappy, you are probably also clinically depressed. Your quality of life could significantly be better than it is right now.

If you are not already in treatment you should consult a mental health professional.

If you would like to visualize where you stand relative to each of the ten core values you can plot your scores and connect the dots on the grid which displays your Profile of Life Satisfaction.

PROFILE OF LIFE SATISFACTION

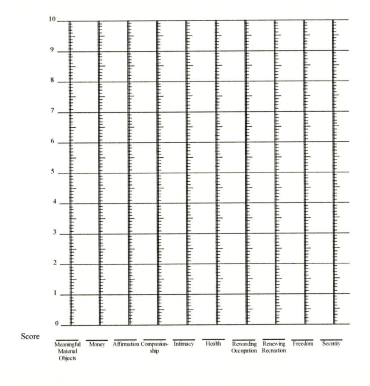

Calculating a GELS score is sort of like using a thermometer. Just as your body temperature provides some indication of the degree to which you are healthy, a GELS score indicates the degree to which you are happy. Yet neither of these measurements tells you anything about how you got to be as healthy or as happy as you are. What's more, neither provides information about what you can do to become healthier or happier.

Up to this point we have been reviewing what we must have in order to become and remain happy. The rest of this book deals with how we go about getting and holding on to happiness. If you are currently less than satisfied with your overall quality of life, you are now going to learn about how to improve your level of happiness. If you are generally satisfied, you will learn how to hold on to your high-quality life.

## MENTAL PROCESSES

Research reveals that how we perceive, evaluate, and think about the things, people, and the events of daily living impacts our contentment and satisfaction with life. Being able to recognize the role priorities, expectations, attitudes, and certain patterns of thought play in how we deal with core values enables you to determine whether and to what degree these mental processes are influencing your current level of happiness. Insight into these mental processes may also give you the power to actually enhance your quality of life.

While we all need to get and keep all ten core values in order to be content and satisfied, not all values have the same priority for each of us. Money has a higher priority than recreation for Morgan, while recreation has a higher priority than money for Craig. This means Morgan will have to have more money than Craig in order to be happy while Craig's happiness will require more recreation than Morgan's.

Sometimes being less than fully satisfied with life results from the relative priority we place on a particular core value. Phoebe had been an outstanding tennis player in high school. She won several trophies, and she was voted most valuable player two years in a row. When she went to college, she received a partial scholarship to be a member of the tennis team. After graduation she found a job as a high school English teacher, got married, had two children, and settled down to life in the suburbs.

Since tennis was so important to her, Phoebe joined a highly competitive women's tennis league. Although initially she held her own, her competitive capacities deteriorated as she began to get older, and she found herself playing against younger women who were in better shape. In order to keep up, Phoebe practiced two hours two nights a week while her husband stayed at home to watch the kids and help them with their homework. When Phoebe finally got home, she was frequently stressed trying to spend time with her children, keep up with her share of the housework, complete her lesson plans, and get her students' papers graded.

Calculating her GELS score, Phoebe was shocked to discover that it was 68. Looking over her Profile of Life Satisfaction, she was surprised to find her renewing recreation score was 2.5. In looking at what she endorsed on the items in this section of the GILS, she realized that even though tennis took up nearly twelve hours a week, her responses indicated she did not enjoy the time she was playing tennis, and she was no longer looking forward to practice and competitions.

In analyzing her scores Phoebe recognized she was placing too much priority on tennis. She realized that while this sport used to be very important to her, it had now become a source of discontent and dissatisfaction. She concluded she was at a stage in her life when other aspects of living should have a higher priority than they had for her up till then.

Deciding to shift her priorities, Phoebe started playing tennis with a group of women who were roughly her age and who were significantly less skilled and less aggressive. Quitting her twice-a-week practices, she was able to spend more time with her family. This change in her priorities also resulted in a more leisurely attitude towards the tasks of homemaking and what she needed to be doing for work.

After a few months, Phoebe filled out another GILS and calculated her GELS. To her surprise, her GELS score had risen to 86. Not only had the rewarding recreation score gone from 2.5 to 10, but her scores on companionship, intimacy, and rewarding occupation were also higher than they had been.

If you are generally satisfied with life, your priorities are probably more or less appropriate. If you are less than fully satisfied, you might want to reflect on the relative priority you are giving to each of your core values. Like Phoebe, you may conclude that a change in the priority you are placing on any of your core values may make a difference in your overall quality of life.

Expectations are other mental processes affecting our overall satisfaction and contentment in living. Expectations are ideas about how the things, people, and events of daily life are supposed to be. Realistic expectations are based on an understanding of what typically occurs given the actuality of the circumstances within which we are situated. When we have realistic expectations, we tend to be relatively happy as long as what we have is relatively consistent with those expectations.

Asked whether her marriage fulfilled her expectations, Theresa enthusiastically responded, "It's everything I thought it would be." Having grown up in a family where continuous marital conflict eventually led to divorce, Theresa entered marriage hoping she and Chris would get along better than her parents. She was convinced she could do a better job holding up her end of the relationship, and she expected Chris to treat her better than her dad had treated her mom. Although what went on between them wasn't always the stuff of romance novels, her marriage was more or less consistent with the way she thought it was supposed to be.

Unrealistic expectations are based on hopes, dreams, fantasies, or idealizations which are not well-rooted in what typically occurs. When we operate on unrealistic expectations, the things, people, and events we encounter in daily living do not conform to the way we believe they are supposed to be. Consequently, we frequently find ourselves becoming disappointed, discontent, and dissatisfied.

One year after the wedding, Audrey was relatively unhappy with Bruce. While he was quite attentive before they got married, as the months passed he paid less and less attention to her. Even though Bruce continued to frequently tell Audrey he loved her, to take her out every Saturday night, and to spend at least half an hour talking with her every day, she was constantly unhappy. Her marital discontent was rooted in the disappointment she experienced because she expected Bruce to kiss her as much as he did when they were dating, to spend most of every evening and all day Sunday with her, and to take her out dancing on Friday as well as on Saturday nights.

If you are currently satisfied with life, your expectations are probably fairly realistic. On the other hand, if you are less than fully satisfied, you may want to look at where and how your expectations are playing a role in your current level of discontent. One way of doing this consists of reviewing your Profile of Life Satisfaction to identify your greatest sources of discontent. Next, look at the items of the GILS which contributed to your lowest scores and ask yourself what you expect relative to what you have. Once you have identified your expectations make some effort at evaluating the degree to which they are realistic.

Determining whether your expectations are realistic may involve doing some homework in order to find out what the norms are with respect to these expectations. This may consist of looking at other people who are similarly situated and examining what you have or are doing relative to what they have or what they do. This could also involve consulting a professional who has specialized knowledge in the area where you suspect an expectation may not be well-rooted in reality.

If you have been operating with unrealistic expectations, making them more realistic can actually enrich your overall level of happiness. When Audrey and Bruce consulted a marriage counselor, she was informed that some of her expectations about how her husband should treat her were relatively unrealistic. She learned that as marriages mature, levels of affection typically decline as does the amount of time the couples spend together. As Audrey discovered that what was happening in her marriage did not indicate Bruce was losing interest, her scores on the items of the GILS measuring her levels of satisfaction in terms of affirmation, companionship, and intimacy significantly improved. She was more content in her marriage, and she was more satisfied with life.

Attitudes are a more basic mental process affecting our overall level of happiness. Attitudes are relatively enduring ways we approach the things, people, and events we encounter in daily life. In the broadest sense, we tend to approach life with either positive or negative attitude.

When we approach the world with positive attitude, we pay attention to what is present. When we look at the glass of water, we see it as being half full. We focus our attention on the good things in our circumstances, and we overlook what's not there. We are optimistic about the future, and we approach the world with confidence we can get and hold on to what we need to become and remain happy.

Theresa is a person with positive attitude. She appreciates the apartment she shares with Chris as well as their furniture and the car they drive. She is very aware of how much she enjoys the time she spends with Chris, and she is conscious of the fact that he frequently compliments her and demonstrates his affection in a number of other ways. Even though she had been unable to get a position where she would be paid for having her bachelor's degree, she finds her job as a waitress rewarding. She appreciates the degree of freedom she finds in her work as well as in her marriage. She is grateful for the overall level of security she enjoys.

When we approach life with negative attitude, our attention is focused on what is not present. We describe that glass as being half empty. We tend to focus on what we want but do not have. We are pessimistic about the future, and we approach life expecting to be forever discontent and dissatisfied.

When Jerry calculated his GELS, he obtained a score of 48. Although he earns enough money to provide for his family, he is dissatisfied because he does not have a bigger home on a larger lot. Even though he makes six figures, he is unhappy with his income because a friend he went to college with is making at least twice what he earns. Despite several promotions and consistent positive performance appraisals, Jerry broods over not having been further advanced and the reality that he does not have a larger office. Having been repeatedly assured his job is secure, Jerry also frets over the possibility he may be terminated if the corporation decides to downsize.

The fact that Jerry is dissatisfied despite having obtained and maintained several of the ten core values indicates his attitude is playing a significant role in his overall level of happiness. A change in attitude would result in him being much more satisfied even though objectively his circumstances remain the same. He could accomplish this change in attitude by making an effort to focus his attention on the benefits of his current situation and trying to appreciate what he has rather than on what he has yet to obtain.

If you are currently relatively satisfied you probably already have a generally positive attitude toward living. If you are less than fully satisfied, it would be useful to consider whether negative attitude is playing some role in your current level of discontent.

One way to explore this possibility consists of reflecting on the way your parents approached the world when you were a child. If they were typically talking about what they didn't have, if they were frequently pointing out shortcomings in themselves and others, if they were generally pessimistic, or if they thought that happiness was unattainable, you were probably influenced by negative attitude when you were young. There is a good chance you have internalized some of this negativity and that it is playing a significant role in your ability to find contentment and satisfaction in life.

Another way of looking into whether this mental process may be affecting your happiness consists of asking people you trust to give you honest feedback in terms of whether they observe you typically displaying negative attitude. Share the description of negative attitude contained in this book with some people who know you fairly well and ask for their sense of how well it fits your typical day-to-day approach to life. Only go through this process with a good friend, a family member, or a romantic partner who does not themselves display negativity in their own approach to the things, people, and events of daily living.

A third way to determine whether negative attitude is impacting your happiness involves consulting a mental health professional who has training in cognitive psychotherapy. This type of clinician can efficiently diagnose negativity. He or she can give you feedback with respect to the degree negative attitude is contributing to your overall level of discontent and dissatisfaction with life.

If you find negative attitude is undermining your capacity to obtain contentment and satisfaction in living, consulting a mental health professional trained in cognitive psychotherapy can also be a useful way of enhancing your overall quality of life. These practitioners can help you to clearly identify where and how negativity is playing some role with respect to your ability to appreciate each of the ten core values you already have obtained. They also have a number of methods to assist you in developing a more positive outlook on life.

In addition to priorities, expectations, and attitudes, certain self-defeating patterns of thought can also play a role in how the things, people, and events of daily living impact overall happiness. If you are currently satisfied with life, the thought processes you typically employ probably enable you to recognize you have all or almost all of the core values. If you are less than satisfied, you may be thinking in ways which undermine your ability to appreciate core values you have already obtained.

One of these self-defeating ways of thinking is referred to as *discounting the positive*. Marcus has low self-esteem in part because he believes others do not think of him as an adequate, competent, or acceptable fellow. He has harbored this opinion for as long as he can remember, and he continues to hold it despite the fact that those who live in his neighborhood see him as a good neighbor and those he encounters on the job are impressed with the quality and quantity of his work. His wife provides numerous indications he is a good husband, and his kids, on more than one occasion, have told him they are glad to have him as their dad. Marcus continues to feel inadequate, incompetent, and unacceptable because each time he is affirmed by any of these people, he tells himself the positive feedback doesn't really count because those who provide it are either lying or trying to manipulate him in some way.

Other self-defeating ways of thinking include *all-or-nothing reasoning* and *overgeneralization*. Ginger has had a series of failed romantic relationships. With each new boyfriend she hoped she had found the man with whom she could share the rest of her life. Despite the relatively normal amount of time and interest each of these fellows invested in their relationship, Ginger repeatedly found herself complaining that the man "never" wanted to spend "any" time with her and insisting that he was "only" interested in her for sex. Each of her boyfriends became so frustrated with her complaints and accusations that he eventually called it quits.

Sometimes it's difficult to determine whether our ways of thinking are undermining our capacity to find and hold on to happiness. One way to explore this possibility involves purchasing a self-help book on cognitive psychology. In reading it, you will become familiar with self-defeating thought processes, and you can get a better sense of whether they are playing some role in your current discontent and dissatisfaction with life. These books also provide several methods for reducing or eliminating tendencies to engage in self-defeating ways of thinking. You may also benefit from consulting a mental health professional who has had training in the theory and practice of cognitive psychotherapy.

## BIRTH AND BEHAVIOR

While mental processes impact how we experience the core values we encounter in daily living, two other factors play an equally, if not more, significant role in our ability to become and remain happy.

Early in life how we are situated with respect to core values is determined by circumstances of birth. When Dean was born, his father was an upper-level executive in a multimillion-dollar corporation. As a child, Dean lived in a palatial home, he was taken on a number of trips to foreign countries, and he spent several months in the winter at the family's second home in Boca Raton. When he was young he had every toy he wanted, and as an adolescent he was provided with stylish clothes, an elaborate sound system, and a state-of-the-art personal computer. When he was sixteen, his father handed him the keys to a brand-new BMW. While growing up, Dean was constantly affirmed by his parents, other family members, teachers, and friends. He was healthy, and he spent most of his leisure time honing his game of golf and socializing with girls at the country club pool. All in all, Dean was very happy as a child.

Holly was born into entirely different circumstances. Conceived out of wedlock, she never knew her dad. She started life in a public-housing apartment with an alcoholic mother. Because her mom spent most of her money on booze, Holly grew up with few of the meaningful material objects she desired. Her mother was constantly disaffirming and provided virtually no companionship or intimacy. When Holly was ten, her mother dropped dead from a cerebral aneurysm.

Taken into the custody of a child welfare agency, Holly thereafter began a series of placements in a number of foster homes. In addition to experiencing little affirmation, companionship, or intimacy from any of her foster families, she had little positive feedback from teachers or students she met in a succession of new schools. Because she was always behind academically, Holly never obtained any satisfaction from her schoolwork. She had limited opportunities for recreation, she had much less freedom than the average teenager, and she had virtually no security because any day her caseworker could show up, tell her to pack her things, and take her to another foster home. In the absence of several of the ten core values Holly was fairly unhappy as a child.

As we mature, whether and to what degree we are able to obtain and maintain core values becomes more and more a matter of what we do or fail to do.

Dean's parents sent him to a prestigious university even though he had mediocre grades in high school. As the next three years unfolded, he failed out of three different colleges. Eventually, his father stopped paying for school. Dean next went through a series of jobs. None paid very well, and he never enjoyed the work. He changed jobs because he was repeatedly fired for poor attendance and inefficiency. Alienated from his family, Dean found his friends from high school drifting away once he was out of college and living in a low-rent apartment. His health deteriorated, and he could no longer afford to golf. His ability to do what he wanted to do when he wanted to do it eventually faded away as did his overall sense of security. By the time he was in his late twenties Dean was clinically depressed.

Although Holly always had difficulty with reading, writing, and arithmetic, she had an eye for color and possessed a knack for doing hair. She enrolled in the vo-tech program in tenth grade, and despite attending a number of different high schools she eventually mastered the skills of a cosmetologist. Once she graduated, Holly got a job in a styling salon where she worked at developing her abilities. Acquiring the know-how to work with tints and dyes, she eventually became the local go-to gal for color. Holly was able to earn enough money to rent a modest apartment and furnish it the way she wanted. To keep her figure, she began working out, and she started paying attention to what she ate. She developed a number of friendships, and within a few years she met a fellow and fell in love. He showered her with affirmation and provided companionship and intimacy.

On the weekends they would go dancing, and she found she looked forward to Saturday nights. By the time she was twenty-eight Holly had more freedom and security than she had ever had before. She was generally content and satisfied with life.

If you are currently satisfied, you are probably already doing what you need to do to get and keep each of the ten core values. If you are less than satisfied, you may be able to improve your overall contentment and satisfaction in living by doing what you can to get what you need in order to become and remain happy. A review of your Profile of Life Satisfaction can help you identify where to invest time and energy in an effort to improve your overall quality of life.

If one of your sources of discontent is *meaningful material objects*, improving your level of satisfaction involves finding some way to get the things you want but do not have. This may consist of spending time and energy actually constructing or producing something which would render you more content than you are right now. But, since we purchase most of our meaningful material objects, obtaining what will enhance the quality of your life will probably involve pursuing some course of action aimed at getting the money to buy them.

There are a number of ways of obtaining more *money*. If you currently do not have a job, you could look for employment. If you are already working part-time, you could find a full-time job. If you are working full-time, you might be able to pick up some overtime, take on a side job, or start some sort of supplemental self-employment to increase your income above your current wage.

Another means of making more money consists of pursuing courses of action which will enhance your earning capacity. This may involve further education or training. Or, it may involve investing more time and energy in an existing position or in your own business with the expectation of eventually earning a promotion or creating further business opportunities thereby generating greater income.

You can get more money by soliciting a raise. You could look for another position for which you are currently qualified and which offers better pay and benefits. In addition to earning more money you could sell or refinance something you already possess. You can take some of what you've earned and make investments which provide a productive rate of return. You can also make more money available by figuring out how to cut back on some of your current expenses.

If *affirmation* is a source of discontent, you can begin to pursue courses of action which are likely to provide more opportunities to get positive feedback. The most effective means of achieving this goal is to begin, or recommit, yourself to making a consistent and concerted effort to treat other people the way you would like to be treated. In addition, you can obtain greater levels of affirmation by doing what other people in your network of social relationships consider to be desirable or appropriate behavior.

In community relations, finding affirmation typically involves doing something which benefits the neighborhood or the community as a whole. In commercial relationships, affirmation results from doing what the organizations you work for consider to be desirable employee behavior. If you are self-employed, affirmation is achieved by providing a quality product or service in a reasonably timely manner for a price perceived to be fair.

In friendships, you can typically obtain greater affirmation by pursuing courses of action which demonstrate you are invested in the well-being of the person you refer to as a friend, companion, or chum. In family relations, affirmation follows from fulfilling the expectations with which families define the roles of mother, father, son, daughter, brother, sister, grandma, granddad, aunt, uncle, nephew, niece, and cousins. Within romantic relationships, you will be affirmed by providing what your partner expects from a man or woman who is in love.

You can even improve your level of affirmation by doing more within nonhuman relationships. If you don't have a pet, you might want to consider getting one. If you already have a dog or a cat, you can increase your affirmation by showing the animal more affection than you have been up to now. If you already have a relationship with God, you can get affirmation by pursuing courses of action He wants you to pursue. If you are a nonbeliever, you may want to consider establishing a relationship with Him.

If enhancing your overall level of satisfaction involves finding more *companionship*, you can accomplish this by spending more time sharing experiences with people whose company you enjoy and with whom you have common interests or concerns. You may be able to find more companionship in your community relations by becoming involved, or increasing your involvement, in some sort of religious, civic, or volunteer organization. At work, you could increase companionship by developing a more expressive relationship with one or more of your coworkers. You might be able to find more companionship with friends by making an effort to spend more time with an acquaintance who seems to share common interests or you can take the initiative to spend more time communicating with a person who is already a chum. You can probably obtain more companionship with family members and romantic partners by spending more time with loved ones and making an effort to be emotionally present to them when these get-togethers occur. Increasing the amount of companionship available with a pet may involve spending more time interacting with your animal. Increased companionship with God can be found in regularly spending time in prayer and meditation.

If improving your overall level of *intimacy* will enhance your quality of life, you can find more intimacy by making an effort to share the most personal aspects of yourself in the context of relationships where you already feel safe. In addition to risking self-disclosure, increasing opportunities for intimacy also involves listening to what others have to say and respecting the privacy of the intimate encounter by treating as confidential whatever has been disclosed in the context of the intimate interaction. If you do not find intimacy in a relationship where it should be, you can do something about rectifying what is going on. This may involve raising your partner's level of awareness about your need for intimacy or it may involve obtaining some relationship counseling.

If your *health* is a source of discontent, there are several courses of action you may consider. If you are suffering with an illness or disability which is not improving, you may want to seek a second or third opinion about the treatment you are currently receiving. If you have not been scrupulously following your healthcare provider's treatment plan, you should probably begin making a more concerted effort to do what he or she has prescribed. If you aren't already getting adequate amounts of rest and exercise, eating a healthy diet, and avoiding tobacco and the excessive use of alcohol, you can begin practicing these basic wellness principles. If you are distressed, you can take steps to reduce, or more constructively manage, the level of stress which you deal with in daily living. If you continue to be anxious or depressed, you should consult a clinical psychologist, a psychiatrist, a social worker, or some other type of mental health practitioner.

If you have a less-than-*rewarding occupation*, you can go through the process of evaluating what you don't care for in your current job and seeing if there are any changes which you can make within it to render greater satisfaction with your work. If you do not like the tasks of your current occupation, you could look for another means of making a living. This may be as easy and as simple as finding another job or it may involve going on for further training in order to qualify for a more interesting line of work. If your discontent at work has something to do with your current level of competence, you could obtain additional training or seek supervision or mentoring aimed at improving your level of skill. If you rarely have a sense of accomplishment, you could work on developing processes or procedures which might generate a sense of task completion in your daily routine.

If you currently have little *renewing recreation*, you may need to take more time to play. This could involve scheduling leisurely activities or investing time and energy in developing some new skills. In exploring what to do to recreate you should select something you truly enjoy and it should be an activity you look forward to while you are engaging in the day-to-day tasks of living. If whatever you are already doing for recreation renders you less than renewed when you are done, you may want to consider finding some other way of having fun.

If more *freedom* would enhance your satisfaction with life, you can make an effort to ensure that current constraints on your behavior are reasonable and appropriate. This may involve some type of legal or political action. Or, it may consist of moving to a location where freedom is more available. Within your network of interpersonal relationships, you may have to make others aware of the degree to which you feel what they do limits your ability to express your thoughts and feelings and/or prohibits you from doing what you want to do when you want to do it. If you cannot make headway on your own, you may want to consult a mental health professional trained in relationship and family counseling. Enhancing your overall freedom may ultimately involve ending relationships with people who continue to interfere with your ability to express yourself even after you make an effort at working on this issue with the person or persons involved.

If your level of *security* is less than satisfying, there are a number of ways to become more secure. If it is a matter of physical safety, you could pursue some course of action intended to remove or minimize threats to your physical well-being. If your insecurity has to do with meaningful material objects, you can do what you need to do to protect them from theft or destruction, and you can purchase insurance to compensate you for their possible loss. If it is a matter of money, you can take steps to protect or minimize potential financial loss. You can enhance your level of security within your interpersonal relationships by doing what you can to maximize the potential you will be providing affirmation, companionship, and intimacy to those with whom you want to maintain relationships. You may need to press for a commitment from persons who do not provide sufficient assurance they are interested in maintaining a relationship with you. You can find greater confidence about your health by practicing wellness principles, seeking regular checkups, and getting timely treatment when you are not well. Increasing your job security may involve efforts at improving your job performance or doing what you can to contribute to the stability of the organization where you are employed. It may involve finding another job or line of work which provides greater levels of security. You may need to pursue some sort of legal or political course of action to insure you will be able to retain the level of freedom which you currently enjoy, or you may need to challenge other people who threaten your freedom within your network of day-to-day interpersonal relationships.

Clearly, the process of investing time and energy in any course of action intended to enhance your level of satisfaction with respect to one of the core values will involve diverting these resources from whatever you are already doing to get and keep the others. This means that before pursuing any course of action aimed at improving your quality of life you should take a look at how what you intend to do will impact the balance of your overall matrix of core values. In chapter 10 you will be introduced to a program for Personal Strategic Planning which shows you how to go through this assessment in detail. It will enable you to predict how your efforts at achieving greater satisfaction with respect to one of the core values will impact your level of satisfaction with respect to the other nine.

Whether you intend to improve your overall level of satisfaction using this program or whether you decide to go ahead and use a more rough-and-ready approach, you need to be aware that the course of action you are considering may be one which you think will enhance the quality of your life but which may end up making you much less happy than you are today. In the next chapter I will share with you how to recognize certain types of behavior which frequently have this self-defeating effect. Becoming aware of these patterns of behavior is essential to your pursuit of happiness even if you are currently content and satisfied with life.

# Chapter 6

# SELF-DEFEATING BEHAVIOR

The research described in the foreword of this book reveals how people frequently pursue courses of action intending to enhance their quality of life only to end up becoming much less happy than they were before doing what they did. This research has also resulted in the discovery that all of these courses of action can be classified into seven basic types. Each type of self-defeating behavior *appears* to enhance the pursuit of happiness but *actually* frequently results in a threat to, or loss of, one or more of the ten core values.

## HEEDLESS BEHAVIOR

Heedless behavior consists of pursuing a course of action while, at the same time, being aware it poses a threat to one or more of our core values.

Cigarette smoking is probably the most obvious example of heedless behavior. Every pack of smokes sold in the United States carries a written warning that smoking cigarettes can cause lung cancer, heart disease, and emphysema. Whenever smokers light up they are knowingly pursuing a course of action which is clearly a threat to their health.

Other fairly obvious examples of heedless behavior include driving a car without wearing a seatbelt or while under the influence of alcohol, beginning to use marijuana or cocaine or heroin, and having sexual intercourse with a virtual stranger. Like smoking, each of these courses of action jeopardizes health. But, they are also a much less obvious threat to several other core values.

Even though he knew he had a few too many beers, Geno left the White Horse Tavern as he had every Thursday night for the past several years. He always took the back way home, and he had never seen the police. Although he knew he could be picked up for drunk driving, he couldn't imagine it would ever actually occur.

But, one night as he drove into the intersection of Waterside Avenue and Mount Pleasant Road, another car suddenly appeared in front of him. Stomping on the brake, he hit it broadside. Not quite believing what had occurred and realizing he was not injured, Geno got out of his car only to discover a pregnant woman sitting behind the steering wheel of the other automobile. She was not breathing, and blood was dripping from her nose. When the paramedics arrived, Geno's worst fears were confirmed. In addition to being arrested for driving under the influence, Geno was also charged with vehicular homicide.

A few days later Geno lost his job as a probation officer. In the following months he spent thousands of dollars defending himself, and he did some time in jail. In order to raise money to cover his legal bills and his family's living expenses he had to sell his house. In addition to losing a rewarding occupation, a substantial amount of money and several meaningful material objects, Geno also experienced a significant loss of affirmation, companionship, and intimacy which he formerly found in his relationships with his children and with his wife.

In her senior year, Saundra and three of her sorority sisters went to Cancun for spring break. She saw this as her last big fling before graduating, getting married, and starting life with her fiancé who would be finishing law school in a few months. With her wedding scheduled for June, Saundra originally had some reservations about the trip because Bill was not happy over the prospect of her spending a week with a bunch of drunken college students such a long way from home. But, by mid-February Saundra decided to go, assuring Bill everything would be okay.

On the fourth night in Mexico the girls went to a party with some boys from Chapel Hill. One of the fellows was fairly charming. As he started coming on to her, Saundra found herself becoming increasingly attracted. They continued drinking, and eventually he suggested they take a walk. One thing led to another, and they ended up back in his motel room. Before she knew it they were between the sheets. When it was over, Saundra realized he had not used a condom.

Feeling guilty for the remainder of her vacation, Saundra decided not to let Bill know what happened when she got back to New York. But it didn't take long for him to sense something was wrong. Within a week, he got her to confess. In addition to being emotionally devastated by his reaction, she began experiencing some physical discomfort. Her doctor delivered a diagnosis of genital herpes.

By late May Bill called off the wedding plans. He told Saundra he did not want to live with a woman he couldn't trust and who had a sexually transmitted disease. In losing Bill, Saundra not only lost the affirmation, companionship, and intimacy she once had with him, but she also lost the economic and material benefits she would have had if they had shared a life together. What is more, she was now aware that her opportunities for future romantic relationships were limited because another man may not be willing to marry a woman who would frequently be sexually unavailable and with whom he could not experience the full pleasure of intercourse.

Often heedless behavior is somewhat subtler than these examples imply. For months Amanda had been looking forward to spending a weekend with her husband, Ken. He had been able to get tickets to *Phantom of the Opera* in Toronto, and he reserved a suite at the King Edward Hotel. Planning to knock off early on Friday, they could drive up from Pittsburgh in time to have dinner at the CN Tower. They would have all day Saturday to do some sightseeing before going to the show. After a leisurely Sunday morning, they could leave midday and get home before it got too late on Sunday night.

Unfortunately, Ken's Chrysler blew a head gasket on Thursday afternoon. The parts needed for the repair would not be at the dealership until Saturday. Needing another way to get to where they were going, Amanda suggested they take her company car, even though she knew she was the only authorized driver and even though it was only supposed to be used for work.

All was going according to plan when suddenly Amanda and Ken found themselves in a multiple car accident on the Queen Elizabeth Expressway about fifty miles west of Toronto. Although several people in the other cars were seriously injured, Amanda was unhurt and Ken required only minor medical attention for the lacerations he suffered when the driver's side airbag deployed. The car was so badly damaged the tow-truck driver was sure it would be totaled. Renting another car, Amanda and Ken finished their drive to the city, saw the show, and drove back home Sunday afternoon.

Reporting to work Monday morning, Amanda shared the news with her supervisor, Paulette. When she got to work on Tuesday, Amanda was greeted by Paulette who ushered her into her office and confronted her with the consequences of what occurred. Paulette informed Amanda that since the accident happened in a country where the corporation had no business, there was going to be a major problem filing the insurance claim. Amanda was told she would be personally liable for the repairs to the automobile as well as any bodily injury suits initiated by the people in the car her husband hit. Paulette went on to say a corporate attorney was looking into whether criminal charges needed to be filed against Amanda and her husband as a means of protecting the organization from any exposure to litigation resulting from the accident. Finally, Paula instructed Amanda to immediately clear out her desk and leave.

When we are confronted with the consequences of heedless behavior, we often refer to what we did as stupid, dumb, or foolish. This implies that heedless behavior has something to do with limited intelligence or education. But, research shows there is no statistically significant correlation between heedless behavior and the level of intelligence or education possessed by the people who behave this way. This means that rather than being a matter of limited intelligence or ignorance, heedless behavior simply involves failing to think things through.

Regis was a primary care physician who earned his medical degree from an Ivy League University. He had been married to Peggy for almost twenty years. Although she was relatively happy early in their marriage, she became increasingly discontent as the two of them grew more distant over time. After putting in long hours at the hospital and the office, Regis eventually spent most of his free time in the company of other men he met through the country club. They would golf, go on hunting trips, and attend professional hockey and baseball games once a week or more. Whenever Regis was with Peggy he rarely talked to her. When she tried to communicate that she felt they had drifted apart, he told her she had unrealistic ideas about marriage and that she should grow up and stop reading her romantic novels.

Eventually Peggy went to a psychologist. In psychotherapy she became aware that her emotionally vacant marriage was playing a central role in her depression. In time, she came to the realization she could no longer tolerate living without companionship and intimacy from her spouse. She asked Regis to enter couples counseling with her. After he repeatedly refused, Peggy finally presented him with an ultimatum. Either they would go to counseling and fix their relationship or she was going to file for divorce.

Regis attended two sessions of couples counseling. The therapist informed him he needed to take Peggy's complaints seriously and he needed to make an effort to provide her with more companionship. Regis continued to insist Peggy's complaints had no foundation in reality, and he made no attempt at implementing the psychologist's recommendations. Four months after he dropped out of couples counseling, Regis came home one evening to discover Peggy had moved out.

At this point, Regis realized he needed to do something to save his marriage. He volunteered to return to counseling and do whatever was necessary to get Peggy to come back. Reluctantly Peggy agreed to one more session with the former counselor. In it, she announced that whatever love she once felt for Regis had long since died, and she could never imagine loving him again. As far as she was concerned their marriage was over. She had no interest in doing anything with him other than finalizing their divorce.

Regis found himself lamenting the loss of affirmation, companionship, and intimacy Peggy once provided. He also regretted the loss of his home and a substantial amount of money. He was angry with himself for having failed to heed Peggy's ultimatum. After all, he read about this sort of thing in his family practice professional journals, and over the years a number of female patients who expressed similar complaints to him eventually gave up on their marriages.

## SELF-EFFACING BEHAVIOR

Self-effacing behavior occurs when we pursue a course of action with the intention of making other people happy while ignoring what we need in order to become and remain content and satisfied with life.

Typically, the tendency to engage in self-effacing behavior begins in childhood relationships with parents and peers. It can continue during adolescence when teens defer to others whenever there is some sort of conflict of interest in peer relationships. In adult life this type of behavior can be observed when people regularly try to do whatever will result in someone else's contentment and satisfaction without asserting themselves when it comes to getting what they want and need. The net effect of self-effacing behavior typically becomes most evident in the context of an ongoing relationship with a family member or a romantic partner.

At midlife, Marie entered psychotherapy. She was depressed, and she had good insight into how she got that way. In the initial interview she described a life which revolved around trying to please her father. During childhood she worked hard in school so he would be proud of her. As an adolescent she rarely dated because he disapproved of most of the boys who wanted to go out with her. When she fell in love at college, she broke off the relationship because her father told her he would be unhappy if she married a man who was not Italian.

Although she wanted to be a lawyer, Marie majored in elementary education because her dad preferred that line of work. Since her father thought he would make a good son-in-law she married an Italian fellow, even though she wasn't sure she was really in love. She became disillusioned with her husband when she learned he was fooling around with another woman while she was pregnant with their second child. Wanting to leave him, Marie remained in the marriage because she could not find a teaching job and because her father did not want her to disgrace the family name with a divorce.

Looking back, Marie realized her life would have been different had she not made most of her momentous decisions based on trying to satisfy her dad. If she had married the man she once loved she might have been able to find some happiness in marriage. If she had gone to law school she wouldn't be financially dependent on her husband. If she had divorced him, she might have been able to find another romantic partner who could have provided the affirmation, companionship, and intimacy she wanted in a marriage. If she had made her momentous decisions based on what she needed to become and remain happy, she could have become a forty-five-year-old woman who was actually content and satisfied with life.

Brad was happy the day he married Sharon. He thought living with her would lead to perpetual contentment and lifelong satisfaction. Believing he would be happy as long as she was happy, he made most of his momentous decisions in terms of what he thought mattered to her.

Shortly after the wedding, Brad had an opportunity to take a transfer to southern California. He wanted to relocate, not simply because of career opportunities, but also because he liked sunshine and the beach. But Sharon preferred the Cleveland suburbs where the two of them were living a few miles from her mom and dad. Once he deferred to Sharon's wishes, Brad also went along with buying the house she picked out and her ideas concerning how it should be furnished and decorated even though the expenses involved required selling his boat and forgoing treasured weekends on Lake Erie.

Giving up a number of subsequent potential promotions, which would have required leaving Ohio, limited Brad's earning capacity. When there was any extra money he always went along with what Sharon wanted to do with it. Over the years, Brad was never able to afford another boat.

As he neared fifty-two, Brad became depressed. He had a job which he did not enjoy. He obtained little affirmation, companionship, or intimacy from his wife. And he had no renewing recreational activities. In making Sharon happy, Brad had generally neglected what he required in order to become and remain content and satisfied with life.

Ever since her children were born, Ella tried to make them happy. When they were young, she always prepared meals they liked to eat. Early on she let them pick out the clothes they wanted to wear, even though her daughter often took hours trying on one outfit after another when they shopped. As the children got a little older, Ella signed them up for a variety of sports. As a full-time mom, she invested several hours each week getting them to and from practices and games. She convinced her husband, Simon, they should buy a car for each of the kids when they graduated from high school, and the two of them went deeply into debt with college loans.

Despite the fact her daughter got into drugs and dropped out of school, Ella continued to help her with her living expenses while she and Simon had a hard time paying their own bills. When her son quit school and announced he wanted to start his own business, Ella convinced Simon to cash out the equity in their house to come up with the money to buy an ice cream shop because their son could not qualify for a loan on his own. Within a year the business failed, and Ella and Simon were left servicing the debt.

The consequence of living for the sake of her children caught up with Ella when Simon suddenly suffered a stroke at the age of fifty-five. No longer able to work as a mechanical engineer, he was left relying on disability payments which amounted to roughly half the income he received prior to becoming disabled. Faced with diminished cash flow and having no savings, Ella and Simon were forced to sell their home. In addition, Ella left behind the garden which had been her primary opportunity for rewarding recreation most of her adult life. She and Simon found themselves living in a tiny apartment far removed from her former neighbors and friends. Within a year, Ella was clinically depressed.

## NONPRODUCTIVE BEHAVIOR

Nonproductive behavior consists of spending an excessive amount of time and energy on courses of action which have nothing to do with acquiring or maintaining core values.

The effect of nonproductive behavior on our quality of life is often first evident in adolescence. Teens, who spend countless hours listening to music, watching television, or making phone calls, rather than doing homework and studying for exams, typically get poor grades. They lose affirmation from parents and teachers as well as opportunities for future rewarding occupations, the potential to earn more money, and the meaningful material objects, freedom, and security which that money could provide.

Similar losses are the consequence of nonproductive behavior in adult life. While at work, Justin frequently surfed the Internet when he was supposed to be preparing reports.

When his manager confronted him with statistics indicating he was spending roughly a third of his workday doing something other than the tasks he had been assigned, he found himself suddenly unemployed. In addition to a rewarding occupation, Justin lost affirmation, companionship, and intimacy with his wife who developed a fair amount of resentment over the changes in their lifestyle resulting from his inability to find another position with similar pay and benefits.

Alan quit his job at the brewery to have a more enjoyable occupation by starting his own furniture-reupholstering business. Once he became self-employed, he began getting up at a little later every morning and spending roughly two hours drinking coffee, smoking cigarettes, reading the newspaper, and watching television talk shows before starting his workday. After about two hours of stretching and tacking fabric, he would typically take an hour for lunch. In the afternoon, he would put in three hours of work before knocking off around five. After drinking a few beers, Alan lost whatever momentum he might have had and spent the evening watching television, playing with his kids, or hanging out with his friends at the Elks.

Quite skilled at his work, Alan had little difficulty obtaining furniture to reupholster. But, he was terrible at getting finished pieces back to his customers in a reasonable amount of time. Eventually it became clear that he was unable to make enough money to support himself and his family. Finally, after nearly a year of badgering from his wife, Alan went back to his job on the bottling line. Alan's insufficient investment of time and energy in the tasks required to develop and sustain his business resulted in his failure to acquire a rewarding occupation as well as the money, freedom, and security which comes from being successfully self-employed.

Although most nonproductive behavior is relatively pleasurable, it is not identical with renewing recreation.

Engaging in some activity for the mere pleasure it provides is rewarding recreation when we have already done what needs to be done in order to get and keep what we require in order to become and remain happy. Recreational activity becomes nonproductive behavior when we do what we do for fun at the same time we need to be investing time and energy in a course of action which would enable us to get or keep one or more of the ten core values.

While the negative consequences of nonproductive behavior are fairly obvious in the world of work, they also occur in aspects of our life which have nothing to do with an occupation. Once his first daughter was born Merritt began to do some light carpentry after hours while working as a draftsman in a moderately sized architectural firm. The extra money came in handy, and he and Betsy began to rely on this additional income. As time went on, Merritt began taking on bigger jobs, and eventually he decided to build a house which he could sell for a substantial profit. Although the job did not net as much as he expected, he discovered he could actually handle a project this size and decided to try it again. Within a few years Merritt found himself building a series of homes. He worked nights and weekends while he held on to his day job in order to keep the benefits.

Although Merritt was making good money and he was providing more for his family, he now had little time to spend with his wife and children. Countless opportunities for companionship and intimacy with them slipped away almost every day. His demanding schedule left Merritt with no time for recreation, and he put on nearly one hundred pounds because he invested no effort at working on controlling his weight. As he approached middle age, Merritt had become successful in business, but he was far from content and satisfied with life.

Sometimes nonproductive behavior is a matter of simply not having enough time and energy to complete the tasks required to achieve the value a course of action is intended to provide. As a single mother of three elementary school children who was working full-time as a legal secretary, Carlotta decided to become a part-time real estate agent in order to generate some extra income. After completing her training, she got on with a broker who was sympathetic to her circumstances and agreed to let her work two nights a week and one day on the weekends.

For a while, Carlotta was able to put in a full day at work, come home to make dinner for the kids, oversee the cleanup, and put in a load in the wash or vacuum the living room floor before setting out for the real estate office where she took calls or showed houses between seven and nine on Tuesday and Thursday nights. Every other Saturday, she would try to cultivate clients. On alternating Sundays she would typically handle an open house.

As time went on, Carlotta's scheduled began to take a toll on her. She was too exhausted to get all the housework done, and she was losing contact with her kids. She started calling off a couple of evenings a month and just about every other weekend. Not having the time or energy to cultivate relationships with potential buyers, she failed to make a sale. After nearly two years Carlotta decided to give up trying to sell real estate. She realized that since she could not invest enough time and energy to succeed in this line of work, continuing with it was a nonproductive use of the time and energy she was already investing.

## DISRESPECTFUL BEHAVIOR

Our happiness can only be achieved when we live in a social setting which supports the principle that each person is entitled to the pursuit of happiness. In order to ensure we are not infringing on one another's attempts at becoming and remaining happy, political philosophers have developed the concept of human rights. These are the right to life, freedom, property, and privacy. Disrespectful behavior consists of pursuing a course of action which violates any of these basic rights.

Respect for another person's life is rooted in the realization that we are biological entities. This means we are susceptible to death, injury, and disease. The most obvious violation of the right to life involves pursuing a course of action which causes another person to be killed, to be injured, or to become, in some sense, diseased.

When we engage in homicide or assault or when we act with indifference to the safety of others, we frequently suffer a loss of freedom. In addition, we acquire a criminal record which undermines our ability to get and keep a number of other core values. The suspicion aroused by the mere fact of being identified as a criminal results in a significant loss of affirmation, companionship, and intimacy in community, commercial, family, and romantic relationships. It also tends to limit employment opportunities, thereby interfering with our ability to obtain a rewarding occupation, money, and the meaningful materials objects which that money could provide.

While most of us cannot imagine committing these crimes, not all behavior which threatens or violates another person's bodily integrity is a type of criminal activity.

Edgar exposed his wife to a sexually transmitted disease by having intercourse with her after being with another woman. When his wife discovered she was infected, he lost the affirmation, companionship, and intimacy which had previously been part of their relationship. When she obtained a divorce, Edgar also lost a home which he loved, a fair amount of money, and ongoing contact with his kids.

Candace didn't bother securing her two young sons in infant seats when she jumped into the car to go to the convenience store. At a sudden stop her youngest son flew forward, hit his head, and suffered a neck injury which rendered him permanently confined to a wheelchair. Candace lost a fair amount of affirmation as a mom, as well as a significant level of companionship and intimacy with her husband who was deeply resentful over her role in the injury to their son. In addition, having to deal with her son's daily need for physical care, Candace was rarely able to do what she wanted to do when she wanted to do it.

While driving back from the beach, Calvin and Bridget got into one of their frequent arguments over her former affair with a coworker. As Calvin became increasingly enraged, he started speeding while telling Bridget he was about to take both of them out by driving into a concrete wall. Terrified, Bridget sat helplessly, watching the speedometer hit 125 miles an hour while praying for her life.

In time, Calvin calmed down. They got home without ending up in a wreck. But, for Bridget, things would never be the same. She realized that when driving at such a dangerous speed, Calvin had no respect for her life. Thereafter she found herself thinking about how he could hurt her if he once again became enraged. Concluding she could no longer live with a man who was a threat to her physical well-being, Bridget moved out and filed for divorce a few months later.

Behaviors that fail to respect the freedom of others are those which unnecessarily interfere with their ability to do what they want when they want to do it. The most obvious examples are rape, kidnapping, and imprisonment. While each of these activities results in the threat to, or loss of, core values which are the consequence of being convicted of a crime, otherwise law-abiding citizens sometimes find themselves in serious legal trouble by failing to respect this basic right.

On their second date, Alex and Marian ended up at his apartment. They both had a little too much to drink, and eventually they found themselves entangled with one another on the couch. Sensing Marian wanted to make love, Alex began to attempt intercourse. As she became aware of what was happening, she told him she did not want things to go all the way. Ignoring her resistance, Alex was subsequently charged with indecent assault.

Fritz and his wife, Lena, were having one of their many arguments in the bedroom of their apartment. At some point Lena told Fritz the conversation was over. She expressed an interest in leaving the room. He responded by standing in front of the door and insisting she continue to listen to what he had to say. For nearly an hour Fritz continued to berate his wife with a series of accusations and to recount a number of past incidents in which she did something which made him mad. When he finally let her out, Lena took off for the women's shelter where she was assisted in obtaining a court order barring Fritz from living in their home.

Even if failing to respect another person's freedom has no legal consequences, significant losses can result from engaging in this type of self-defeating behavior.

Isabella and her daughter, Consuela, were in constant conflict. For years they had been fighting over almost everything and, as Consuela got older, the battling became even more intense. When Consuela was sixteen, Isabella took her to a psychologist. She complained that Consuela had been defying her authority since she developed a mind of her own at the age of two. Consuela maintained her mother simply didn't understand teenagers and that she was having a problem recognizing Consuela was growing up.

The psychologist informed Isabella that parenting an adolescent involves progressively permitting greater degrees of freedom and that with his help she could learn how to determine how much freedom was age appropriate. Displeased with his treatment plan, Isabella decided to seek the services of the juvenile court. By embellishing descriptions of Consuela's oppositional behavior and fabricating allegations about her whereabouts and activities, Isabella was able to have Consuela placed on probation. Thereafter, Isabella prevented Consuela from engaging in many age-appropriate behaviors by threatening her with placement in a juvenile facility.

On her eighteenth birthday, Consuela moved out of Isabella's house and went to live with the family of a friend. When she finished high school she got a job as a secretary. She was able to save enough money to move to another state. Wanting nothing to do with her mother, Consuela completely severed communication with Isabella. She never visited, wrote, or called. As a consequence of not respecting Consuela's freedom during adolescence, Isabella lost whatever affirmation, companionship, and intimacy she could have found in a relationship with her daughter as an adult.

Russell and Norma married right after high school. In the early days Russell was able to land a job with the police department, and Norma worked as a sales clerk at a department store. Once they had their first child Norma became a stay-at-home mom. As the years passed and the kids went off to school, Norma found herself becoming bored as a full-time homemaker. She decided to go back to work but quickly discovered she no longer enjoyed retail sales.

Thinking she would like to be a nurse, Norma looked into taking some classes at the community college to see if she could get into nursing school. When she shared her interest with Russell, he became upset. He told her he did not want to spend the money on tuition, and he insisted she was not smart enough to be a nurse. Despite his objections, Norma started school and discovered she was able to succeed.

As time went on, Russell began complaining about the time Norma spent at the college, studying and preparing for exams. He told her she was a lousy mother and wife because she was not keeping the house at the same level of neatness it had been before she started school. He also made fun of her for wanting to better herself, and he began to accuse her of fooling around with other men when she was not at home. When Norma finally became a nurse, she filed for divorce because she was no longer willing to put up with Russell's emotional abuse. As a result of his disrespect for Norma's freedom, Russell lost the affirmation, companionship, and intimacy which he once obtained from her.

Respect for another person's property consists of only taking or doing something with what belongs to another when we have the permission of the owner. Clear examples of failing to respect another person's property include robbery, theft, and vandalism. As with other types of criminal behavior, property crimes bring with them a threat to, or loss of, a number of core values. But not all disrespect for property results in trouble with the law.

Roxanne and Nina had been best friends since second grade. They applied to and were accepted at the same college, and both of them were excited over the prospect of becoming roommates. While they initially enjoyed living together, after the first few weeks, Nina found herself getting annoyed over Roxanne taking clothing from her closet without first asking if she could borrow what she took. Growing increasingly angered, Nina eventually let Roxanne know she would like her to ask permission before taking any of her stuff.

Although Roxanne went along with Nina's request for a while, she once again started wearing Nina's clothes without permission. When Nina discovered what was happening, she lost her temper and began yelling at Roxanne. Thereafter the relationship was never the same. No longer considering Roxanne a friend, Nina announced she had no intentions of rooming with her when it came time to sign up for roommates at the end of their freshman year.

Respect for another person's property also means taking care of what belongs to someone else when the owner permits us to make use of it. It means doing whatever is necessary to repair any damage we cause to borrowed property. Finally, it means replacing whatever we have borrowed if it is somehow lost or destroyed while it is in our care.

Lanny began to become upset with his brother, Toby, after noticing that when Toby borrowed his tools Lanny never seemed to get them back. When he confronted Toby with his complaint, Toby made an effort to return things for a while. But, in time, his tendency to not return what he borrowed began to reoccur.

One day a windstorm dropped a tree across Lanny's driveway preventing him from getting his car out of the garage. Unable to get to work, he called Toby and asked him to return the chainsaw he borrowed months earlier. When Toby showed up, Lanny was infuriated to discover Toby had damaged the saw and made no attempt to fix it even though it had been on his back porch for the past few months. From that day forward, Lanny was no longer willing to lend Toby his tools, and the brothers became estranged. Thereafter, in addition to losing his brother's affirmation and companionship, Toby had to go to the expense of renting or purchasing tools he used to be able to borrow.

Disrespect for another person's privacy consists of doing anything which exposes something about another person which that person considers personal or potentially embarrassing. Obvious examples include listening in on telephone conversations, reading another person's mail, going through personal papers which are kept in a place where there is some attempt to maintain security, audio or video recording in a setting where a person expects not to be observed, and disclosing information obtained in the context of a confidential conversation. When violating another person's right to privacy constitutes a crime, we suffer the loss of core values which are the consequence of being identified as a criminal. But, not all failure to respect another person's privacy results in difficulty with the law.

Sometimes disrespect for privacy is a violation of professional ethics or work rules. Jacqueline was employed as a medical transcriptionist by a gynecologist. While working, she discovered her next-door neighbor had an elective abortion when she was sixteen. Although Jacqueline knew maintaining patient confidentiality was one of the conditions of her employment, she nonetheless shared this information with a girlfriend who lived across the street. In time, Jacqueline's disclosure came to the attention of her employer. Immediately terminating her, Dr. Williamson also informed Jacqueline he would not give her a favorable reference and that he would fight any attempt on her part to obtain unemployment compensation. Not only did Jacqueline lose a rewarding occupation, but she also lost the affirmation, money, and security which it had provided.

On the other hand, failing to respect another person's privacy may have nothing to do with violating any written rules. Dallas disclosed to his friend, Myron, that he was having sexual fantasies involving a female coworker who recently started at the office. Within a week Dallas was confronted with his incensed wife, Lydia. She started interrogating him concerning his intentions toward this woman and whether he had ever had any physical contact with her. Since Myron was the only person with whom Dallas shared his fantasy, he inferred Myron must have mentioned something to his wife, who, in turn, passed the information on to Lydia. Faced with a fair amount of ongoing marital disharmony, Dallas decided Myron really wasn't much of a friend. Myron lost the affirmation, companionship, and intimacy which had, up till then, been part of his friendship with Dallas.

## UNFAITHFUL BEHAVIOR

Unfaithful behavior consists of pursuing a course of action which violates an agreement freely entered into at an earlier point in time.

Sometimes we suffer a loss of values as a result of frequently failing to honor our agreements. After surviving her period of probation as a billing clerk at a community hospital, Stephanie established a pattern of showing up late for work. When Lorna, her supervisor, indicated her tardiness was unacceptable, Stephanie agreed to be more punctual. For a while she showed up when she was supposed to, but, as time went on, she started coming in late once or twice a week. Lorna once again confronted Stephanie, telling her a letter of reprimand was going into her file, and that if she continued to be tardy, she was going to be terminated. Again agreeing to be punctual, Stephanie fell back into her old pattern in about six weeks. When Stephanie was terminated, she pleaded with Lorna to give her another chance. Lorna told Stephanie she no longer saw her as a reliable employee.

Sometimes we suffer a threat to, or loss of, core values as a result of a single instance of unfaithful behavior. One night Kevin was out with one of his friends when a couple of women approached them at the bar. One thing led to another, and in time, Kevin and one of the women ended up going at it in the backseat of his car. His wife was devastated when she discovered what he had done. She no longer saw Kevin as a good husband, and he suffered a significant loss of companionship and intimacy with her.

Sometimes unfaithful behavior constitutes a failure to fulfill an implicit agreement which is nonetheless voluntary. Becoming pregnant during her senior year in high school, Amy had three basic alternatives. She could get an abortion, place the baby for adoption, or raise the child on her own. Choosing to become a mother, Amy qualified for aid to dependent children, food stamps, Medicaid, and a government-subsidized apartment once Rosemary was born.

Fourteen months later a neighbor called the police after listening to Rosemary scream for nearly an hour at two o'clock in the morning. When the officers arrived they found Rosemary alone in the apartment and discovered Amy was down the street at a bar. The child welfare agency immediately assumed custody. Amy's failure to fulfill her agreement to mother Rosemary led to a loss of affirmation, companionship, and intimacy she could have found in the mother-child relationship as well as the money and meaningful material objects she had been receiving while she qualified for government support.

## DECEPTIVE BEHAVIOR

Deceptive behavior consists of intentionally attempting to create an image of reality in another person's mind which does not correspond with what actually exists. Deceptive behavior may involve falsifying written documents, entering false information into a computer database, or doctoring audio or video recordings. It might involve distorting descriptions of things or events, telling half-truths, or utilizing a significant level of bias in making a report. But, in everyday life the most common form of deceptive behavior is telling a garden-variety lie.

The reality that deceptive behavior can result in a threat to, or loss of, one or more of our core values is probably no more vividly illustrated than in the story of the boy who cried wolf.

After repeatedly deceiving those who were willing to help him fend off wild animals, a wolf finally attacked and killed the shepherd boy while those who could have saved him ignored his calls for help. From this story we learn that he who lies is the one who dies.

Sometimes, as in this fable, the negative impact of deceptive behavior on our quality of life results from repeated misrepresentations. During the second semester of his freshmen year, Ron was placed on academic probation after receiving a D-minus grade point average. Continuing to cut classes, doing virtually none of his homework, and rarely studying for exams, he consistently told his father he was making it to class, working on his assignments, and preparing for his tests. The report card for the second semester was essentially no different than it had been for the first.

Disillusioned, disappointed, and indignant, Ron's father told him he was throwing no more money away on tuition and that Ron would have to start supporting himself while living on his own. Horrified by the prospects of having to leave his parents' house and losing the ongoing financial support which his dad provided, Ron pleaded for one more chance. His father refused his request, stating he no longer believed anything Ron said.

Sometimes we can lose several core values as the result of a single deception. Before they were married, Clayton and Carolyn talked about having children. Whenever the subject came up, Carolyn expressed an interest in having two or three kids because she came from a large family and she genuinely enjoyed her relationships with her siblings. In each of these conversations, Clayton gave Carolyn the impression he shared her enthusiasm for having a number of children with her.

Once they got married Clayton began to change his tune. At first, he told Carolyn he was not ready to have kids because he wanted the two of them to have a chance to grow in their marriage. After a couple of years he told her he wanted to put off having children until he was further along in his career. Finally, after five years of marriage, Clayton told Carolyn he was not interested in having a child and that he had only given her the impression he intended to be a father because he wanted her to marry him. When Clayton made this statement, Carolyn agreed that if he had been honest with her before they got married, she would not have gone ahead with the wedding. Thereafter, Clayton's relationship with Caroline went downhill. She lost respect for him, she no longer enjoyed their time together, and her interest in making love with him completely disappeared. Six months later she left Clayton and filed for divorce.

An analysis of deceptive behavior reveals we typically attempt to deceive others about our own behavior in an effort to conceal that we have already engaged in, or that we intend to engage in, some sort of heedless, nonproductive, disrespectful, or unfaithful course of action. Kevin told his wife he quit smoking even though he hadn't, because he did not want to listen to her lectures on how he was killing himself. Antoinette lied to her parents about doing her homework because she knew they would not let her spend hours on the Internet if they actually knew she hadn't finished it. Ned denied stealing an electric drill from his jobsite because he could be fired if he admitted to having taken it home. Sixteen-year-old Marcia lied to her father about continuing to see her nineteen-year-old boyfriend after she agreed to break off the relationship because she knew her father would ground her if he actually knew what was going on.

## ILL-CONSIDERED INTERPERSONAL INTERACTIONS

Ill-considered interpersonal interactions are courses of action which involve another person despite evidence the other person's behavior poses a threat to one or more of our own core values.

Some of the most obvious examples of ill-considered interpersonal interaction involve associating with those who have a tendency to engage in heedless behavior. Knowing Duane was in the habit of driving while under the influence, George agreed to let him drive the two of them to a professional football game. After observing Duane drinking several bottles of beer and taking frequent nips from the flask of bourbon he brought with him, George had good reason to believe Duane was fairly well hammered by the time the game was over. On the way home Duane decided to pass another car he felt was going too slow. In the ensuing crash Duane was killed and George suffered injuries which rendered him in chronic pain and unable to continue working as a steam fitter. In addition to losing his health, George lost a rewarding occupation and a substantial amount of money. He was also no longer able to play softball, a recreational activity he had always enjoyed.

Sometimes ill-considered interpersonal interaction consists of continuing to be involved with persons who repeatedly engage in nonproductive behavior. Despite Sam's failure to meet his sales quota, Gloria, his district manager, kept him on the job. As time went on his poor performance dragged her sales figures down, resulting in significant losses for her.

Another form of ill-considered interpersonal interaction consists of becoming and staying involved with a person whose behavior is disrespectful. Antonio met Joshua, who introduced himself as an unofficial financial advisor, at a mixer sponsored by the Chamber of Commerce. Despite Joshua's reputation for being less than scrupulous with other people's money, Antonio found him to be very engaging, and they rapidly became pals. About three months into their friendship, Joshua told Antonio he could double his money more or less overnight. Joshua suggested investing in some futures he claimed would be going through the roof within a month. Two weeks after Joshua got fifty thousand dollars from Antonio, the value of the investment fell by nearly half. Telling Antonio he wanted to prevent any further loss of principal, Joshua wrote Antonio a check for the current value of the account.

After some investigation, Antonio concluded Joshua probably knew the value of the investment would deteriorate before Joshua got him to pony up his money. He also had good reason to believe Joshua never actually invested the money, but rather simply put it into his own account as a means of making nearly twenty-five thousand dollars. In consulting an attorney, Antonio learned he had been scammed, but he had no legal recourse to recover his loss.

Ill-considered interpersonal interaction may involve continuing to rely on promises made by a person who repeatedly engages in unfaithful behavior. Claudette sought counseling when she realized her depression had risen to the point she was thinking of killing herself. She told her psychologist she began to get depressed after discovering the man with whom she had been having an affair for nearly seven years was sexually involved with his secretary. Claudette could not believe he became involved with this woman since he repeatedly promised to make a life with her once his youngest son graduated from high school and he could leave his wife. Throughout their seven-year relationship Claudette ignored the fact that her boyfriend's infidelity to his wife indicated he probably would not be keeping promises he was making to her.

Another example of ill-considered interpersonal interaction consists of pursuing a course of action with a person who is known to be deceptive. As the years went by Hollis noticed Lyle was constantly talking about things he was going to do but which never seemed to materialize. At some point, Lyle began talking about renting a sailboat in St. Thomas and doing the Islands in the spring. He convinced Hollis to recruit another friend to get the costs down to a level the two of them could afford. Hollis scheduled his annual, two-week vacation for the middle of May. He and the other fellow bought nonrefundable airline tickets and paid a substantial deposit for the sailboat. One week before they were about to leave, Lyle announced he would not be able to go. Since Hollis and his friend could not afford to rent the boat by themselves, they ended up canceling the trip. In addition to losing a fair amount of money, Hollis also lost an opportunity to do anything he really wanted with the only vacation time he was going to have that year.

# Chapter 7

## SELF-DEFEATING BELIEFS

In learning about self-defeating behaviors you may have found yourself wondering why people behave in ways which obviously result in a threat to, or loss of, one or more core values. Reasons they provide for doing what they did reveal that self-defeating behavior is often the result of mistaken ideas about life and how to live. These ideas are referred to as *self-defeating beliefs*.

### HAPPINESS IS A MATTER OF HAPPENSTANCE

Believing happiness is a matter of happenstance involves any way of looking at life which maintains that quality of life is a matter of some force or process over which we have little or no control.

The notion that quality of life is influenced by something other than our own behavior is deeply rooted in Western civilization. In the ancient world it was expressed by the idea that an invisible force, generally referred to as fate, determines whether and to what degree we are able to become and remain happy. It is also found in the theory that quality of life is a matter of the motion of the planets and the stars. Some religious traditions developed the view that God predestines who is going to become and remain content and satisfied with life.

When we believe happiness is a matter of happenstance, we often pursue heedless courses of action because we have no reason to consider the consequences of doing what we do. After playing a round of golf, Keith offered Jake a ride home. As he started the engine, Keith noticed Jake had not buckled his seatbelt. He was surprised when Jake ignored his request to buckle up because, as a physician, Jake spent many years working in a trauma center, treating persons who were seriously injured in automobile accidents. In an attempt to get him to cooperate, Keith asked Jake if he had learned anything from working all those years in the emergency room. "When your number's up, your number's up, and there's nothing you can do about it," Jake replied.

Modern manifestations of believing happiness is a matter of happenstance can be found in the thinking of many who hold a scientific worldview. Some scientists theorize contentment and satisfaction in living is ultimately determined by biochemistry or a person's genes. Others maintain there is a set point for happiness which is rooted in the anatomy of the individual brain. Despite proof that happiness is simply a matter of brain chemistry, genetics, or neurophysiology, many people who hear about these theories begin believing their behavior has nothing to do with whether and to what degree they are able to become and remain happy.

Assuming that what we do does not affect our quality of life perpetuates nonproductive as well as heedless behavior because it supports the view that attempting to make positive changes in the quality of our lives is an exercise in futility.

Grant flunked out of college as a result of significant alcohol abuse and failing to do his school work. He came to the conclusion he simply couldn't handle school and that it was time for him to go to work. After being fired twice from minimum-wage jobs due to alcohol-related absences, Grant's parents offered to pay for him to go through a top-notch rehab program. One week after he was admitted Grant withdrew from treatment stating that trying to get sober was a waste of time and effort. When his parents pleaded with him to go back, he responded, "I'm not wasting my time working this twelve-step stuff. I'll always be a drunk anyway. You know, I've got the alcoholic gene."

## NOTHING BAD WILL REALLY HAPPEN TO ME

Believing nothing bad will ever really happen is a process psychologists refer to as denial. Denial occurs when we recognize the possibility some undesirable event may occur but dismiss this possibility as so unlikely that it is not a source of concern. Denial can also be described as a refusal to imagine an undesirable event will ever actually become a reality.

Denial frequently plays a role in heedless behavior. As a probation officer, Geno recognized drinking and driving could have devastating consequences because many of the people on his caseload had been arrested for this offense. After his arraignment he told his attorney, "I still can't believe this happened to me. I never thought I could be in this much trouble. I always thought this sort of thing happened to someone else."

Assuming nothing bad will happen to me can also contribute to nonproductive behavior. As a cost accountant for a manufacturing company, Justin always had a good relationship with his supervisors. Once he discovered he could surf the Internet and engage in a fair amount of email correspondence while in his office, he spent more and more of his workday on these non-work-related activities. Justin was shocked when his supervisor told him that persons higher in the chain of command decided to let him go due to his low level of productivity. "I knew what I was doing *could* create a problem at work, but I never thought this *would* happen to me. I thought maybe I would get a reprimand or something from my boss, but I never imagined they'd get rid of me for doing what I did."

Sometimes believing nothing bad will ever happen contributes to disrespectful and deceptive behavior. After her apartment was burgled, Charlotte came up with the idea of making some extra money by exaggerating her losses to the insurance company. She got her boyfriend to obtain a blank receipt from an electronics store where his cousin was employed. She filled it out to look like she purchased a three-thousand-dollar computer a year before the break-in. When the adjuster contacted the store, he discovered it had not yet opened at the time the alleged purchase had been made. A few weeks later Charlotte was arrested for fraud. Astounded by this turn of events, Charlotte bemoaned, "I knew what I was doing was illegal, but I never thought I'd get caught. And, even if they figured out what I did, I thought they would just deny the claim. I can't believe I was arrested. After all, I'm no criminal; this sort of thing doesn't happen to people like me."

Denial can also play a role in ill-considered interpersonal interactions. After discovering he had been scammed, Antonio shared some thoughts with his attorney. "I heard people talk about Joshua being a con man, but he seemed like such a nice guy I had a hard time believing what they were saying could be true. After we became buddies, I found myself defending him when I ran into people who knew we were paling around. Occasionally I would think maybe he was setting me up somehow. But then I would tell myself he wouldn't really do that kind of thing to me."

## WE SHOULD FOLLOW OUR FEELINGS

Believing we should use emotions as the primary means of making decisions is expressed in a number of ways. Sometimes it shows up as the idea that we should rely on intuitions or gut reactions when dealing with things, people, and events encountered in daily living. Often this belief is embodied in the notion that we should listen to our hearts as a means of deciding how we should behave.

When we believe following feelings is an effective means of pursuing happiness, we tend to engage in heedless behavior because this belief suggests there is something good about obtaining immediate gratification and there is something wrong with thinking about the consequences of doing what our emotions mobilize us to do. When asked to explain her behavior the night she got herpes, all Sandra could say was that she was following her feelings. Regis dropped out of couples counseling because he didn't enjoy listening to his wife's complaints and because he didn't feel comfortable talking to a psychologist.

Assuming we should act on emotion often supports self-effacing behavior. Cleo and Emmett would frequently disagree over where to take their summer vacations. Fond of the heat, Cleo always wanted to go south while Emmett was interested in camping and fishing trips up north. Year after year Cleo gave in to her husband because she felt his contentment and satisfaction was more important than her own. After thirty years of marriage, she was deeply resentful because she was never able to vacation in a location she enjoyed.

Presuming we should do what we feel like doing also motivates nonproductive behavior because work is typically not as emotionally appealing as other available alternatives. Alan was unable to support himself with his reupholstering business because he frequently felt like doing something other than working on furniture. Following his feelings he spent most of his day reading the paper, watching television, playing with his kids, or hanging out at a club instead of investing his time and energy on what he had to do in order to be successfully self-employed.

Supposing emotions are effective guides to action can also result in some type of disrespectful behavior. Acting on a gut reaction, Otis attacked another driver who had given him the finger. Camille took a watch from a jewelry store because she felt like taking it. Chet began making recordings of his wife's telephone conversations because he had a feeling she was involved with another man.

Believing we should follow our feelings often also plays a role in unfaithful behavior. While talking with her pastor about how much frustration she experienced in her marriage, Vernice found herself falling in love. She had never met a man who was so sensitive, sympathetic, and understanding. Guided by these feelings, she eventually became sexually involved with him.

Following feelings can even contribute to perpetuating ill-considered interpersonal interactions. Rita continued in her romantic relationship with Lewis despite the fact he was typically inconsiderate and took her, more or less, for granted. She was frequently disappointed when he failed to call after he said he would and when he stood her up for dates. At times Rita's frustration would become so overwhelming she told Lewis she was through with their relationship. But, then, he would come around promising to treat her right, and she would start feeling better. Listening to her heart, Rita would take him back only to once again become unhappy as Lewis reverted to his habitual pattern of failing to follow through with what he said he would do.

## IT'S WRONG TO JUDGE OTHERS

Believing it's wrong to make judgments about other people is a frequent factor in ill-considered interpersonal interactions.

Even though Claudette knew her boyfriend was being deceptive and unfaithful with his wife as he carried on his affair with her, she never really thought of him as cheating on and lying to the woman he married. Reflecting on her failure to think about him this way, she realized she never wanted to be accused of being judgmental. Every time she began to think he was doing something wrong or that he might not really be a nice guy, Claudette would tell herself it wasn't right to make moral judgments. Her failure to recognize that he was repeatedly unfaithful and deceptive with his wife enabled her to remain in a relationship with a man who eventually broke her heart. Her refusal to see him as someone who was not a good person for her meant she spent several years in a dead-end relationship when she could have been developing one with another romantic partner who might have been willing to commit himself to her.

Many people assume it's wrong to judge others because of what they've heard in church. Looking back on time spent with her boyfriend, Claudette explained, "I didn't want to think what he was doing was wrong because Jesus said we shouldn't judge other people." Like many who harbor this self-defeating belief, she somehow lost the rest of the sentence. Scripture records Jesus saying, "Judge not, lest you be judged; for the way you judge you will be judged and with what yardstick you measure you will be measured." This means that if we are going to make judgments about other people, we should be prepared to be judged according to the same set of ideas about what's right and wrong. Far from maintaining that it's wrong to judge others, Jesus was saying we should apply the same standards in judging the behavior of others as we use to evaluate our own behavior.

Many others believe it's wrong to make judgments about other people because they view any type of interpersonal discrimination as a form of injustice. This attitude is rooted in the reality that people are often injured as a result of discrimination based on gender, race, or ethnicity. Those who hold this view frequently point to situations where one person judges another person in a way which has an undeserved negative impact on that person's quality of life.

After thirty-five years of running his own jewelry store, Ward decided to make one of his employees the manager so he could go into semi-retirement. Having worked with Edna for several years, he knew she was his most conscientious worker. She always showed up on time, and she continuously waited on customers when she was on the clock. She always managed to do what she said she was going to do when she said she was going to do it. When she closed the store the register always balanced. Ward could not recall ever catching Edna in a lie.

While working with Ralph, Ward also had an opportunity to observe his behavior. He frequently came in late, took long breaks in the middle of his shift, and often failed to follow through with what he said he was going to do. Those evenings Ralph closed out, the register was often short by five or ten dollars. Despite these observations and the fact that Ward caught him in a number of lies over the years, Ward decided to make Ralph his manager because he believed the person in charge should be a man.

In this situation, Edna clearly suffered a loss as a result of Ward's decision to promote Ralph. But, at the same time, this example illustrates how making judgments about others based on the features determined at conception is actually a form of ill-considered interpersonal interaction. By failing to judge Ralph in terms of his habitual, nonproductive, disrespectful, unfaithful, and deceptive behavior, Ward was pursuing a course of action which threatened his own ability to enjoy contentment and satisfaction with life.

## SINCE EVERYBODY'S DOING IT, IT MUST BE OKAY

Believing we should do what the majority of people are doing is fairly popular these days. It is a way of thinking which results from the tendencies of behavioral scientists to identify the frequency with which people engage in a specific behavior and then making reference to the degree a particular person's behavior deviates from that norm. The notion that we ought to do what's normal is referred to as norm-based reasoning.

Norm-based reasoning contributes to heedless behavior because it focuses our attention on the present and away from thinking about the consequences of doing what we do. Even though Loretta learned about the long-term consequences of regularly using marijuana and binge drinking while she was in high school, she discarded most of what she had been taught when she got to college. She didn't see anything bad happening to any of her friends, all of whom were frequently getting high. After she failed out of school, Loretta realized that despite the fact that most of her friends were regularly using drugs and alcohol, none of them were actually becoming and remaining happy as a result of doing what they did.

Norm-based reasoning can also contribute to nonproductive behavior. The day he was hired as a carpenter, Orlando observed other members of the crew taking extended breaks and spending a fair amount of time on their cell phones while they were supposed to be hammering nails. Within a week he also began to work about half the time he was getting paid. Although he thought he could get away with this level of nonproductivity because all the other guys were doing what he did, Orlando found himself out of work when the owner of the construction company filed bankruptcy a few months after he was hired.

We often resort to norm-based reasoning when we are pursuing courses of action which are generally considered bad or wrong. The sense of guilt which often sets in when we lie, cheat, or steal can be reduced when we remind ourselves that these are *normal* patterns of behavior. Yet, simply being able to avoid subjective discomfort does not mean we are able to escape the negative effect deceptive, unfaithful, and disrespectful behavior can have on our ability to become and remain happy.

Although Austin initially felt uncomfortable fooling around on his wife, he was able to feel a little better by reminding himself that most of his friends cheat a little now and then. Viewing his behavior as normal helped Austin overcome his early reservations about his infidelity. It also enabled him to manage his guilt as he continued with his affair. At the same time, his norm-based reasoning did not provide any protection from the losses he suffered when his wife discovered what was going on.

Irving was fired from his job as a manufacturing representative after he was caught filling out a number of falsified expense reports. He was not sure how he got into the habit of padding his expenses, but in discussing what happened with his psychotherapist, he remembered beginning to misrepresent what he spent after reading an article in the *Times*. "The story talked about how some study showed nearly eighty percent of people polled admitted to routinely lying at work. I guess I thought if so many people were doing this sort of thing, I could do it too."

## MORALITY HAS NO REALITY

During childhood most of us are introduced to a set of ideas about what's right by parents, teachers, and other figures of authority. As children, we are told that using moral principles as guidelines for making choices in daily living will affect the subsequent quality of our lives. As long as we believe acting on moral principles actually makes a difference in terms of our overall level of happiness we tend to try to avoid deceptive, unfaithful, and disrespectful behavior. If we come to believe moral principles have nothing to do with our personal pursuit of happiness, the incentive to refrain from these self-defeating patterns of behavior disappears.

When Charlotte came up with her scheme of filing a fraudulent insurance claim she realized people that went to church would think what she was doing was wrong. But she hadn't been to church since eighth grade, and by the time she finished college none of what went on there had much meaning for her anymore. In talking to her therapist, Charlotte recalled the day one of her psychology professors told the class how Freud proved God was simply an illusion people dreamed up as a means of reassuring themselves they were not alone in a cold and uncaring universe. She remembered reasoning that since God didn't exist nothing in the Bible could actually be true. For her, this meant ideas about what's right and wrong she got from church had nothing to do with reality. Thereafter, she thought they were irrelevant to making decisions in daily life.

While some conclude morality has no reality because they believe religion is a myth, others discount morality as outdated and naive. After Clayton's marriage to Carolyn fell apart, he realized it never dawned on him to think about whether deceiving her was wrong. He recalled what he learned in his college course on ethics. The professor described moral principles as ideas about how people are supposed to behave that are held by the majority of people in a specific community. He maintained moral principles simply exist in people's heads and that they actually have no connection to reality. At that point in his life Clayton decided it was stupid to engage in any type of moral reasoning because at the end of the day none of it really mattered anyway.

## GOD WILL SAVE ME FROM MY SINS

While believing religion is an outdated relic leads some to conclude morality has no reality, certain interpretations of Christianity lead others to believe there is no reason to avoid deceptive, unfaithful, or disrespectful behavior because God will protect a person of faith from the natural negative consequences which may result from these types of self-defeating behaviors.

Vernice sought counseling after her romantic relationship with her minister became a source of scandal resulting in his resignation. She was clinically depressed, not only over the loss of her lover, but also because her husband had left their home along with her two teenage sons. Reflecting on what happened, Vernice realized she had no idea she would eventually suffer the losses with which she was now confronted when she originally became involved with the pastor.

At first Vernice felt terribly guilty. She knew adultery was a sin. But, as time passed, her sense of guilt eased and eventually went away. The reverend reminded Vernice that God loved her, that Jesus Christ died for her sins, and that, as a result, she was automatically forgiven for any immoral act. To her this meant God would not punish her for cheating on her husband. It also meant God would protect her from any of the negative consequences that could result from the affair.

The error of this way of understanding her faith became evident when the pastor's wife figured out what was going on. Looking back, Vernice recognized she began to see God more or less as a permissive parent. "I guess I supposed He never was serious about the rules he set up, and I just thought He would do whatever was necessary to take care of me if I did wrong," she told her psychologist.

## WHAT'S RIGHT IS ONLY THAT WHICH BENEFITS OTHERS

Another way of thinking about morality which contributes to a tendency to engage in deceptive, unfaithful, and disrespectful behavior involves believing right moral action is that which enhances the well-being of others. This belief is rooted in the notion that morality is based on our capacity to empathize with other people and the reality that other people can be hurt when we lie, cheat, or steal. Advocates of this way of looking at morality maintain we should only be motivated to avoid doing what's wrong because others are injured when we engage in deceptive, unfaithful, and disrespectful behavior.

At one level, focusing exclusively on the potential harm which results to others when we lie, cheat, or steal discourages us from attempting to avoid these types of behaviors when we cannot see how a course of action brings harm to another person. When John lied to Vicky about his relationship with Mona, he thought what he was doing was right because he was protecting his wife from the pain she would experience if she knew he was involved in an extramarital affair. When Saundra had her one-night stand in Cancun, she reasoned that what her fiancé didn't know wouldn't hurt him. Working for a multinational construction company, Ned didn't see how he was hurting anyone when he stole a drill from his work site.

On another level, believing we should not lie, cheat, or steal simply because of its potential effect on others tends to undermine motivation for avoiding these types of behaviors. Numerous studies reveal the reason most people attempt to do what's right is rooted in their belief that they will personally benefit as a result. This research indicates that people tend to be more likely to tell the truth, keep their promises, and respect the property of others when they think they will be rewarded or avoid some undesirable consequence. When people begin to believe the only reason to do what's right is the benefit others will receive, many tend to view moral principles as obstacles to, rather than guidelines for, the effective pursuit of happiness.

Finally, believing what's right is only that which benefits other people tends to support perpetual self-effacing behavior. When Ella ended up talking to a psychologist after she and Simon found themselves living in their small apartment, she expressed a tremendous amount of anger. "You know, I always put my kids' needs before my own because I always thought I should be doing what I could to help other people. I remember when Billy wanted us to take out the loan for that ice cream shop. Simon really put up a fight. He told me we should be concerned with our own future at that point in life, but I told him he shouldn't be so selfish. Now I think if I had listened to Simon, I wouldn't be thinking about killing myself these days."

## THERE'S NOTHING REALLY WRONG WITH DOING WRONG

Believing there's nothing really wrong with doing wrong is rooted in the reality that we can frequently lie, cheat, or steal without suffering a threat to, or loss of, core values. When we get some sort of benefit from self-defeating behavior, that benefit is positively reinforcing. The more we are positively reinforced by self-defeating behaviors, the more we tend to view them as an effective means of becoming and remaining happy. This, in turn, results in repeated patterns of self-defeating behavior which raises the likelihood we will eventually suffer a threat to, or loss of, core values as a result of doing what we did.

When Ron first deceived his father about the amount of time he was studying and preparing for exams, he knew it was wrong to lie to his dad. But as it became obvious that his deceptive behavior enabled him to continue partying more or less continuously, Ron began to see stringing his father along was a method of getting what he wanted. He continued to believe there was nothing wrong with deceiving his father until he was confronted with a man who no longer trusted him and who would no longer support his nonproductive way of life.

When Amelia began cheating on her husband, she thought what she was doing was wrong. But as the days and weeks went on and there was no negative consequence to her affair, her sense of guilt gradually disappeared. By the time her husband discovered what she was up to, she had gotten to the point of believing there was nothing wrong with her infidelity as long as she didn't get caught.

Carl began fleecing change while working in his cousin's hardware store. Although he initially recognized this was a form of theft, he was happy to have a few extra dollars in his pocket at the end of each shift. After a while, in addition to cheating his customers, Carl began to steal from the till. By the time he was arrested he no longer saw that what he was doing was any real threat to his quality life.

In addition to perpetuating deceptive, unfaithful, and disrespectful behavior, the positive reinforcement we often experience as a result of self-defeating behavior also tends to perpetuate heedless, nonproductive, and self-effacing behavior as well as ill-considered interpersonal interactions.

Even though Geno knew drunk driving wasn't right, he continued to drive under the influence because he did it frequently and he had never been pulled over by the police. Although Orlando knew he should be working while on the job, he got used to drinking coffee and shooting the bull with the fellows at the construction site while they were on the clock.

Rita maintained her relationship with Lewis because she enjoyed the companionship and intimacy it provided despite evidence he was continuing to be deceptive and unfaithful with her.

Stuart was a gifted student who was enrolled in advanced placement and honors classes. At seventeen, his father took him to a psychologist because he was concerned with Stuart's use of chewing tobacco. Stuart was very angry about what was going on and told the psychologist he had no intention of giving up his chew. He enjoyed the taste, and he liked the way it made him feel.

The psychologist asked Stuart what he had learned in health class about the consequences of chewing tobacco. He responded by telling the psychologist it could cause tooth decay, gum disease, and cancer of the mouth. When asked whether any of this caused him any concern, Stuart indicated he only worried about the possibility of cancer. But, he insisted he had the situation under control. He described a morning ritual in which he would get up, go into the bathroom, and look at his mouth in the mirror. He would use his fingers to feel around in an effort to find any open sores. "If I can't find any cancer, I know I can chew another day," he explained.

While most of us can see the lack of logic in Stuart's reasoning, many do not recognize their own thinking is similarly flawed when believing there is nothing really wrong with continuing to engage in any of the seven self-defeating patterns of behavior as long as there is no perceptible negative effect on their quality of life.

# Chapter 8

## PRINCIPLES FOR THE
## PURSUIT OF HAPPINESS

$B$eing aware of self-defeating behaviors and beliefs is an important aspect of the pursuit of happiness. Our ability to avoid self-defeating behavior is essential to becoming and remaining happy. Fundamentally, this ability is a matter of how we make choices in daily living.

Life is a series of choices because we are continually confronted with alternatives and because we have the capacity to select among them. When our alternatives involve potential courses of action, there are three ways of choosing which one to pursue. Each method of making choices involves a specific type of reasoning.

Emotional reasoning is the most basic. It consists of relying on feelings, intuitions, or gut reactions as a means of selecting among alternative potential courses of action. When we use emotional reasoning to choose an alternative, we pursue the course of action which has the greatest emotional appeal.

Fifteen-year-old Dan is spending the night with Ed, his fourteen-year-old friend. After midnight, the boys sneak out of the house. Ed suggests they take the neighbor's car for a joyride. At this point Dan has two alternatives—he can go along with what Ed wants to do or he can let Ed know he isn't willing to take the car. If Dan uses emotional reasoning, he will go for the ride because he feels like driving the neighbor's car.

The second method of making choices is referred to as consequential reasoning. This process consists of considering the consequences of alternative potential courses of action and choosing the one with the most desirable consequence. If Dan looks at the potential for getting caught with the neighbor's car and concludes there is a good likelihood he and Ed will end up on juvenile probation, he may decide not to go along with Ed's suggestion because this anticipated outcome is less desirable than the short-lived thrill they would experience in taking the ride.

On the other hand, in considering the consequences of his alternatives Dan may arrive at a different conclusion. He might question Ed about how they could get the car out of the driveway without waking up the owner, whether the police patrol the roads they would be driving, and whether other people who might recognize them would be on the road when they are out. If the answers to these questions lead Dan to think they could take the joyride without getting caught, he may agree to take a spin in the neighbor's car.

Principled reasoning is the third method of selecting among alternative potential courses of action. Principled reasoning consists of evaluating a potential course of action in terms of whether it is right or wrong. It then involves pursuing a potential course of action which is determined to be right or rejecting one which is determined to be wrong.

If Dan utilizes principled reasoning to decide how to deal with Ed's suggestion, he will look at the prospect of taking the neighbor's car in terms of whether this potential course of action is right or wrong. He will conclude it would be wrong to go for the ride because it is not right to take or use what belongs to someone else without first obtaining the owner's permission. Having come to this conclusion, he will tell Ed he isn't willing to go along with what Ed wants to do.

As it turned out, whether Dan used emotional or consequential reasoning was relatively irrelevant. Having decided to go for the joyride, the two boys ended up in a serious accident. Dan was arrested, charged with auto theft, and later placed on probation by the juvenile court judge

Principled reasoning is superior to emotional and consequential reasoning because the use of principles allows us to avoid courses of action which *appear* to contribute to our happiness but which *actually* frequently have the opposite effect. If Dan used principled reasoning as a means of selecting which alternative to pursue, he would not have been involved in the accident—an event neither of the other two types of reasoning would have enabled him to foresee. Dan could have avoided being arrested and suffering the loss of freedom he experienced as a result of being placed under the supervision of the court.

Since the dawn of history many people have recognized principled reasoning as superior to the other two means of making choices. They realized principles enable people to distinguish between those potential courses of action which appear to enhance the quality of life, but which often result in a negative effect on overall contentment and satisfaction in living. They understood that learning about principles and using them to make choices in daily living is essential to the personal pursuit of happiness.

Religion has always been one source of principles for making choices in daily life. The Bible contains several ideas about what's right and wrong and encourages people to act on principle when choosing between alternative potential courses of action. Believing these principles have been given to humankind by the Creator and Sustainer of the universe, many persons of faith assume acting on them will result in happiness in this world as well as in a life hereafter.

Until now the other source of principles has been the field of philosophy. Rather than relying on God to provide principles of daily living, philosophers have always assumed the human mind has the ability to distinguish between what's right and wrong. Most philosophers maintain that a handful of great minds—Aristotle, Immanuel Kant, August Compte, and John Stuart Mill—had the ability to formulate principles which are superior to anything the rest of us could come up with on our own.

Today there is a third alternative. The scientific study of the connection between happiness and human behavior has discovered a set of behaviors which appear to enhance our happiness but actually frequently have the opposite effect. Utilizing this discovery, it has been possible to formulate a set of principles which enable us to avoid self-defeating behavior and thereby to maximize our potential to become and remain happy.

## SELF-RESPECT

Self-respect consists of embarking on a course of action only after concluding it does not pose a threat to one or more of our core values.

Self-respect is the alternative to heedless behavior. Having a family history of heart disease and dangerously high cholesterol, Monroe felt like ordering a cheeseburger and fries for lunch. In looking at his alternatives, he considered how eating this meal would perpetuate a pattern of behavior rendering him a good candidate for a heart attack or a stroke. He thought about how either of these events would mean spending time in the hospital and going through a series of anxiety provoking tests. He also thought about the prospect of life-threatening surgery and subsequent restrictions which could affect his job and his ability to compete in contact sports which he very much enjoyed. Since he recognized eating the burger and fries posed a threat to his health, a rewarding occupation, and renewing recreation, he decided that pursuing this course of action would not be the right way for him to behave. Acting on the principle of self-respect, Monroe decided to order a low-fat turkey sandwich.

Self-respect is also the alternative to self-effacing behavior. Emma's husband was offered a promotion which would require that they relocate from Atlanta to Chicago. Teaching in an elementary school, Emma liked her job and enjoyed the people with whom she worked. In doing some research, Emma discovered she would probably not be able to find a similar position if she moved to Illinois. Acting on the principle of self-respect, she let her husband know how their move would impact on her ability to maintain a rewarding occupation. She refused to relocate until they could work out some plan which would be less threatening to her overall contentment and satisfaction with life.

In addition to being an alternative to heedless and self-effacing behavior, the principle of self-respect is the alternative to ill-considered interpersonal interaction. Self-respect includes recognizing that when we are involved with people who regularly engage in self-defeating behaviors, we expose ourselves to a threat to, or loss of, one or more of our core values. Self-respect involves evaluating the other persons involved in a potential course of action in terms of the likelihood they will engage in heedless, disrespectful, unfaithful, or deceptive courses of action. Acting on the principle of self-respect consists of pursuing a course of action which eliminates or reduces the potential negative effect the self-defeating behavior of others could have on the values which determine the quality of our lives.

Sometimes acting on the principle of self-respect consists of protecting ourselves from another person's heedless behavior. Randy worked in a chemical factory with Aaron who frequently lit cigarettes in areas designated as no-smoking zones. Each time Randy confronted Aaron with his concern for their safety, Aaron would simply dismiss his complaint. Acting on the principle of self-respect, Randy finally told Aaron he was going to report him to their supervisor if he didn't stop putting both their lives in danger.

Acting on the principle of self-respect may involve taking steps to protect ourselves from other people's nonproductive or deceptive patterns of behavior. When Ron failed his second semester at college, his father realized Ron had been lying to him about how much effort he was putting into school. He also recognized that in the absence of any evidence Ron had any intention of behaving differently, continuing to pay Ron's tuition and living expenses would simply result in a further loss of his money. Acting on the principle of self-respect Ron's father announced his decision to discontinue funding Ron's education.

On some occasions acting on the principle of self-respect involves refusing to go along with a person's unfaithful pattern of behavior. Roy failed to follow through with numerous dates he made with Anita. On more than one occasion she turned down invitations from other fellows because Roy told her he would take her out on Saturday night only to cancel at the last minute. Anita ended up at home feeling lonely, hurt, and angry.

Despite Anita's numerous complaints and Roy's repeated promises that he would not stand her up again, he continued to fail to fulfill his agreements. Acting on the principle of self-respect, Anita finally told Roy she would no longer make plans to go out with him, and she effectively terminated their relationship.

In addition to serving as an alternative to three types of self-defeating behavior, the principle of self-respect is also a realistic alternative to a number of self-defeating beliefs. Because self-respect requires considering how a potential course of action may impact on what we require in order to become and remain happy, it negates the notion that happiness is a matter of happenstance as well as the fallacy that nothing bad will ever really happen to me. By directing us to think about the consequences of doing what we are emotionally mobilized to do, this principle stands in stark contrast to believing we should simply follow our feelings. Because it requires that we look at how what we do will likely affect the quality of our lives at some future point in time, self-respect is also a corrective to believing if everybody's doing it, it must be okay.

Since the principle of self-respect involves considering how the behavior of others is likely to impact on our own quality of life, it contradicts the notion that it's wrong to judge others. What's more, this principle provides appropriate criteria for making interpersonal discriminations. Self-respect requires that we judge others based on what they actually do or fail to do rather than on the basis of gender, race, or ethnicity. According to the principle of self-respect it is right, proper, and appropriate to judge others in terms of their potential to persist in heedless, nonproductive, disrespectful, unfaithful, and/or deceptive patterns of behavior.

Finally, the principle of self-respect is an effective alternative to believing that what's right is only that which benefits others.

Evaluating a potential course of action in terms of the principle of self-respect is a means of affirming our own right to become and remain happy. Acting on the principle of self-respect is asserting that it is right, proper, and appropriate to value our own happiness and to do what is needed to become and remain happy.

Some of those who believe what's right is only that which benefits others have difficulty with the principle of self-respect. Believing life should be lived for the sake of others, they see acting on the principle of self-respect as a self-centered and a self-absorbed approach to life. In holding this view, they do not recognize the difference between selfishness and self-respect.

*Selfishness* consists of evaluating a potential course of action in terms of its probable benefit to ourselves while ignoring how it is likely to affect what other people require in order to become and remain happy. When we behave selfishly, we pursue a course of action with no concern for how what we are doing could result in a threat, or loss of, that which another person requires for satisfaction and contentment in living. Acting on the principle of self-respect is not an act of selfishness.

Although the principle of self-respect requires considering how what we might do affects our own quality of life, it does not require ignoring how a potential course of action is likely to affect others. When Emma told her husband she did not want to give up her teaching job, the two of them did some brainstorming to see whether other career-development opportunities for him might be available in Georgia. Working with Emma, he was able to eventually secure a promotion with a competitor in Atlanta. His new position enabled Emma to keep her job while he was able to advance his career. Acting on the principle of self-respect, Emma was able to maintain her own contentment and satisfaction in living while, at the same time, assisting her husband in his efforts to enhance his quality of life.

When Ron's father cut off funding for his education, he informed Ron he would be willing to pay for further schooling if Ron met a series of conditions. He told Ron that if he paid his own tuition at a community college and obtained B's or better in at least two classes, he would be willing to fund Ron's tuition at a junior college until he finished a two-year program with better-than-average grades. He indicated that if Ron accomplished this goal he would pay for him to finish his degree as a full-time student at a four-year school.

Eventually getting his act together, Ron attended the community college where he was able to earn two A's. His father followed through with the promises he made. After finishing college, Ron went on to law school and eventually became a practicing attorney. In acting on the principle of self-respect, Ron's father protected himself from Ron squandering more of his money while, at the same time, he required Ron to take an active role in assuming responsibility for his own quality of life.

## INDUSTRY

Industry consists of investing the time and energy necessary to acquire and maintain what we require to become and remain happy.

As the alternative to nonproductive behavior, industry involves initiating and sustaining productive effort aimed at getting and keeping core values even though another more appealing alternative is available. Shortly after being hired as a secretary at a travel agency, Elizabeth observed that when the owner was out of the office the rest of the clerical staff goofed off. Rather than working at their computers, making phone calls, or filing, some of her coworkers would talk to one another about what was going on in their families while others made personal phone calls or read magazines. Acting on the principle of industry, Elizabeth continued working on the tasks of her job rather than doing what the other employees did when the owner was away.

The principle of industry also involves investing time and energy to get or keep what we require to become and remain happy as opposed to attempting to acquire core values in some nonproductive way.

Shortly after establishing his law office, Ron realized he could bill against his clients' retainers for work he had not actually performed. He could charge twice the amount of time he actually put into case review and hearing preparation. His clients would have no way of determining whether his records were accurate. At the same time, he did not realize billing clients for work he had not done would undermine his efforts to become successfully self-employed since he would eventually get a reputation for being an overpriced attorney. Applying the principle of industry, Ron concluded it would not be right for him to pad his bill even though he could probably get away with this subtle form of larceny. Acting on this principle, Ron decided to accurately charge his clients. As a result, he gained a reputation as a reasonably priced, effective lawyer which, in turn, generated more than enough business to provide the money he required to become content and satisfied with life.

Once Martha's live-in boyfriend moved out, she found herself faced with two potential courses of action. The first involved spending time with a series of men who would help her out with rent, buy her groceries, and pay for her utilities. She could also rely on her mother's compassion to provide her with a couple hundred dollars a month. Her second alternative consisted of getting a job, paying her own way, and entering into a training program where she could improve her earning power over time. Acting on the principle of industry, she decided to pursue this course of action. She was able to obtain more money, get better meaningful material objects, find new sources of affirmation and companionship, and experience greater levels of freedom and security than she would have obtained if she decided to simply rely on charity.

Ollie wanted to have a nicer car than the one he had been driving for the past five years. Stocking shelves in a grocery store, he realized he would not be able to buy a better car simply by relying on what he earned. He could have dealt with this desire by spending some of his earnings on lottery tickets, wagering at the track, or betting on football games, hoping he would be able to win enough money to buy another car. Ollie's second alternative involved earning more money. Acting on the principle of industry, Ollie approached his supervisor with a request for more overtime. Since the odds of winning are stacked against anyone who bets with organized gambling, Ollie increased the likelihood he would be able to get his car by choosing to work for what he wanted rather than relying on luck.

Like self-respect, the principle of industry is an effective alternative to believing happiness is a matter of happenstance because it helps us focus on the reality that whether and to what degree we are able to find happiness is a matter of our willingness to work at enhancing the quality of our lives. Since industry encourages us to look at the consequences of what we do, it renders us unable to approach life supposing if everybody is doing it, it must be okay. This principle is a life-enhancing alternative the fallacy we should simply follow our feelings because work is typically less emotionally appealing than the other alternatives available when making choices in daily living.

## EQUITY

Equity consists of respecting the rights of others and honoring our agreements. It is the alternative to disrespectful and unfaithful behavior.

Sonya was a cigarette smoker who had recently given birth. She read about the effect of secondhand smoke on an infant's respiratory system, and she knew smoking around her newborn son was a hazard to his health. Acting on the principle of equity, Sonya decided to stop smoking in her home.

Lamar felt uncomfortable about his seventeen-year-old daughter going on dates with her nineteen-year-old boyfriend. Remembering what he was up to at that age, he was concerned his daughter might become pregnant. Acting on the principle of equity, Lamar decided to counsel his daughter rather than unreasonably restricting her freedom to date.

After spending a week at the beach with Cora, Jessica discovered five of Cora's compact discs in her case. Jessica realized Cora had no way of knowing what happened to her CDs, and Jessica realized she could keep them for herself. Acting on the principle of equity, Jessica returned Cora's CDs.

Patrick and Cherrie had not been getting along since he discovered she had a one-night stand with a coworker. Despite insisting she was having no further contact with the other man, Patrick had a hard time believing her. His friend who was aware of what happened and who was also a computer whiz volunteered to hack into Cherrie's email. Although Patrick was tempted to violate Cherrie's privacy, he acted on the principle of equity when he declined his friend's offer.

Things had not been going well at home for Charlie. After five years of marriage, he and Sadie were fighting over everything and their sexual relationship had deteriorated to the point where they made love no more than once every two or three months. One evening, when Charlie went to watch Monday Night Football with a couple of buddies, three women joined them at the bar. By the fourth quarter there was no doubt the home team was going to lose. The woman who had been talking with Charlie suggested they get a room in a nearby motel. Although the prospect of making love with her was quite appealing, Charlie acted on the principle of equity when he walked away from this opportunity.

Like self-respect and industry, the principle of equity provides a corrective alternative to a number of self-defeating beliefs. Because equity confirms that it is not right to cheat and steal, we cannot act on this principle while believing morality has no reality. It is also more realistic than believing what's right is only that which benefits other people. As the alternative to two types of self-defeating behavior, equity is a way of thinking about what's right which clearly benefits the person who acts on this principle when making choices in daily living.

## HONESTY

Honesty is the alternative to deceptive behavior. Acting on the principle of honesty consists of rendering an accurate description of reality.

For several days after his twenty-year-old son was arrested for selling heroin, Barry spent most of his workday locating a good attorney, securing bail, and attending hearings, rather than calling on his customers or responding to their phone calls. Within a week he was confronted by his manager who wanted to know why Barry hadn't returned any of the twelve calls which came in from one of his top accounts. Barry was tempted to make up a story about how he tried to return these calls and how he somehow couldn't connect. His other alternative consisted of admitting he had been neglecting his work and telling his boss he had been preoccupied with personal problems. Acting on the principle of honesty, Barry retained his manager's affirmation because he already knew what was going on, and he would have lost respect for Barry if Barry lied to him.

One afternoon Tina questioned Alice concerning whether an outfit she just purchased made her look fat. Horrified by what she saw, Alice could not believe her best friend picked an article of clothing in which she looked like she had gained twenty pounds. Not wanting to hurt Tina's feelings, Alice thought about telling a little white lie. Acting on the principle of honesty, Alice told Tina what she really thought. Even though Tina did not like the feedback she received, she considered Alice a friend because she cared enough to tell the truth.

When we are regularly honest, we maintain the trust of others and increase the potential for affirmation, companionship, and intimacy which is available in significant interpersonal relationships. Becoming known as a person who tells the truth also contributes to our ability to find rewarding occupation, to make money, and to acquire those meaningful material objects which we are able to purchase with it. In addition, acting on the principle of honesty enhances our security because we do not have to worry about the consequences of getting caught in a lie.

Beyond these benefits, the principle of honesty enables us to insure that what we are doing is consistent to the other three principles of the formula. The fact that we are frequently deceptive because we want to conceal some other sort of self-defeating behavior suggests that when we are tempted to deceive there is a good chance we have already, or we intend to, engage in some sort of heedless, nonproductive, disrespectful, or unfaithful pattern of behavior. This means that when we act on the principle of honesty, we may also be avoiding undetected self-defeating pattern of behavior.

If Monroe tried to tell himself that eating a cheeseburger and fries was not heedless behavior, knowing he would lie to his wife about what he ate for lunch signaled that what he wanted to do was a self-defeating course of action. If Elizabeth somehow failed to recognize that making personal phone calls while her employer was away was nonproductive behavior, realizing she would have to be deceptive in accounting for how she spent her time would have awakened her to the reality that what she was doing was not right. Had Jessica not recognized keeping Cora's CDs was a disrespectful course of action, realizing she would have to lie to Cora would have alerted Jessica to the reality that what she wanted to do was a form of disrespectful behavior.

Sometimes the principle of honesty is the only clue we have that we are about to engage in some sort of self-defeating course of action. Wanting to purchase a carpet cleaning franchise, Gordon was willing to invest everything he had. Despite re-mortgaging his house and selling his car he could not raise enough cash to qualify. To solve this problem, a friend who worked at a bank offered to write a letter indicating Gordon would have a line of credit which he could not actually secure. Although Gordon was tempted to pursue this course of action, he recognized using the letter would be deceptive. Acting on the principle of honesty, he was able to avoid the substantial losses he would have suffered if he actually started a business which was undercapitalized.

In addition to deterring us from virtually all of the self-defeating patterns of behavior, the principle of honesty also serves as a corrective alternative to a number of self-defeating beliefs. Since honesty has always been considered a moral principle, the fact that it is an alternative to self-defeating behavior reveals the fallacy of believing morality has no reality. It also constitutes an alternative to believing if everybody's lying, it must be okay, and assuming there is nothing really wrong with lying because the principle of honesty is based on research about the causal connection between deceptive behavior and our subsequent quality of life. Finally, this principle is a life-enhancing alternative to believing what's right is only that which benefits others because it is based on research which documents the clear and tangible benefits to ourselves when we render an accurate description of reality.

# Chapter 9

# FOLLOWING THE FORMULA
# FOR HAPPINESS

Y ou now have the formula for happiness. It is a blueprint by which you can maximize your potential for constructing and maintaining a high-quality life. It identifies the ten core values essential to becoming and remaining happy as well as the four core principles which enable us to get and keep them. Following the formula consists of looking at your life in terms of where and how you are able to get and keep core values, evaluating potential courses of action in terms of whether they are consistent with the four principles, and acting on those principles when making choices in daily living.

The first step in following the formula involves reflecting on where and when you suffered a threat to, or loss of, one or more of your core values in an attempt to see whether what your were doing at the time was some type of self-defeating behavior. If it was, you can probably now see that if you had acted on the principle which is the alternative to that type of self-defeating behavior, you probably could have avoided the unhappiness resulting from doing what you did. You may also want to reflect on your past to see if you are in the habit of repeatedly engaging in any particular type of self-defeating behavior. If you are, following the formula requires that you pay particular attention to acting on the principle which is the alternative to your habitual pattern of self-defeating behavior.

As you face your future, it is important to realize that regardless of whether you are focusing on any one of the core principles, you need to apply all four of the principles when evaluating any particular potential course of action.

When Gordon was considering whether to use the letter stating he had a line of credit which did not actually exist, he believed he was acting on the principle of self-respect because he could not foresee how what he was going to do posed a threat to any of his core values. He also assumed he was being industrious because using the letter would enable him to get a business where he was willing to invest a tremendous amount of his own time and effort. He thought he was being equitable because he was not actually taking any money that belonged to someone else. Only when he also considered this course of action in terms of the principle of honesty was he able to make a decision which enabled him to avoid personal bankruptcy.

One way to ensure you are acting on all of the core principles consists of asking a series of questions about any potential course of action. These questions can be organized into a decision tree made up of a series of steps which result in determining whether a potential course of action is a viable alternative with respect to the likelihood it will enhance your quality of life. To see how this works, evaluate a potential course of action you are currently considering in terms of the decision tree for the pursuit of happiness.

*Decision Tree for Pursuit of Happiness*

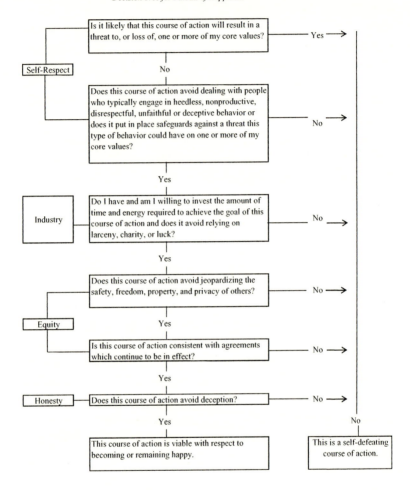

For practice, you may benefit from taking a few potential courses of action you encounter in the next few days through this decision tree. You will find that fairly quickly you have internalized this way of thinking about your alternatives, and the process will become more or less automatic. In the future, if you find yourself confronted with alternative potential courses of action which result in some confusion, you can always refer to this decision tree for assistance in figuring out which alternative to pursue.

While following the formula involves evaluating any particular course of action in terms of all four core principles, it also requires that you consistently apply these principles as you go about the process of making choices in daily living.

Alan's efforts at making a living reupholstering furniture did not work out because he repeatedly failed to act on the principle of industry. As each day unfolded he had countless opportunities to stretch and tack fabric, but instead he read the newspaper, watched television talk shows, played with his kids, and hung out with the fellows at the club. In addition to a pattern of nonproductive behavior, he also failed to act on the principles of equity and honesty by not completing his jobs when he told his customers he would have them done and by fabricating excuses to cover up his nonproductive and unfaithful behavior. Had he consistently acted on the principles of self-respect, industry, equity, and honesty, Alan might have been able to make a go of his business rather than having to return to a job which, for him, was not a rewarding occupation.

Like Alan, Holly had numerous opportunities to engage in nonproductive behavior. Throughout high school and once she graduated, most of her friends spent much of their time hanging out, listening to music, and getting high. Rather than going along with them she did her homework when it needed to be done, she studied for her exams, and she practiced what she learned in class by styling hair for her friends. When she started to work as a cosmetologist, Holly spent some of her free time observing more experienced operators and asking questions about their techniques. In addition to acquiring skills, she kept her promises and told the truth. By regularly choosing self-respecting, industrious, equitable, and honest behavior, Holly was able to become successful in a vocation she found genuinely rewarding.

One way to remember the importance of consistently acting on all of the core principles of the formula involves a visual representation which looks like the pyramid of foods you can find on packaging for loaves of bread and boxes of cereal.

*Pyramid of Principles for the Pursuit of Happiness*

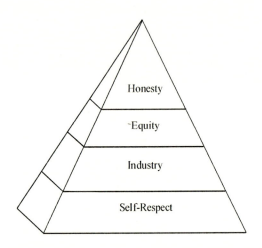

The base of the pyramid is the principle of self-respect because the pursuit of happiness is rooted in the conviction that your happiness has a value and that you are the only one who can take responsibility for finding and holding on to your own happiness. Since your happiness is the product of the time and energy you put into obtaining and maintaining core values, industry is at the next level of the pyramid. Equity occupies the third because you can only find and hold onto happiness when you function as a responsible and reliable member of society. Honesty is at the pinnacle of the pyramid because the successful pursuit of happiness is always a matter of maintaining an abiding respect for reality.

The pyramid of principles may also assist in your efforts at following the formula because it reminds us that applying all of the principles in daily living is much like attempting to practice wellness principles. We know that when we consistently eat a low-fat, high-fiber diet, avoid tobacco and the excessive use of alcohol, and get adequate amounts of rest and exercise, we maximize our potential for becoming and remaining healthy. Likewise, when we regularly act on the principles of self-respect, industry, equity, and honesty, we maximize our potential for becoming and remaining happy.

Carrying this analogy a step further, it is useful to remember that just as practicing wellness principles results in physical well-being, following the formula contributes to our emotional well-being. Since emotions reflect how the things, people, and events of daily living affect what is essential to our contentment and satisfaction in life, whether we can get and keep core values makes a difference with respect to our overall emotional adjustment. By consistently acting on the four principles of the formula, we are able to effectively manage our overall emotional well-being.

When we follow the formula we have greater opportunities for love because we are able to obtain and maintain relationships with those people and things which actually enrich and enhance the quality of our lives. We more frequently experience joy because we have regular access to those things, people, and events which we love. We often experience pride because we have the ability to get what we want and need.

When we follow the formula, we lessen the frequency with which we experience negative emotions because we minimize the threat to and loss of things, people, and conditions of existence which enhance the quality of our lives. By minimizing threats to those core values we already have, we reduce those occasions on which we become fearful and anxious. Being able to hold on to core values we rarely experience disappointment and depression. Because our relationships are relatively stable and since we rarely do anything which would result in a threat to our core values, we infrequently experience envy, jealousy, or guilt.

In the next two chapters I will be giving you tools you can use to thoroughly apply the formula if you want to develop a plan of action for improving your overall level of happiness or if you are confronted with a decision which you know will have significant long-term consequences with respect to your ability to become and remain happy. These programs will show you whether what you are going to do is likely to actually contribute to your contentment and satisfaction in living. But, before you look at them, I want to show you how following the formula can enrich the quality of your life in a number of other ways.

## MASTERY, OPTIMISM, AND ENHANCED SELF-ESTEEM

Research reveals a correlation between subjective reports of contentment and satisfaction with life and a sense of mastery, optimism, and self-esteem. As you follow the formula, you will be cultivating each of these desirable personality traits. This is going to happen because you will be operating on a scientifically based, comprehensive, and a systematic approach to living which is firmly rooted in reality.

These days many people always use some sort of personal pronoun when talking about core values. They refer to "my" core values, "your" core values, "her" core values, "his" core values, "our" core values, or "their" core values. They assume core values are essentially subjective, that they are relative to the individual, and that they are basically a matter of personal choice. Those who make these assumptions fail to distinguish between core values and core beliefs.

*Core beliefs* are basic ideas about what is important in life and how to live. Core beliefs exist within the mind of an individual, and they can exist in the minds of several of the individuals in a group. Since core beliefs are a matter of what we think, they may have little, if anything, to do with reality.

Believing he could find contentment and satisfaction by getting high, Richie began using cocaine when he was in his mid-thirties. He has several friends who share this belief about life and how to live. They think they are enhancing their quality of life by investing a fair amount of time and money in getting and using cocaine. But, simply because Richie and his friends believe using this substance will make them happy does not mean they will actually achieve their intended goal.

As Richie continues to maintain his core belief he will probably lose many of his core values. In all likelihood he will experience several frustrations, disappointments, and catastrophes. There is a good chance he will become fairly pessimistic, he will feel his life is out of control, and he will suffer a loss of self-esteem. We know all of this will probably happen despite what Richie believes about cocaine because we have objective evidence that these are some of the consequences of regular cocaine use.

The core values of the formula are not simply a set of ideas. They exist outside the human skull. They are the things, interpersonal interactions, and conditions of human existence we encounter in the course of daily living. We know they *actually* make a difference in terms of becoming and remaining happy because we have *objective evidence* that they enhance the quality of human life.

Likewise, the core principles of the formula are not some arbitrary opinions about good behavior or simply someone's notion about what we ought to do. They were formulated from what research has revealed about the *actual* relationship between happiness and human behavior. These principles identify patterns of behavior which *really* determine whether and to what degree we are able to become and remain happy.

If you adopt the core concepts of the formula as your set of core beliefs, you will organize your life around a set of ideas which will enable you to actually become and remain happy. Rather than viewing your life as the result of events which are beyond your control, you will be playing a central role in determining your own destiny. Instead of going through life with a sense of incompetence, inadequacy, and failure, you will have a sense of mastery which comes with the power to effectively manage your own quality of life.

When Ginger entered treatment she was demoralized. At twenty-nine she had not been able to hold onto a job for more than six months at a time, and she recently suffered the loss of a boyfriend who was the last of a lifelong series of failed relationships. Reflecting on her past, Ginger realized how her pattern of nonproductive, unfaithful, and deceptive behavior contributed to her inability to hold on to a rewarding occupation, companionship, and intimacy. Coming to the realization that if she acted on the core principles of the formula, she would stand a much better chance of keeping a job and a romantic partner had a profound effect on her outlook on life. "Now I actually know what I have to do to get what I want. I really believe I can make it now. I know how to spot my weaknesses and what to do to overcome them. For the first time in my life, I feel like I'm really in control." As she acted on the principles of the formula and as she was able to hold on to her next job and her next boyfriend, Ginger's sense of mastery continued to solidify.

Since the formula identifies the basic elements of happiness and provide reality-based guidelines which enable you to actually get and keep them, you will become more confident in your capacity to become and remain happy as you follow it in daily living. When you operate on a set of beliefs which actually reflects what is important in life and how you should be living, you may immediately become more optimistic because you know you have improved the likelihood you will be able to get and keep what you need to find contentment and satisfaction in living. As you follow the formula for happiness, this sense of optimism will grow as you recognize how operating on these core beliefs actually enhances your quality of life.

Evan was fairly hopeless when he started psychotherapy. At the age of thirty-five he was contemplating his third divorce. Over the course of treatment, he was able to recognize how his unhappiness with his current wife was the result of the same pattern of self-effacing behavior which had led to his desire to flee from his first two marriages. When he learned about the importance of self-respect and he began asserting himself with his wife, his marriage and his mood began to improve. "A few months ago I thought I would never be happily married," he reported to his psychotherapist. "But now it seems things are working out. In fact, now that I'm letting Lorraine know what I want, I actually think things are going to be okay."

Self-esteem is the conviction we are entitled to the pursuit of happiness combined with confidence in our capacity to become and remain happy. When you choose to follow the formula for happiness, you are operating on a set of ideas about what's important in life which will actually enhance your overall self-esteem. By adopting the core concepts of the formula as your set of core beliefs you are affirming your right to the pursuit of happiness. Following a set of guidelines which you know will lead to happiness almost immediately provides you with greater self-confidence. As you discover how following the formula enhances your quality of life, you will begin to see yourself as a reliable resource for becoming and remaining happy.

## ENRICHING THE LIVES OF OTHERS

Several studies show a correlation between happiness and behavior which enhances the lives of other people. When we follow the formula for happiness, we are contributing to the happiness of others in a number of significant ways.

Many people benefit when we make an effort at obtaining what we require to become and remain happy. We earn money by creating or contributing to the creation of products or services which enhance the lives of those who purchase what we have produced. Their lives may be enriched because our efforts have provided one of their meaningful material objects or because the services we have rendered contribute to their health, freedom, or security.

If we work for someone else, our time and energy makes money for our employer or the shareholders of the corporation where we are employed. The money we pay in taxes provides meaningful material objects and medical care for those who are dependent, disabled, and poor. Our taxes also support police and fire departments, emergency services, courts of law, and the military, all of which contribute to the health, freedom, and security of people in our community, our state, and our nation.

When we buy meaningful material objects, we provide money to those who produce, transport, and sell whatever we are purchasing. This money enables them to get those meaningful material objects they need for their personal pursuit of happiness. In addition, we are contributing to their opportunities for rewarding occupations as well as their health and security, assuming their employers provide health insurance and pension plans.

Other people also benefit when we make an effort to get and keep interpersonal values. Armando is affirmed by Mr.

Dominges because his ability to sell real estate increases Mr. Dominges's income as well as the reputation of Dominges Realty. Going the extra mile to find good homes and the financing to purchase them, Armando is affirmed by his clientele. He is also affirmed by his wife and children, in part, because he provides them with meaningful material objects, money, affirmation, companionship, intimacy, freedom, and a fair amount of security.

We contribute to the happiness of others when we make efforts to obtain and maintain companionship. Armando is able to share his experiences with Manuela because he is interested in her sharing her experiences with him. Theresa gets companionship from Chris because she provides companionship to him.

We get our intimacy from a relationship in which our partner is also obtaining this value from us. Theresa finds that she can disclose the most personal aspect of herself with Chris because he feels he can share the most personal aspects of himself with her. He benefits from her intimacy with him as much as she benefits from his intimacy with her.

We help others by maintaining our health because when we are healthy, we are not utilizing medical services which can be provided to those who are not well. When we enjoy our work and return to the tasks of our occupation refreshed and renewed, we tend to provide quality products and services which contribute to other people's satisfaction and contentment with life. We enrich the lives of others when we have freedom because they can benefit from our individual creativity. When we have a sense of security, we have more time and energy to consider how we can enhance the lives of others than we do when we are continuously preoccupied with fear, anxiety, and doubt.

Acting on the principle of self-respect requires becoming involved with others in doing what we can do to ensure the greatest number of people have the greatest opportunity to become and remain happy. Acting on this principle also means working within communities to develop, support, and maintain quality public education, healthcare institutions, libraries, and emergency services as well as places where people have the ability to find renewing recreation. In addition, self-respect entails supporting politicians and public policies which balance agricultural, mining, and manufacturing interests with environmental concerns. It includes supporting candidates and government officials in their efforts at ensuring fair law enforcement, protecting the integrity of the court system, and maintaining military readiness so we can all benefit from the freedom and security effective government provides.

When we act on the principle of industry, we are doing what we can to meet our own needs rather than being or becoming burdens to others. When we invest the time and energy necessary to get and keep what our own happiness requires, we are typically generating more than we actually need to find contentment and satisfaction in living. As a result, we have the wherewithal to give to others in need as well as to donate to charitable organizations which provide for those who are unable to acquire what they require on their own.

Other people benefit in a number of important ways when we act on the principle of equity. By respecting life we are protecting others from potential hazards to their health and safety. When we respect the freedom of others, we contribute to one of the basic elements of their happiness. By respecting property rights we enable others to hold on their meaningful material objects and money. When we respect the right to privacy, we permit other people to experience intimacy and thereby contribute to their emotional well-being. When we keep our agreements, other people obtain what they count on getting from us.

Others benefit when we act on the principle of honesty because we are providing them with an accurate image of reality. They have a realistic view of their circumstances, and they know what we have done, what we are doing, or what we intend to do. When they have accurate information, they can realistically evaluate their potential courses of action in terms of how their alternatives are actually most likely to impact their personal pursuit of happiness.

## FOSTERING FAITH

Research reveals that people of faith tend to be more content and satisfied than those who see no value in religion. If you are already a person of faith, following the formula may enhance your relationship with God. If you are not already a person of faith, following the formula may awaken in you the value of establishing and cultivating this type of relationship.

The Bible contains a tremendous amount of practical advice for daily living. It provides instructions on how to deal with a number of issues such as what to do with money, how to handle food and alcohol, how to manage sexuality, and how to deal with negative emotions and difficult people. Virtually all of this advice has something to do with avoiding heedless, nonproductive, disrespectful, unfaithful, and deceptive behavior which was just as much a threat to core values in biblical times as it is for us today.

But, beyond this advice, the Judeo-Christian tradition has also always emphasized the importance of acting on principle. The Ten Commandments are the basic principles for both Judaism and Christianity. Christians include two more which are referred to as the Great Commandments of Christ.

All of these basic biblical principles fall into two groups. One, which includes the first great commandment of Christ and the first four of the Ten Commandments, describes how God wants us to relate to Him. The other, which includes the second great commandment and the remaining Ten Commandments, refers to how we are to deal with one another.

When you follow the formula for happiness, your behavior is consistent with the second group of principles. Acting on the principle of equity, your behavior is in line with the second great commandment of Christ because you are treating other people the way you would like to be treated. You are also acting in accord with the commandments condemning murder, theft, and adultery. When you act on the principle of honesty, your behavior is consistent with the commandment which maintains it is wrong to lie.

Some people of faith find the consistency between the core principles of the formula for happiness and biblically based moral principles enhances their faith in God. They view the fact that the principles of the formula are the product of scientific reasoning and research as confirmation of their belief that biblically based moral principles are actually firmly rooted in reality. For them the formula's scientifically formulated principles of morality are further proof that God is, and has always been, a valid and reliable source of knowledge about life and how to live.

Some people of faith who learn about this consistency experience a new way of thinking about their relationship with God. Raised in a church, Inez had been taught she should act on principle in order to please God. She was told that when she failed to act on principle she was offending God and making Him angry with her. She also learned that if He were angry, He would do something to make her unhappy or eventually send her to hell.

When Inez learned about the formula for happiness and the consistency between its principles and some of those she learned at church, her view of God began to change. "You know, up 'til now I always thought of God as a sort of a killjoy. You know, He gave us the commandments to take the fun out of life. I also thought He was kind of selfish because I was always told we should do what makes Him happy. But now I see things the other way around. You know, it's like when I tell my kids they should tell the truth. I don't want them to do it for me, I want them to be honest so other people will believe them and so other people won't label them as liars. Now I think it must be like that with God. You know, it's not all about Him. He loved us so much He gave us these commandments to show us how to behave so we can be happy. For the first time I think I really understand what Jesus meant when he talked about God being a loving father."

For some people who are not already persons of faith, following the formula can give rise to appreciating how a relationship with the Creator and Sustainer of the universe can enhance the likelihood of becoming and remaining happy.

Anthropologists tell us the roots of religion are found in a primitive insight that there are limits to what human beings are able to manage and control. Finding themselves at the mercy of storms, floods, swarms of insects, earthquakes, and volcanoes, our distant ancestors saw some willful intent in these powerful forces of nature. Religion began with their efforts at communicating and negotiating with these supernatural forces in an attempt to somehow obtain favorable treatment. Prayer, rituals, and sacrifices were intended to stay on the right side of the spirits controlling the forces of nature which influenced people's ability to get and hold on to what they required in order to become and remain satisfied with life.

As time went on, the people of Israel realized that rather than being influenced by a number of different supernatural forces, the world in which they lived was managed by one willful force which had the power to control and influence everything on earth. Referring to this force as the one true God and recognizing there was only so much they could do to manage their circumstances, they came to depend on Him to help them with those aspects of reality which were beyond their control. For Christians, this divine force eventually took on human form in the person of Jesus Christ. He announced to humanity that the Creator and Sustainer of the universe is actually interested in our personal quality of life and that He is available to assist in our personal pursuit of happiness.

Even though all of this occurred thousands of years ago, the reality that there are limits to what we can manage and control remains the same today. Following the formula for happiness *only* maximizes our potential for becoming and remaining happy. The outcome is *never* guaranteed.

Malina was a happily married mother of two children. She had a clear sense of what she needed to become and remain happy, and her behavior was consistent with the core principles of the formula. At the same time, she had no control over her circumstances when a drunk driver plowed into the car carrying her husband and children while they were on their way to get ice cream.

Persons of faith who follow the formula do what they can to take care of themselves while relying on God to manage those aspects of reality which are beyond their own control. Coping with a life-threatening heart condition, Mark found himself facing surgery. Acting on the principle of self-respect, he selected the most qualified physician he could find, and he followed the instructions he had been given up to the day he was hospitalized. Having done all he could do, Mark turned to God for help in taking care of what would happen when he went under the knife. Going into surgery, he relied on God to guide the doctor's hands, to protect the sterile field, and to maintain the proper mechanical functioning of the apparatus involved in the procedure throughout the operation so he could survive, regain his health, and return to a rich and rewarding life with his wife and family.

If you are not already a person of faith, you could ask God to help in your personal pursuit of happiness. As you follow the formula, you can pray for help in managing those things, people, and events which affect your quality of life but over which you have little or no control. You may discover you are linking your abilities with a powerful ally in your effort to get and keep core values. You can enhance your relationship with God by paying attention to the group of commandments which describe how He wants you to deal with Him. If you do, you may discover how following the formula for happiness while maintaining a relationship with God is the most effective and reliable method for becoming and remaining content and satisfied with life.

# Chapter 10

# PERSONAL STRATEGIC PLANNING

This program for personal strategic planning is designed to assist you in developing a plan of action aimed at improving your overall level of happiness. It requires you to refer to your responses to the *General Inventory of Life Satisfaction*. If you recently completed the GILS in chapters 3 through 5 of this book, you may use your responses there to begin the process of personal strategic planning. If it has been some time since you responded to the GILS, fill out the General Inventory of Life Satisfaction provided in chapter 12. If you think you may want to fill out another GILS at some point in the future, you should make photocopies of chapter 12. You may also want to photocopy the pages of this chapter before you begin to write your responses in this book.

This process of strategic planning differs from other approaches with which you may be familiar. Unlike those that begin by encouraging you to clarify your personal values, this program is designed to identify goals which are rooted in the ten core values of the formula for happiness. It then gives you the ability to forecast whether achieving these goals is actually likely to enhance your overall quality of life. Once you have determined that achieving your goals is likely to improve your level of happiness, you will develop a plan of action for attaining them.

This process of personal strategic planning consists of six steps.

*Step 1*     Identifying Sources of Dissatisfaction
*Step 2*     Formulating Goals
*Step 3*     Developing Potential Courses of Action
*Step 4*     Evaluating Potential Courses of Action
*Step 5*     Forecasting the Effect of Potential Courses of Action
*Step 6*     Developing a Plan of Action

## *STEP 1*

### IDENTIFYING SOURCES OF DISSATISFACTION

Developing a strategy for improving your level of happiness begins with identifying what changes are likely to improve your overall satisfaction in living. This is accomplished by looking at the Profile of Life Satisfaction which you obtained on your most recently completed GILS. Circle the lowest core value score on your profile. Next, turn to the section of the GILS which measures that value and circle the item number or numbers which reflect the greatest degree of personal dissatisfaction with respect to that value. Once you have completed this process, go to the next lowest core value score and circle the number or numbers on the GILS which reflect the greatest degree of dissatisfaction in that section. Continue this process until you have identified up to four item numbers which reflect your greatest degree of discontent.

Once you have circled four items on the inventory, write the number of the items you have circled next to the value category in the *Table of Identified Sources of Dissatisfaction*. An example of how this is done is presented on the following page.

| Table of Identified Sources of Dissatisfaction | | | |
|---|---|---|---|
| *Value* | *Item Number/s* | *Value* | *Item Number/s* |
| MM Objects | ___ ___ ___ ___ | Health | ___ ___ ___ ___ |
| Money | ___ ___ ___ ___ | Rewarding Occupation | ___ ___ ___ ___ |
| Affirmation | ___ ___ ___ ___ | Renewing Recreation | ___ ___ ___ ___ |
| Companionship | ___ ___ ___ ___ | Freedom | ___ ___ ___ ___ |
| Intimacy | ___ ___ ___ ___ | Security | ___ ___ ___ ___ |

# EXAMPLE OF IDENTIFYING SOURCES
# OF DISSATISFACTION

In reviewing his responses to the GILS, a forty-three-year-old man discovered his lowest value scaled score was Companionship. His responses to the items in this section of the GILS were as follows:

A  SA  SD  D  NA                                     Companionship
● O O O O 1. I am satisfied with the level of companionship I receive from the people in my community.
O O ● O O 2. I am satisfied with the level of companionship I receive from coworkers.
● O O O O 3. I am satisfied with the level of companionship I receive from my friends.
O O O ● O 4. I am satisfied with the level of companionship I receive from my children.
O O O O ● 5. I am satisfied with the level of companionship I receive from my parents.
O O O ● O 6. I am satisfied with the level of companionship I receive from my spouse or romantic partner.
O O ● O O 7. I am satisfied with the level of companionship I receive from my extended family.
O O O O ● 8. I am satisfied with the level of companionship I receive from my pet.
O O O O ● 9. I am satisfied with the level of companionship I receive through my relationship with God.

Companionship Score  4.2

Since his two lowest scores on Companionship were his responses to item numbers 4 and 6, he wrote those numbers on the *Table of Identified Sources of Dissatisfaction*. He then went on to look at his scores on Intimacy where he discovered low scores on items numbered 2 and 5. He next wrote these item numbers in the appropriate places on his *Table of Identified Sources of Dissatisfaction*.

### *Table of Identified Sources of Dissatisfaction*

| Value | Item Number/s | Value | Item Number/s |
|---|---|---|---|
| MM Objects | | Health | |
| Money | | Rewarding Occupation | |
| Affirmation | | Renewing Recreation | |
| Companionship | 4  6 | Freedom | |
| Intimacy | 2  5 | Security | |

# *STEP 2*

### FORMULATING GOALS

On the next ten pages you will find ten *Goal Formulation Worksheets*, each of which deals with one of the ten core values. Turn to the worksheets which correspond to the values which have item numbers listed on the *Table of Identified Sources of Dissatisfaction*. Circle the questions at the top of each worksheet corresponding to the numbers listed next to the value in *The Table of Identified Sources of Dissatisfaction*. Once this process is completed, answer the questions on those worksheets containing circled questions. Continue this process until you have identified up to three goals.

For example, once the forty-three-year-old man filled in items numbered 4 and 6 on the *Table of Identified Sources of Dissatisfaction*, he completed the goal-setting worksheet for Companionship on the next page. Circle these numbers and follow what he did:

## GOAL FORMULATION WORKSHEETS

### COMPANIONSHIP

1. What would bring about more companionship with people in my community?
2. What would bring about more companionship with my coworkers?
3. What would bring about more companionship with my friends?
4. What would bring about more companionship with my children?
5. What would bring about more companionship with my parents?
6. What would bring about more companionship with my spouse or romantic partner?
7. What would bring about more companionship with my extended family?
8. What would bring about more companionship with my pet?
9. What would bring about more companionship with God?

Answer the first question you have circled in the space below. If you cannot imagine anything which would bring about greater companionship in the context of this relationship, move on to answer the next question with a circled number.

*Spending more time with the kids on the weekends*

*What else might have a similar result?*
*Coaching the kids' softball team*
√ *Working with the kids on their homework after dinner*

Now make a check by the answer you think is the most realistic means of bringing about an increase in your satisfaction. For purposes of strategic planning this will be a goal. Now use five words or less to describe this goal in the space below.

*Do homework with kids*

If you have other circled questions about Companionship, use as many additional sheets of paper as necessary to repeat this procedure. Once you have identified up to two more goals, describe each in five words or less on the spaces below.

*Alone time with wife*

## GOAL FORMULATION WORKSHEET

### MEANINGFUL MATERIAL OBJECTS

1. What would bring about more satisfaction with my housing situation?
2. What would bring about more satisfaction with the furnishings in my home?
3. What would bring about more satisfaction with my wardrobe?
4. What would bring about more access to reliable transportation?
5. What would bring about more satisfaction with electronic devices which save time and effort?
6. What would bring about greater access to stores where I can find an adequate varitety of reasonably priced necessities?

Answer the question next to the first number you have circled in the space below. If you cannot imagine anything in answer to this question, move on to the next question with a circled number.

_____

_____

What else might have a similar result?

_____

_____

_____

Now make a check by the answer you think is the most realistic means of bringing about an increase in your satisfaction. For purposes of strategic planning this will be a goal. Now use five words or less to describe this goal in the space

_____

If you have circled other questions about Meaningful Material Objects, use as many additional sheets of paper as necessary to repeat this procedure. Once you have identified up to two more goals, describe each in five words or less on the spaces below.

_____

_____

## GOAL FORMULATION WORKSHEET

### MONEY

1. What would bring about enough money to acquire and maintain material objects that make my life satisfying?
2. What would bring about income or assets sufficient to secure the respect , and perhaps admiration, of those people who are important to me?
3. What would bring about enough money for interesting interpersonal activities?
4. What would bring about enough money for intimate interpersonal experiences?
5. What would bring about enough money to enable me to participate in activities that enhance my health and prevent illness?
6. What would bring about enough money to obtain quality health care?
7. What would bring about a fair and reasonable level of compensation for my work?
8. What would bring about enough money for rewarding recreational activities?
9. What would bring enough money for adequate options in daily living?
10. What would bring enough income for me to feel safe?

Answer the question next to the first number you have circled in the space below. If you cannot imagine anything in answer to this question, move on to the next question with a circled number.

_____
_____

What else might have a similar result?

_____
_____
_____

Now make a check by the answer you think is the most realistic means of bringing about an increase in your satisfaction. For purposes of strategic planning this will be a goal. Now use five words or less to describe this goal in the space below.

_____

If you have other circled questions about Money, use as many additional sheets of paper as necessary to repeat this procedure. Once you have identified up to two more goals, describe each in five words or less on the spaces below.

_____
_____

## GOAL FORMULATION WORKSHEET

### AFFIRMATION

1. What would bring about greater affirmation from people in my community?
2. What would bring about greater affirmation from my coworkers?
3. What would bring about greater affirmation from my supervisors?
4. What would bring about greater affirmation from my friends?
5. What would bring about greater affirmation from my children?
6. What would bring about greater affirmation from my parents?
7. What would bring about greater affirmation from my extended family?
8. What would bring about greater affirmation from my spouse or romantic partner?
9. What would bring about greater affirmation from my pet?
10. What would bring about greater affirmation from God?

Answer the question next to the first number you have circled in the space below. If you cannot imagine anything in answer to this question, move on to the next question with a circled number.

_____

_____

What else might have a similar result?

_____

_____

_____

Now make a check by the answer you think is the most realistic means of bringing about an increase in your satisfaction. For purposes of strategic planning this will be a goal. Now use five words or less to describe this goal in the space below.

_____

If you have other circled questions about Affirmation, use as many additional sheets of paper as necessary to repeat this procedure. Once you have identified up to two more goals, describe each in five words or less on the spaces below.

_____

_____

## GOAL FORMULATION WORKSHEET

### COMPANIONSHIP

1. What would bring about greater companionship from people in my community?
2. What would bring about greater companionship from my coworkers?
3. What would bring about greater companionship from my friends?
4. What would bring about greater companionship from my children?
5. What would bring about greater companionship from my parents?
6. What would bring about greater companionship from my spouse or romantic partner?
7. What would bring about greater companionship from my extended family?
8. What would bring about greater companionship from my pet?
9. What would bring about greater companionship from God?

Answer the question next to the first number you have circled in the space below. If you cannot imagine anything in answer to this question, move on to the next question with a circled number.

_____

_____

What else might have a similar result?

_____

_____

_____

_____

Now make a check by the answer you think is the most realistic means of bringing about an increase in your satisfaction. For purposes of strategic planning this will be a goal. Now use five words or less to describe this goal in the space below.

_____

If you have other circled questions about Companionship, use as many additional sheets of paper as necessary to repeat this procedure. Once you have identified up to two more goals, describe each in five words or less on the spaces below.

_____

_____

## GOAL FORMULATION WORKSHEET

### INTIMACY

1. What would bring about more intimacy with friends?
2. What would bring about more intimacy with my children?
3. What would bring about more intimacy with my parents?
4. What would bring about more intimacy with my extended family?
5. What would bring about more intimacy with my spouse or romantic partner?
6. What would bring about more intimacy in a professional relationship, such as with a pastor, rabbi, or mental health professional?
7. What would bring about more intimacy with God?

Answer the question next to the first number you have circled in the space below. If you cannot imagine anything in answer to this question, move on to the next question with a circled number.

_____

_____

What else might have a similar result?

_____

_____

_____

_____

Now make a check by the answer you think is the most realistic means of bringing about an increase in your satisfaction. For purposes of strategic planning this will be a goal. Now use five words or less to describe this goal in the space below.

_____

If you have other circled questions about Intimacy, use as many additional sheets of paper as necessary to repeat this procedure. Once you have identified up to two more goals, describe each in five words or less on the spaces below.

_____

_____

## GOAL FORMULATION WORKSHEET

### HEALTH

1. What would bring about a greater sense of physical well-being?
2. What would lessen or eliminate my physical pain or discomfort?
3. What would lessen or eliminate my feelings of depression?
4. What would lessen or eliminate my feelings of worry or anxiety?
5. What would bring about a greater confidence that I will continue to experience physical and emotional well-being?

Answer the question next to the first number you have circled in the space below. If you cannot imagine anything in answer to this question, move on to the next question with a circled number.

_____

What else might have a similar result?

_____
_____
_____
_____

Now make a check by the answer you think is the most realistic means of bringing about an increase in your satisfaction. For purposes of strategic planning this will be a goal. Now use five words or less to describe this goal in the space below.

_____

If you have other circled questions about Health, use as many additional sheets of paper as necessary to repeat this procedure. Once you have identified up to two more goals, describe each in five words or less on the spaces below.

_____
_____

## GOAL FORMULATION WORKSHEET

### REWARDING OCCUPATION

1. What would bring about greater mastery of the skills required to successfully complete the tasks of my occupation?
2. What would bring about a greater level of enjoyment in performing the tasks required by my occupation?
3. What would bring about a greater sense of accomplishment in the tasks required by my occupation?

Answer the question next to the first number you have circled in the space below. If you cannot imagine anything in answer to this question, move on to the next question with a circled number.

_____

What else might have a similar result?

_____
_____
_____
_____

Now make a check by the answer you think is the most realistic means of bringing about an increase in your satisfaction. For purposes of strategic planning this will be a goal. Now use five words or less to describe this goal in the space below.

_____

If you have other circled questions about Rewarding Occupation, use as many additional sheets of paper as necessary to repeat this procedure. Once you have identified up to two more goals, describe each in five words or less on the spaces below.

_____
_____

## GOAL FORMULATION WORKSHEET

### RENEWING RECREATION

1. What would bring about more opportunities to engage in activities which have the primary purpose of pleasing me in some way?
2. What sort of pleasurable activities would send me back to tasks of living with a sense of being refreshed and renewed?
3. What pleasurable activities could I look forward to when engaged in the tasks of living?

Answer the question next to the first number you have circled in the space below. If you cannot imagine anything in answer to this question, move on to the next question with a circled number.

_____

_____

What else might have a similar result?

_____

_____

_____

Now make a check by the answer you think is the most realistic means of bringing about an increase in your satisfaction. For purposes of strategic planning this will be a goal. Now use five words or less to describe this goal in the space below.

_____

If you have other circled questions about Renewing Recreation, use as many additional sheets of paper as necessary to repeat this procedure. Once you have identified up to two more goals, describe each in five words or less on the spaces below.

_____

_____

## GOAL FORMULATION WORKSHEET

### FREEDOM

1. What would reduce unacceptable restraints on my actions?
2. What would bring about more freedom with those in my community?
3. What would bring about more freedom with those I interact with at work?
4. What would bring about more freedom with my friends?
5. What would bring about more freedom with my parents?
6. What would bring about more freedom with my spouse or romantic partner?

Answer the question next to the first number you have circled in the space below. If you cannot imagine anything in answer to this question, move on to answer the next question with a circled number.

_____

_____

What else might have a similar result?

_____

_____

_____

_____

Now make a check by the answer you think is the most realistic means of bringing about an increase in your satisfaction. For purposes of strategic planning this will be a goal. Now use five words or less to describe this goal in the space below.

_____

If you have circled more than one question about Freedom, use as many additional sheets of paper as necessary to repeat this procedure. Once you have identified up to two more goals, describe each in five words or less on the spaces below.

_____

_____

## GOAL FORMULATION WORKSHEET

### SECURITY

1. What will enable me to maintain my meaningful material objects?
2. What will provide enough money to maintain a satisfying life?
3. What will enable me to perpetuate relationships providing affirmation?
4. What will enable me to perpetuate relationships providing companionship?
5. What will enable me to perpetuate relationships providing intimacy?
6. What will enable me to maintain the degree of health I currently enjoy?
7. What will enable me to maintain the degree of occupational satisfaction I currently enjoy?
8. What will enable me to maintain the degree of satisfaction from recreational activities I currently enjoy?
9. What will enable me to maintain the level of freedom I currently have in relation to people in my community, my workplace, my family, my friends, and my romantic relationship?

Answer the question next to the first number you have circled in the space below. If you cannot imagine any answer to this question, move on to answer the next question with a circled number.

_____

What else might have a similar result?

_____
_____
_____
_____

Now make a check by the answer you think is the most realistic means of bringing about an increase in your satisfaction. For purposes of strategic planning this will be a goal. Now use five words or less to describe this goal in the space below.

_____

If you have other circled questions about Security, use as many additional sheets of paper as necessary to repeat this procedure. Once you have identified up to two more goals, describe each in five words or less on the spaces below.

_____
_____

# STEP 3

## DEVELOPING POTENTIAL COURSES OF ACTION

If, at this point, you have no goals, repeat step 1 by adding those items to your *Table of Identified Sources of Dissatisfaction* which have the next lowest scores on your GILS and then proceed with them through step 2. Once you have identified one or more goals you are ready to develop a potential course of action to achieve each of them. This is accomplished by filling out *Potential Course of Action Worksheets.*

The next page shows how the forty-three-year-old man in the previous example filled out one of these worksheets. Once you understand this example, fill out a *Potential Course of Action Worksheet* for up to three of the goals you have identified.

# POTENTIAL COURSE OF ACTION WORKSHEET NO. 1

Write the first goal you formulated in the previous section on the space below.

Goal No. 1 *Do homework with kids*

Now describe a course of action which would enable you to achieve this goal.

*Give up golf league on Tuesday night.*

Are there other ways in which this goal could be achieved?

*Give up position as treasurer of the VFW and stay home on nights to do homework with the kids instead of dealing with the duties of that office.*
√ *Work less overtime the nights the kids have school the next day.*

Place a check mark in front of the potential course of action you believe is most likely to enable you to achieve your goal. Describe that course of action in eight words or less in the space below. This will be a shorthand way of referring to this potential course of action.

*Work less overtime on school nights*

If you have another goal, proceed to the next page which is almost identical to this one. Use it to formulate another potential course of action designed to achieve a second goal. Continue this process until you have identified up to three potential courses of action.

## POTENTIAL COURSE OF ACTION WORKSHEET No. 1

Write the first goal you formulated in step 2 on the space below.

Goal No. 1 _____

Now describe a course of action which would enable you to achieve this goal.

_____
_____
_____
_____

Are there other ways in which this goal could be achieved?

_____
_____
_____
_____
_____
_____

Place a check mark in front of the potential course of action you believe is most likely to enable you to achieve your goal. Describe that course of action in eight words or less in the space below. This will be a shorthand way of referring to this potential course of action.

_____

If you have another goal, proceed to the next page which is almost identical to this one. Use it to formulate another potential course of action designed to achieve another goal. Continue this process until you have identified up to three potential courses of action. If you have no other goals, please proceed to step 4.

## POTENTIAL COURSE OF ACTION WORKSHEET NO. 2

Write the second goal you formulated in step 2 on the space below.

Goal No. 2 _____

Now describe a course of action which would enable you to achieve this goal.

_____
_____
_____
_____

Are there other ways in which this goal could be achieved?

_____
_____
_____
_____
_____

Place a check mark in front of the potential course of action you believe is most likely to enable you to achieve your goal. Describe that course of action in eight words or less in the space below. This will be a shorthand way of referring to this potential course of action.

_____

If you have another goal, proceed to the next page which is almost identical to this one. Use it to formulate another potential course of action designed to achieve another goal. Continue this process until you have identified up to three potential courses of action. If you have no other goals, please proceed to step 4.

## POTENTIAL COURSE OF ACTION WORKSHEET NO. 3

Write the third goal you formulated in step 2 on the space below.

Goal No. 3 _____

Now describe a course of action which would enable you to achieve this goal.

_____
_____
_____
_____

Are there other ways in which this goal could be achieved?

_____
_____
_____
_____
_____

Place a check mark in front of the potential course of action you believe is most likely to enable you to achieve your goal. Describe that course of action in eight words or less in the space below. This will be a shorthand way of referring to this potential course of action.

_____

Now that you have identified up to three potential courses of action designed to achieve your goals, proceed to step 4.

## STEP 4

### EVALUATING A POTENTIAL COURSE OF ACTION

Answer the following questions with respect to each of the courses of action you are considering in order to determine whether any of them are self-defeating. Any course of action which turns out to be some type of self-defeating behavior should be discarded as a nonviable course of action.

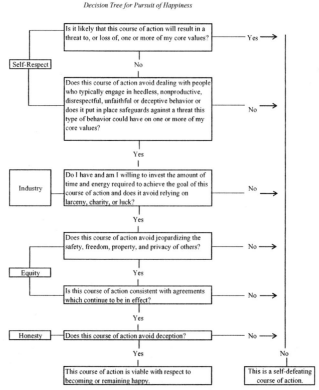

*Decision Tree for Pursuit of Happiness*

## STEP 5

### FORECASTING THE EFFECT OF
### A POTENTIAL COURSE OF ACTION

Once you have determined each of the potential courses of action you are considering is not some type of self-defeating behavior, you can combine them into a comprehensive course of action. This is accomplished by including all the courses of action under consideration within a single sentence.

The forty-three-year-old man who has been our example is considering two courses of action. The first is *working less overtime on school nights.* The second is *taking his wife out to dinner every Saturday night.* A comprehensive course of action consists of *working less overtime on school nights and taking his wife out to dinner every Saturday night.* In the space below write your comprehensive potential course of action.

---

---

---

---

In order to determine how pursuing your comprehensive course of action is likely to impact on your overall contentment and satisfaction in living you can next complete a *Forecasted Inventory of Life Satisfaction* (FILS). Since the impact of your comprehensive course of action may be different at different times in your future, completing your FILS requires that you idenify a future point in time to serve as a reference for your forecast. For example, the effect attending college or vocational school will have on a person's overall quality of life will probably change depending on whether he or she is looking at this potential course of action one year from now or five years down the road. If you are considering potential courses of action that will be completed in sequence, you may want to complete a FILS for each of the points in time at which you expect each segment of the course of action to be completed. In the space below write the future point in time at which you wish to consider how your comprehensive potential course of action will affect your quality of life.

*Future Point in Time* _____

If you intend to make multiple forecasts, photocopy the FILS and the scoring and profile sheets on the next few pages before filling out the FILS in this book.

The process of answering the FILS may take some time because you may need to do some research before you can respond to some of the items. Remember, the reliability of your forecast depends on the accuracy of the information you utilized in completing this inventory.

## THE FORECASTED INVENTORY OF LIFE SATISFACTION

*This questionnaire is designed to measure future satisfaction in living. Complete each sentence with the potential comprehensive course of action you are considering. Your responses should be based on your best estimate of how engaging in this potential courses of action is likely to impact your ten core values. Indicate your level of agreement or disagreement as follows:*

A  = Agree
SA = Somewhat Agree
SD = Somewhat Disagree
D  = Disagree
NA = Not Applicable

*You will be provided instructions for scoring once you have completed your responses.*

| A | SA | SD | D | NA | | *Meaningful Material Objects* |
|---|----|----|---|----|---|---|
| O | O | O | O | O | 1. | I will be satisfied with my housing situation if I . . . |
| O | O | O | O | O | 2. | I will be satisfied with the furnishings in my home if I . . . |
| O | O | O | O | O | 3. | I will be satisfied with my wardrobe if I . . . |
| O | O | O | O | O | 4. | I will be satisfied with my access to reliable transportation if I . . . |
| O | O | O | O | O | 5. | I will be satisfied with the electronic devices which provide entertainment or save time and effort if I . . . |
| O | O | O | O | O | 6. | I will be satisfied with my access to stores where I can find an adequate variety of reasonably priced products which I consider essential to my quality of life if I . . . |

Meaningful Material Objects Score  _____

| A | SA | SD | D | NA | | *Money* |
|---|----|----|---|----|---|---|
| O | O | O | O | O | 1. | I will have sufficient money to acquire and maintain those material objects that make my life satisfying if I . . . |
| O | O | O | O | O | 2. | My level of income and/or assets will be sufficient to secure the respect and perhaps admiration of those people who are important to me if I . . . |
| O | O | O | O | O | 3. | I will have enough money to engage in the interpersonal activities that interest me if I . . . |
| O | O | O | O | O | 4. | Money will not block me from participating in close and revealing interpersonal interactions if I . . . |
| O | O | O | O | O | 5. | I will be able to afford to participate in activities that enhance my health and prevent illness if I . . . |
| O | O | O | O | O | 6. | I will have sufficient money to obtain quality healthcare when I need it if I . . . |
| O | O | O | O | O | 7. | My level of income will be fair and reasonable for the work I do if I . . . |
| O | O | O | O | O | 8. | I will be able to afford to participate in a sufficient variety of renewing recreational activities if I . . . |
| O | O | O | O | O | 9. | My income and/or assets will be sufficient to provide me with an adequate number of options in everyday living if I . . . |
| O | O | O | O | O | 10. | My income or assets will be sufficiently reliable to make me feel safe if I . . . |

Money Score  _____

*Indicate your level of agreement or disagreement:*

A = Agree
SA = Somewhat Agree
SD = Somewhat Disagree
D = Disagree
NA = Not Applicable

*You will be provided instructions for scoring once you have completed your response*

| A | SA | SD | D | NA | | *Affirmation* |
|---|----|----|---|----|---|---|
| O | O | O | O | O | 1. | I will be satisfied with the affirmation I get from people in my community if I . . . |
| O | O | O | O | O | 2. | I will be satisfied with the affirmation I get from coworkers if I . . . |
| O | O | O | O | O | 3. | I will be satisfied with the affirmation I get from my supervisors if I . . . |
| O | O | O | O | O | 4. | I will be satisfied with the affirmation I get from friends if I . . . |
| O | O | O | O | O | 5. | I will be satisfied with the affirmation I get from my children if I . . . |
| O | O | O | O | O | 6. | I will be satisfied with the affirmation I get from my parents if I . . . |
| O | O | O | O | O | 7. | I will be satisfied with the affirmation I get from my extended family if I . . . |
| O | O | O | O | O | 8. | I will be satisfied with the affirmation I get from my spouse or romantic partner if I . |
| O | O | O | O | O | 9. | I will be satisfied with the affirmation I get from my pet if I . . . |
| O | O | O | O | O | 10. | I will be satisfied with the affirmation I get from God if I . . . |

Affirmation Score _____

| A | SA | SD | D | NA | | *Companionship* |
|---|----|----|---|----|---|---|
| O | O | O | O | O | 1. | I will be satisfied with the level of companionship I receive from the people in my community if I . . . |
| O | O | O | O | O | 2. | I will be satisfied with the level of companionship I receive from coworkers if I . . . |
| O | O | O | O | O | 3. | I will be satisfied with the level of companionship I receive from my friends if I . . . |
| O | O | O | O | O | 4. | I will be satisfied with the level of companionship I receive from my children if I . . . |
| O | O | O | O | O | 5. | I will be satisfied with the level of companionship I receive from my parents if I . . . |
| O | O | O | O | O | 6. | I will be satisfied with the level of companionship I receive from my spouse or romantic partner if I . . . |
| O | O | O | O | O | 7. | I will be satisfied with the level of companionship I receive from my extended family if I . . . |
| O | O | O | O | O | 8. | I will be satisfied with the level of companionship I receive from my pet if I . . . |
| O | O | O | O | O | 9. | I will be satisfied with the level of companionship I receive from God if I . . . |

Companionship Score _____

| A | SA | SD | D | NA | | *Intimacy* |
|---|----|----|---|----|---|---|
| O | O | O | O | O | 1. | I will be satisfied with the intimacy I have with my friends if I . . . |
| O | O | O | O | O | 2. | I will be satisfied with the intimacy I have with my children if I . . . |
| O | O | O | O | O | 3. | I will be satisfied with the intimacy I have with my parents if I . . . |
| O | O | O | O | O | 4. | I will be satisfied with the intimacy I have with my extended family if I . . . |
| O | O | O | O | O | 5. | I will be satisfied with with the intimacy I have with my spouse or romantic partner if I . . . |
| O | O | O | O | O | 6. | I will be satisfied with the intimacy I have within a professional relationship, such as with a pastor, rabbi, or mental health practitioner if I . . . |
| O | O | O | O | O | 7. | I will be satisfied with the intimacy I have with God if I . . . |

Intimacy Score ——————

*Indicate your level of agreement or disagreement:*

| A | = Agree |
|---|---|
| SA | = Somewhat Agree |
| SD | = Somewhat Disagree |
| D | = Disagree |
| NA | = Not Applicable |

*You will be provided instructions for scoring once you have completed your responses.*

| A | SA | SD | D | NA | | *Health* |
|---|----|----|---|----|---|---|
| O | O | O | O | O | 1. | I will have a general sense of physical well-being if I . . . |
| O | O | O | O | O | 2. | I will rarely feel physical pain or discomfort if I . . . |
| O | O | O | O | O | 3. | I will rarely feel depressed if I . . . |
| O | O | O | O | O | 4. | I will rarely feel anxious or worried if I . . . |
| O | O | O | O | O | 5. | I will be confident that I will continue to experience physical and emotional well-being if I . . . |

Health Score ——————

| A | SA | SD | D | NA | | *Rewarding Occupation* |
|---|----|----|---|----|---|---|
| O | O | O | O | O | 1. | I will have mastered the skills required to successfully complete the tasks of my occupation if I . . . |
| O | O | O | O | O | 2. | I will enjoy performing the tasks required by my occupation if I . . . |
| O | O | O | O | O | 3. | Completing the tasks required by my occupation will give me a sense of accomplishment if I . . . |

Rewarding Occupation Score ——————

| A | SA | SD | D | NA | | *Renewing Recreation* |
|---|----|----|---|----|---|---|
| O | O | O | O | O | 1. | I will have sufficient opportunities to engage in activities which have the primary purpose of pleasing me in some way if I . . . |
| O | O | O | O | O | 2. | The recreational activities I choose will send me back to the tasks of living with a sense of being refreshed and renewed if I . . . |
| O | O | O | O | O | 3. | I will look forward to my recreational activities when I am involved in the tasks of living if I . . . |

Rewarding Recreation Score _____

## *You will be provided instructions for scoring once you have completed your response*

*Indicate your level of agreement or disagreement:*

| | |
|---|---|
| A | = Agree |
| SA | = Somewhat Agree |
| SD | = Somewhat Disagree |
| D | = Disagree |
| NA | = Not Applicable |

| A | SA | SD | D | NA | | *Freedom* |
|---|----|----|---|----|---|---|
| O | O | O | O | O | 1. | Any constraints that restrict my actions will be reasonable, appropriate, and acceptable if I . . . |
| O | O | O | O | O | 2. | I will be able to express my thoughts and feelings without fearing I will be rejected, ridiculed, or punished in some way by people in my community if I . . . |
| O | O | O | O | O | 3. | At work, any constraints on my actions and the expression of my thoughts and feelings will be reasonable, appropriate, and acceptable if I . . . |
| O | O | O | O | O | 4. | Among friends, I will be able to express my thoughts and feelings without fear I will jeopardize the relationship in some way if I . . . |
| O | O | O | O | O | 5. | With my parents, I will be able to express my thoughts and feelings without fear I will jeopardize the relationship in some way if I . . . |
| O | O | O | O | O | 6. | With my spouse or romantic partner, I will be able to express my thoughts and feelings without fear I will jeopardize the relationship in some way if I . . . |

Freedom Score _____

| A | SA | SD | D | NA | | *Security* |
|---|----|----|----|----|---|---|
| O | O | O | O | O | 1. | I will be able to maintain possession of or access to those material objects which I currently enjoy if I . . . |
| O | O | O | O | O | 2. | I will be confident I have enough money to maintain a reasonably satisfying quality of life if I . . . |
| O | O | O | O | O | 3. | I will be able to maintain those interpersonal relationships which provide affirmation if I . . . |
| O | O | O | O | O | 4. | I will be able to maintain those interpersonal relationships which provide companionship if I . . . |
| O | O | O | O | O | 5. | I will be able to maintain those interpersonal relationships which provide intimacy if I . . . |
| O | O | O | O | O | 6. | I will be confident I can continue to have the degree of health and emotional well-being I currently enjoy if I . . . |
| O | O | O | O | O | 7. | I will continue to experience at least the degree of occupational satisfaction I currently enjoy if I . . . |
| O | O | O | O | O | 8. | I will be able to continue at least the degree of enjoyment that my recreational activities currently provide if I . . . |
| O | O | O | O | O | 9. | I will be confident that constraints on my actions and behavior will be reasonable and appropriate with members of my community, workplace, and family as well as with friends and my romantic partner without fear of jeopardizing those relationships as a result if I . . . |

Security Score   _____

## Forecasted Inventory of Life Satisfaction
## Scoring Sheet

Use a calculator to figure out your score on each section of the FILS according to the following procedure:

Count the number of items marked "A" and then multiply that number by 10.
Count the number of items marked "SA" and then multiply that number by 7.5.
Count the number of items marked "SD" and then multiply that number by 2.5.
Count the number of items marked "D" and multiply that number by zero.

Add all of these numbers together and divide that sum by the number of items in the category minus the number of items marked "NA."

*Score*

1. *Meaningful Material Objects* ..............................................._____

2. *Money* ................................................................................._____

3. *Affirmation* .........................................................................._____

4. *Companionship* ...................................................................._____

5. *Intimacy* .............................................................................._____

6. *Health* ................................................................................._____

7. *Rewarding Occupation* ........................................................._____

8. *Renewing Recreation* ..........................................................._____

9. *Freedom* .............................................................................._____

10. *Security* .........................…………...............................…............_____

*The sum is your FELS Score\** ...................................…..……...………._____

*If one of the value scores is zero because all items were marked NA, a prorated FELS score can be obtained by multiplying the sum of the other value scores by 1.1. If two or more value scores are zero because all items were marked NA, no FELS score can be obtained.

Plot your current GELS score and your obtained FELS on the *Range of Life Satisfaction Scale* in order to see whether your potential course of action is likely to enhance your overall level of happiness.

*Range of Life Satisfaction Scale*

| 0 | 25 | 50 | 75 | 100 |
|---|----|----|----|-----|

|  | Somewhat | Somewhat |  |
|---|---|---|---|
| Dissatisfied | Dissatisfied | Satisfied | Satisfied |

Plot your core value scores on the *Forecasted Estimate of Life Satisfaction Profile* in order to see how your potential course of action impacts your matrix of core values.

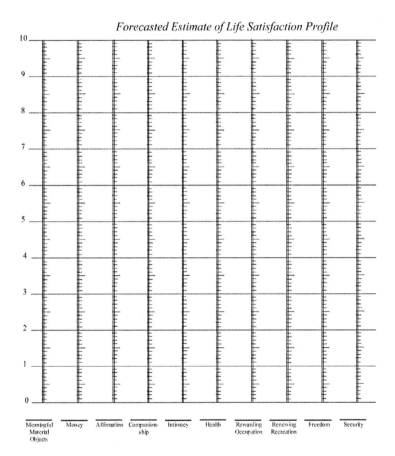

*Forecasted Estimate of Life Satisfaction Profile*

## *STEP 6*

### DEVELOPING A PLAN OF ACTION

If the potential comprehensive course of action under consideration **is not** likely to improve your overall satisfaction in living, return to the *Goal Formulation Worksheets* and rework the program utilizing other goals developed from your responses to the GILS.

If the course of action you have been considering **is** likely to improve your overall satisfaction in living, you are now ready to develop of the steps required to achieve its goal.

On the lines below or elsewhere list the activities necessary to complete your potential comprehensive course of action. These activities should be listed according to the sequence in which they need to occur. Next, indicate the time frame in terms of the weeks, months, or years it will take to complete each of the activities you have identified. Once you have completed this process, review your list and identify specific dates when each activity should begin and the dates by which it should be completed.

| | Activity | Time frame | Start Date | End Date |
|---|---|---|---|---|
| 1. | | | | |
| 2. | | | | |
| 3. | | | | |
| 4. | | | | |
| 5. | | | | |
| 6. | | | | |

Now go to your calendar and insert the activities you have identified on the actual days of the week and month on which you intend to have them occur. You have now completed your action plan. Implementing your plan of action is the next step in your attempt at improving your contentment and satisfaction with life. As you move forward you may want to secure the services of a psychologist or a motivational coach.

Before beginning, please remember that the primary purpose of the program is to assist you in your personal pursuit of happiness. If the plan of action you intend to follow involves other people who are important to your quality of life, there may be a value in having them fill out a GILS and a FILS. This will provide an opportunity to explore how your plan of action is likely to impact on their quality of life. Based on what you discover you may want to modify your plan.

It is also important to realize that your FELS score only indicates the degree to which the course of action you are considering is probably *likely* to affect your personal contentment and satisfaction over time. Your forecasted level of life satisfaction is *not guaranteed* because the future is always never certain. The reliability of your FELS score depends on the accuracy of information used in completing your FILS. Flawed assumptions, misunderstandings, misrepresentations by others, and unforeseen events may invalidate some of that information thereby affecting the reliability of your forecast.

Changing circumstances as well as the discover that your prediction has been based on flawed assumptions, misunderstandings and/or misrepresentations by others may require that you make changes in your plan of action, and you may need to reevaluate your goals. Even if faced with frustration and discouragement, persist in your pursuit of happiness, confident that using this method for personal strategic planning you stand a good chance of enhancing your overall quality of life.

# Chapter 11

# MOMENTOUS DECISION
# MAKING

This program is designed to assist you in sorting out which of your alternatives is most likely to enhance your happiness when you are faced with a decision which will have significant long-term impact on your overall contentment and satisfaction in living. It can be used when dealing with a number of momentous decisions such as what to major in at college, which career to pursue, whether to take a particular job, whether to remain in a romantic relationship, whether to get married, whether to have a child, whether to get a divorce, or whether and when to retire. It can also be used any time you are confronted with any other major decisions in life.

Prior to working through this program, it is useful to determine your current level of happiness. If you have recently filled out the portions of the *General Inventory of Life Satisfaction* contained in chapters 2 through 4 of this book, you may use the *Global Estimate of Life Satisfaction* score you obtained in chapter 5. If it has been some time since you completed a GILS and calculated your GELS, you will find a *General Inventory of Life Satisfaction* you can use in chapter 12. Before you start, you may want to make photocopies of the pages of chapter 12 and the pages of this chapter so you can rework this program at some future point in time.

This method of making momentous decisions consists of working through the following steps:

*Step 1* Identifying Alternatives
*Step 2* Evaluating Potential Courses of Action
*Step 3* Listing Viable Alternatives
*Step 4* Forecasting the Effects of Viable Alternatives
*Step 5* Calculating Your Forecasted Estimate of Life Satisfaction Score
*Step 6* Plotting FELS Scores
*Step 7* Interpreting the Results

## STEP 1

### IDENTIFYING ALTERNATIVES

The first step in momentous decision making consists of identifying the alternatives with which you are currently confronted. When identifying your alternatives be sure to state them in terms of potential courses of action. For example, a man who has been offered a position with his employer's competitor may see one of his alternatives as "taking a new job" and another as "not taking it." His second alternative can be stated as a potential course of action by describing it as "continuing to work for current employer."

Next to the letters below list each alternative available to you in terms of a potential course of action.

A. _____

_____

B. _____

_____

C. _____

_____

In the context of many momentous decision-making situations only two alternatives appear to be available. For example, a woman considering marriage may see her alternatives as getting married or remaining in an ongoing relationship with her romantic partner. It is quite possible a third alternative exists. For example, in addition to the possibility of getting married, this woman could also consider terminating the relationship with her romantic partner and looking for another potential spouse.

Before proceeding to *step 2*, consider whether there may be more than two alternatives available in the situation with which you are currently confronted. If a third alternative exists, add it to the list of alternatives you have already identified.

Once you have identified all of your alternatives, use five words or less to describe each of them on the lines below.

A. _____

B. _____

C. _____

## *STEP 2*

### EVALUATING POTENTIAL COURSES OF ACTION

Answer the following questions in order to determine whether any of the courses of action you are considering is some sort of self-defeating behavior. Any alternative which turns out to be self-defeating behavior should be considered nonviable.

*Decision Tree for Pursuit of Happiness*

| | | |
|---|---|---|
| | Is it likely that this course of action will result in a threat to, or loss of, one or more of my core values? | — Yes → |
| **Self-Respect** | No | |
| | Does this course of action avoid dealing with people who typically engage in heedless, nonproductive, disrespectful, unfaithful or deceptive behavior or does it put in place safeguards against a threat this type of behavior could have on one or more of my core values? | — No → |
| | Yes | |
| Industry | Do I have and am I willing to invest the amount of time and energy required to achieve the goal of this course of action and does it avoid relying on larceny, charity, or luck? | — No → |
| | Yes | |
| | Does this course of action avoid jeopardizing the safety, freedom, property, and privacy of others? | — No → |
| Equity | Yes | |
| | Is this course of action consistent with agreements which continue to be in effect? | — No → |
| | Yes | |
| Honesty | Does this course of action avoid deception? | — No → |
| | Yes | No |
| This course of action is viable with respect to becoming or remaining happy. | | This is a self-defeating course of action. |

## *STEP 3*

### LISTING VIABLE ALTERNATIVES

In the space below list all of the alternatives which remain viable at the end of working through the *Decision Tree for the Pursuit of Happiness.*

*List of Viable Alternatives*

A. _____

B. _____

C. _____

At this point you may have eliminated all but one of your alternatives. If this has occurred, it will appear that the remaining alternative is the only course of action you should pursue. However, before arriving at this conclusion, it is important to consider whether other alternatives exist. Take some time to think about whether there is an alternative which has not yet been identified.

If you can identify another alternative, work it through the *Decision Tree for the Pursuit of Happiness.* If it turns out to be a viable alternative, describe it in five words or less and include it above on your *List of Viable Alternatives.*

**If at this point you still have only one alternative**, there is no purpose in going further with this program. It is reaonable to conclude that your remaining alternative is the one which will result in the greatest likelihood of enhancing or ensuring your overall satisfaction and contentment in living. At the same time, it is important to realize that this likelihood should not compel you to pursue this course of action. It only indicates that the remaining viable alternative is the one which is most likely to enhance your personal happiness, contentment, and satisfaction in living. You may want to consider other factors in ultimately deciding what to do.

If you have two or more viable alternatives, continue with this program by forecasting the effect each is likely to have on your overall contentment and satisfaction in living.

## *STEP 4*

### FORECASTING THE EFFECTS OF VIABLE ALTERNATIVES

Now that you have identified two or more viable alternatives, you can consider how each of them is likely to impact your long-term happiness by completing a *Forecasted Inventory of Life Satisfaction* (FILS).

Because the effect of a potential course of action on your quality of life may be different at different points in your future, you first need to identify the future point in time you will be using as a point of reference for your forecast. This can be done by specifying a time when it is reasonable to expect a course of action to be completed. You can also consider how one of your potential courses of action is going to impact on quality of life at two different points in the future. This can be done by considering the potential course of action at each future point in time as a separate alternative. For example, a woman considering marriage may want to evaluate the effect of this course of action five years from now and then again at ten. In order to do this, one of her alternatives should be listed as *getting married, five years*. The other would be *getting married, ten years*.

On the next page list your viable alternatives and the future points in time at which you want to consider the effect of each on your quality of life.

|  | Viable Alternative | Future Point in Time |
|---|---|---|
| A. | _____ | _____ |
| B. | _____ | _____ |
| C. | _____ | _____ |

As you complete the FILS there are separate columns identified by letters at the top. Read each sentence on the inventory with the alternative on your *List of Viable Alternatives* and respond to it in the column headed by the letter which precedes it on your list. For example, if alternative A is getting married, read item number 1 under Meaningful Material Objects as follows: "I will be satisfied with my housing situation if I . . . get married." If alternative B is breakup with my boyfriend, respond in column B as follows: "I will be satisfied with my housing situation if I . . . breakup with my boyfriend." If you are considering the effects of a potential course of action at two different future points in time, add the time frame to the beginning of the sentence for each of the alternatives. In our example one alternative should be read as, "Five years from now I will be satisfied with my housing situation if I . . . get married." The next, "Ten years from now I will be satisfied with my housing situation if I . . . get married."

# THE FORECASTED INVENTORY
# OF LIFE SATISFACTION

Your answers to this inventory should be based on your best estimate of how engaging in potential courses of action are likely to impact on your life. If you do not have enough information to make a realistic estimate, please take the time to obtain it before completing the items on this rating sheet. Indicate your level of agreement or disagreement in terms of each of your alternatives as follows:

A  = Agree
SA = Somewhat Agree
SD = Somewhat Disagree
D  = Disagree
NA = Not Applicable

|  | ALTERNATIVES | | |
| --- | --- | --- | --- |
| *Meaningful Material Objects* | A<br>A SA SD D NA | B<br>A SA SD D NA | C<br>A SA SD D NA |
| 1. I will be satisfied with my housing situation if I . . . | O O O O O | O O O O O | O O O O O |
| 2. I will be satisfied with the furnishings in my home if I . . . | O O O O O | O O O O O | O O O O O |
| 3. I will be satisfied with my wardrobe if I . . . | O O O O O | O O O O O | O O O O O |
| 4. I will be satisfied with my access to reliable transportation if I . . . | O O O O O | O O O O O | O O O O O |
| 5. I will be satisfied with the electronic devices which provide entertainment or save time and effort if I . . . | O O O O O | O O O O O | O O O O O |
| 6. I will be satisfied with my access to stores where I can find an adequate variety of reasonably priced products which I consider essential to my quality of life if I . . . | O O O O O | O O O O O | O O O O O |
| *Scores for Meaningful Material Objects* | A _____ | B _____ | C _____ |

|  | ALTERNATIVES | | | | | | | | | | | | | | |
|---|---|---|---|---|---|---|---|---|---|---|---|---|---|---|---|
| *Money* | A | | | | | B | | | | | C | | | | |
|  | A | SA | SD | D | NA | A | SA | SD | D | NA | A | SA | SD | D | NA |
| 1. I will have sufficient money to acquire and maintain those material objects that make my life satisfying if I . . . | O | O | O | O | O | O | O | O | O | O | O | O | O | O | O |
| 2. My level of income and/or assets will be sufficient to secure the respect and perhaps the admiration of those people who are important to me if I . . . | O | O | O | O | O | O | O | O | O | O | O | O | O | O | O |
| 3. I will have enough money to engage in the interpersonal activities that interest me if I . . . | O | O | O | O | O | O | O | O | O | O | O | O | O | O | O |
| 4. Money will not block me from participating in close and revealing interpersonal interactions if I . . . | O | O | O | O | O | O | O | O | O | O | O | O | O | O | O |
| 5. I will be able to afford to participate in activities that enhance my health and prevent illness if I . . . | O | O | O | O | O | O | O | O | O | O | O | O | O | O | O |
| 6. I will have sufficient money to obtain quality healthcare when I need it if I . . . | O | O | O | O | O | O | O | O | O | O | O | O | O | O | O |
| 7. My level of income will be fair and reasonable for the work I do if I . . . | O | O | O | O | O | O | O | O | O | O | O | O | O | O | O |
| 8. I will be able to afford to participate in a sufficient variety of renewing recreational activities if I . . . | O | O | O | O | O | O | O | O | O | O | O | O | O | O | O |
| 9. My income and/or assets will be sufficient to provide me with an adequate number of options in everyday living if I . . . | O | O | O | O | O | O | O | O | O | O | O | O | O | O | O |
| 10. My income or assets will be sufficiently reliable to make me feel safe if I . . . | O | O | O | O | O | O | O | O | O | O | O | O | O | O | O |
| *Scores for Money* | A _____ | | | | | B _____ | | | | | C _____ | | | | |

*Indicate your level of agreement or disagreement:*

| | |
|---|---|
| A | = Agree |
| SA | = Somewhat Agree |
| SD | = Somewhat Disagree |
| D | = Disagree |
| NA | = Not Applicable |

*ALTERNATIVES*

| Affirmation | A | | | | | B | | | | | C | | | | |
|---|---|---|---|---|---|---|---|---|---|---|---|---|---|---|---|
| | A | SA | SD | D | NA | A | SA | SD | D | NA | A | SA | SD | D | NA |
| 1. I will be satisfied with the affirmation I get from people in my community if I . . . | O | O | O | O | O | O | O | O | O | O | O | O | O | O | O |
| 2. I will be satisfied with the affirmation I get from coworkers if I . . . | O | O | O | O | O | O | O | O | O | O | O | O | O | O | O |
| 3. I will be satisfied with the affirmation I get from my supervisors if I . . . | O | O | O | O | O | O | O | O | O | O | O | O | O | O | O |
| 4. I will be satisfied with the affirmation I get from friends if I . . . | O | O | O | O | O | O | O | O | O | O | O | O | O | O | O |
| 5. I will be satisfied with the affirmation I get from my children if I . . . | O | O | O | O | O | O | O | O | O | O | O | O | O | O | O |
| 6. I will be satisfied with the affirmation I get from my parents if I . . . | O | O | O | O | O | O | O | O | O | O | O | O | O | O | O |
| 7. I will be satisfied with the affirmation I get from my extended family if I . . . | O | O | O | O | O | O | O | O | O | O | O | O | O | O | O |
| 8. I will be satisfied with the affirmation I get from my spouse or romantic partner if I . . . | O | O | O | O | O | O | O | O | O | O | O | O | O | O | O |
| 9. I will be satisfied with the affirmation I receive from my pet if I . . . | O | O | O | O | O | O | O | O | O | O | O | O | O | O | O |
| 10. I will be satisfied with the affirmation I get from God if I . . . | O | O | O | O | O | O | O | O | O | O | O | O | O | O | O |
| *Scores for Affirmation* | A _____ | | | | | B _____ | | | | | C _____ | | | | |

*Indicate your level of agreement or disagreement:*

| | |
|---|---|
| A | = Agree |
| SA | = Somewhat Agree |
| SD | = Somewhat Disagree |
| D | = Disagree |
| NA | = Not Applicable |

ALTERNATIVES

*Companionship*

| | A | | | | | B | | | | | C | | | | |
|---|---|---|---|---|---|---|---|---|---|---|---|---|---|---|---|
| | A | SA | SD | D | NA | A | SA | SD | D | NA | A | SA | SD | D | NA |
| 1. I will be satisfied with the level of companionship I receive from people in my community if I . . . | O | O | O | O | O | O | O | O | O | O | O | O | O | O | O |
| 2. I will be satisfied with the level of companionship I receive from coworkers if I . . . | O | O | O | O | O | O | O | O | O | O | O | O | O | O | O |
| 3. I will be satisfied with the level of companionship I receive from my peers, particularly my friends if I . . . | O | O | O | O | O | O | O | O | O | O | O | O | O | O | O |
| 4. I will be satisfied with the level of companionship I receive from my children if I . . . | O | O | O | O | O | O | O | O | O | O | O | O | O | O | O |
| 5. I will be satisfied with the level of companionship I receive from my parents if I . . . | O | O | O | O | O | O | O | O | O | O | O | O | O | O | O |
| 6. I will be satisfied with the level of companionship I receive from my spouse or romantic partner if I . . . | O | O | O | O | O | O | O | O | O | O | O | O | O | O | O |
| 7. I will be satisfied with the level of companionship I receive from my extended family if I . . . | O | O | O | O | O | O | O | O | O | O | O | O | O | O | O |
| 8. I will be satisfied with the level of companionship I receive from my pet if I . . . | O | O | O | O | O | O | O | O | O | O | O | O | O | O | O |
| 9. I will be satisfied with the level of companionship I receive from God if I . . . | O | O | O | O | O | O | O | O | O | O | O | O | O | O | O |

*Scores for Companionship*    A _____    B _____    C _____

*Indicate your level of agreement or disagreement:*

| | |
|---|---|
| A | = Agree |
| SA | = Somewhat Agree |
| SD | = Somewhat Disagree |
| D | = Disagree |
| NA | = Not Applicable |

*ALTERNATIVES*

| Intimacy | A | | | | | B | | | | | C | | | | |
|---|---|---|---|---|---|---|---|---|---|---|---|---|---|---|---|
| | A | SA | SD | D | NA | A | SA | SD | D | NA | A | SA | SD | D | NA |
| 1. I will be satisfied with the intimacy I have with my friends if I . . . | O | O | O | O | O | O | O | O | O | O | O | O | O | O | O |
| 2. I will be satisfied with the intimacy I have with my children if I . . . | O | O | O | O | O | O | O | O | O | O | O | O | O | O | O |
| 3. I will be satisfied with the intimacy I have with my parents if I . . . | O | O | O | O | O | O | O | O | O | O | O | O | O | O | O |
| 4. I will be satisfied with the intimacy I have with my extended family if I . . . | O | O | O | O | O | O | O | O | O | O | O | O | O | O | O |
| 5. I will be satisfied with the intimacy I have with my spouse or romantic partner if I . . . | O | O | O | O | O | O | O | O | O | O | O | O | O | O | O |
| 6. I will be satisfied with the intimacy I have within a professional relationship such as with a pastor, rabbi, or mental health practitioner if I . . . | O | O | O | O | O | O | O | O | O | O | O | O | O | O | O |
| 7. I will be satisfied with the intimacy I have with God if I . . . | O | O | O | O | O | O | O | O | O | O | O | O | O | O | O |

*Scores for Intimacy*    A _____    B _____    C _____

| | ALTERNATIVES | | |
|---|---|---|---|
| | A | B | C |
| Health | A SA SD D NA | A SA SD D NA | A SA SD D NA |
| 1. I will have a general sense of physical well-being if I . . . | O O O O O | O O O O O | O O O O O |
| 2. I will rarely feel physical pain or discomfort if I . . . | O O O O O | O O O O O | O O O O O |
| 3. I will rarely feel depressed if I . . . | O O O O O | O O O O O | O O O O O |
| 4. I will rarely feel anxious or worried if I . . . | O O O O O | O O O O O | O O O O O |
| 5. I will be confident that I will continue to experience physical and emotional well-being if I . . . | O O O O O | O O O O O | O O O O O |
| Scores for Health | A _____ | B _____ | C _____ |

| | ALTERNATIVES | | |
|---|---|---|---|
| Rewarding Occupation | A | B | C |
| | A SA SD D NA | A SA SD D NA | A SA SD D NA |
| 1. I will have mastered the skills required to successfully complete the tasks of my occupation if I . . . | O O O O O | O O O O O | O O O O O |
| 2. I will enjoy performing the tasks required by my occupation if I . . . | O O O O O | O O O O O | O O O O O |
| 3. Completing the tasks required by my occupation will give me a sense of accomplishment if I . . . | O O O O O | O O O O O | O O O O O |
| Scores for Rewarding Occupation | A _____ | B _____ | C _____ |

*Indicate your level of agreement or disagreement:*

| A | = Agree |
|---|---|
| SA | = Somewhat Agree |
| SD | = Somewhat Disagree |
| D | = Disagree |
| NA | = Not Applicable |

|  | ALTERNATIVES | | |
|---|---|---|---|
| *Renewing Recreation* | A | B | C |
| | A  SA  SD  D  NA | A  SA  SD  D  NA | A  SA  SD  D  NA |

1. I will have sufficient opportunities
to engage in activities which have the
primary purpose of pleasing me in
some way if I . . .                          O  O  O  O  O        O  O  O  O  O        O  O  O  O  O

2. The recreational activities I choose
will send me back to the tasks of living
with a sense of being refreshed and
renewed if I . . .                          O  O  O  O  O        O  O  O  O  O        O  O  O  O  O

3. I will look forward to my recreational
activities when I am involved in the
tasks of living if I . . .                  O  O  O  O  O        O  O  O  O  O        O  O  O  O  O

*Scores for Renewing Recreation*     A _____     B _____     C _____

*Indicate your level of agreement or disagreement:*

| A | = Agree |
|---|---|
| SA | = Somewhat Agree |
| SD | = Somewhat Disagree |
| D | = Disagree |
| NA | = Not Applicable |

| | ALTERNATIVES | | |
|---|---|---|---|
| _Freedom_ | A | B | C |
| | A SA SD D NA | A SA SD D NA | A SA SD D NA |

1. Any constraints that restrict my actions will be reasonable, appropriate, and acceptable if I . . .

    O O O O O    O O O O O    O O O O O

2. I will be able to express my thoughts and feelings without fearing I will be rejected, ridiculed, or punished in some way by people in my community if I . . .

    O O O O O    O O O O O    O O O O O

3. At work, any constraints on my actions and the expression of my thoughts and feelings will be reasonable, appropriate, and acceptable if I . . .

    O O O O O    O O O O O    O O O O O

4. Among friends, I will be able to express my thoughts and feelings without fear I will jeopardize the relationship in some way if I . . .

    O O O O O    O O O O O    O O O O O

5. With my parents, I will be able to express my thoughts and feelings without fear I will jeopardize the relationship in some way if I . . .

    O O O O O    O O O O O    O O O O O

6. With my spouse or romantic partner, I will be able to express my thoughts and feelings without fear I will jeopardize the relationship in some way if I . . .

    O O O O O    O O O O O    O O O O O

_Scores for Freedom_    A _____   B _____   C _____

_Indicate your level of agreement or disagreement:_

A   = Agree
SA  = Somewhat Agree
SD  = Somewhat Disagree
D   = Disagree
NA  = Not Applicable

| Security | ALTERNATIVES | | | | | | | | | | | | | | |
|---|---|---|---|---|---|---|---|---|---|---|---|---|---|---|---|
| | A | | | | | B | | | | | C | | | | |
| | A | SA | SD | D | NA | A | SA | SD | D | NA | A | SA | SD | D | NA |
| 1. I will be able to maintain possession of or access to those material objects which I currently enjoy if I . . . | O | O | O | O | O | O | O | O | O | O | O | O | O | O | O |
| 2. I will be confident I have enough money to maintain a reasonably satisfying quality of life if I . . . | O | O | O | O | O | O | O | O | O | O | O | O | O | O | O |
| 3. I will be able to maintain those interpersonal relationships which provide affirmation if I . . . | O | O | O | O | O | O | O | O | O | O | O | O | O | O | O |
| 4. I will be able to maintain those interpersonal relationships which provide companionship if I . . . | O | O | O | O | O | O | O | O | O | O | O | O | O | O | O |
| 5. I will be able to maintain those interpersonal relationships which provide intimacy if I . . . | O | O | O | O | O | O | O | O | O | O | O | O | O | O | O |
| 6. I will be confident I can continue to have the degree of health and emotional well-being I currently enjoy if I . . . | O | O | O | O | O | O | O | O | O | O | O | O | O | O | O |
| 7. I will continue to experience at least the degree of occupational satisfaction I currently enjoy if I . . . | O | O | O | O | O | O | O | O | O | O | O | O | O | O | O |
| 8. I will be able to continue at least the degree of enjoyment that my recreational activities currently provides if I . . . | O | O | O | O | O | O | O | O | O | O | O | O | O | O | O |
| 9. I will be confident that constraints on my actions and behavior will be reasonable and appropriate with members of my community, workplace, and family as well as with friends and my romantic partner without fear of jeopardizing those relationships as a result if I . . . | O | O | O | O | O | O | O | O | O | O | O | O | O | O | O |

*Scores for Security*      A _____      B _____      C _____

# *STEP 5*

## CALCULATING YOUR FORECASTED ESTIMATE OF LIFE SATISFACTION SCORE FOR ALTERNATIVE "A"

Use a calculator to figure out your score for alternative "A" on each of the ten core values according to the following procedure:

Count the number of items marked "A" and then multiply that number by 10.
Count the number of items marked "SA" and then multiply that number by 7.5.
Count the number of items marked "SD" and then multiply that number by 2.5.
Count the number of items marked "D" and multiply that number by zero.
Add all of these numbers together and divide that sum by the number of items in the category minus the number of items marked "NA."

*Score*

1. *Meaningful Material Objects* ......................................................._____

2. *Money* ........................................................................................_____

3. *Affirmation* ................................................................................._____

4. *Companionship* ..........................................................................._____

5. *Intimacy* ....................................................................................._____

6. *Health* ........................................................................................_____

7. *Rewarding Occupation* ................................................................_____

8. *Renewing Recreation* .................................................................._____

9. *Freedom* ....................................................................................._____

10. *Security* .........................… …….........................................….............._____

Add them together to compute your FELS* score for alternative "A". _____

*If one of the value scores is zero because all items were marked NA, a prorated FELS score can be obtained by multiplying the sum of the other value scores by 1.1. If two or more value scores are zero because all items were marked NA, no FELS score can be obtained.

## CALCULATING YOUR FORECASTED ESTIMATE OF LIFE SATISFACTION SCORE FOR ALTERNATIVE "B"

Use a calculator to figure out your score for alternative "B" on each of the ten core values according to the following procedure:

Count the number of items marked "A" and then multiply that number by 10.
Count the number of items marked "SA" and then multiply that number by 7.5.
Count the number of items marked "SD" and then multiply that number by 2.5.
Count the number of items marked "D" and multiply that number by zero.
Add all of these numbers together and divide that sum by the number of items in the category minus the number of items marked "NA."

*Score*

1. *Meaningful Material Objects* ........................................................_____

2. *Money* ............................................................................................_____

3. *Affirmation* ....................................................................................._____

4. *Companionship* .............................................................................._____

5. *Intimacy* ........................................................................................._____

6. *Health* ............................................................................................._____

7. *Rewarding Occupation* .................................................................._____

8. *Renewing Recreation* ....................................................................._____

9. *Freedom* .........................................................................................._____

10. *Security* .....................................…………...........................................…............._____

Add them together to compute your FELS* score for alternative "B". _____

*If one of the value scores is zero because all items were marked NA, a prorated FELS score can be obtained by multiplying the sum of the other value scores by 1.1. If two or more value scores are zero because all items were marked NA, no FELS score

## CALCULATING YOUR FORECASTED ESTIMATE OF
## LIFE SATISFACTION SCORE FOR ALTERNATIVE "C"

Use a calculator to figure out your score for alternative "C" on each of the ten core values according to the following procedure:

Count the number of items marked "A" and then multiply that number by 10.
Count the number of items marked "SA" and then multiply that number by 7.5.
Count the number of items marked "SD" and then multiply that number by 2.5.
Count the number of items marked "D" and multiply that number by zero.
Add all of these numbers together and divide that sum by the number of items in the category minus the number of items marked "NA."

*Score*

1. *Meaningful Material Objects* .................................................._____

2. *Money* .............................................................................._____

3. *Affirmation* ......................................................................._____

4. *Companionship* ................................................................._____

5. *Intimacy* ..........................................................................._____

6. *Health* .............................................................................._____

7. *Rewarding Occupation* ......................................................_____

8. *Renewing Recreation* ........................................................._____

9. *Freedom* ..........................................................................._____

10. *Security* ............................................................................_____

Add them together to compute your FELS* score for alternative "C". _____

*If one of the value scores is zero because all items were marked NA, a prorated FELS score can be obtained by multiplying the sum of the other value scores by 1.1. If two or more value scores are zero because all items were marked NA, no FELS score can be obtained.

## *STEP 6*

### PLOTTING FELS SCORES

Plot your FELS score for each of your alternatives on the *Range of Life Satisfaction Scale* using a different-colored pencil or pen for each score.

*Range of Life Satisfaction Scale*

| 0 | 25 | 50 | 75 | 100 |
|---|----|----|----|-----|
| Dissatisfied | Somewhat Dissatisfied | Somewhat Satisfied | Satisfied | |

On the next page plot your scores on each of the core value scales using a different-colored pencil or pen for each alternative on the *Forecasted Inventory of Life Satisfaction Profile Sheet* in order to see how each of your alternatives impacts each of your core values.

*Forecasted Inventory of Life Satisfaction Profile Sheet*

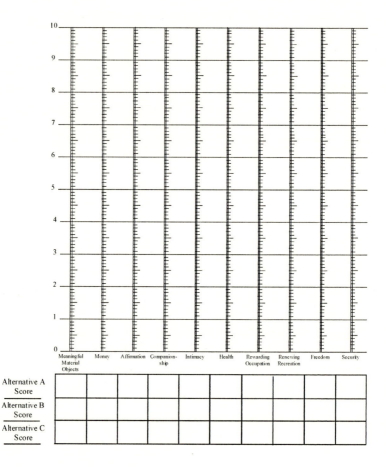

## *STEP 7*

### INTERPRETING THE RESULTS

A glance at where your FELS score falls with respect to each alternative under consideration on the *Range of Life Satisfaction Scale* will give you a general sense of which alternative is most likely to lead to your greatest satisfaction over time. Your *Forecasted Inventory of Life Satisfaction Profile Sheet* reflects how each of your alternatives is likely to impact on each of your core values.

As you discover which one of your alternatives is most likely to enhance your quaility of life, remember that you may want to consider factors other than your own contentment and satisfaction in living when making momentous decisions. If the alternatives you are considering involve significant others, there may be a value in having them fill out a *Forecasted Inventory of Life Satisfaction Score* and calculate a *Forecasted Estimate of Life Satisfaction* with respect to each of your alterantives. This will provide an opportunity to explore how your alternatives are likely to impact on their quality of life over time.

Hopefully your *Forecasted Estimate of Life Satisfaction* is useful information with respect to making the momentous decision with which you are currently confronted. Remember, your FELS scores only indicate the degree to which the alternatives you are considering are probably *likely* to affect your personal contentment and satisfaction in living over time. Your forecasted levels of life satisfaction are *not guaranteed* because the future is always never certain. The reliability of your FELS scores depend on the accuracy of the information you used in completing your FILS. Flawed assumptions, misunderstandings, misrepresentations by others, and unforeseen events may invalidate some of this information thereby affecting the reliability of your forecast. If you discover that any of this has occurred, you can make use of this method for momentous decision making to consider the alternatives with which you are confronted with at that time.

# Chapter 12

# THE GENERAL INVENTORY OF
# LIFE SATISFACTION

This chapter contains the *General Inventory of Life Satisfaction* (GILS) which you had an opportunity to respond to as the core values were described in chapters 2, 3, and 4. In this chapter the GILS is displayed in a format which enables you to evaluate your contentment and satisfaction with life whenever you want to measure your level of happiness. If you think you will want to take and score another GILS at some future point in time, you should make photocopies of the pages in this chapter before filling out the inventory.

## GENERAL INVENTORY OF LIFE
## SATISFACTION RATING SHEET

*Please respond to the following statements as indicated. Your answers should be based on realistic expectations for the specific area of life indicated and the importance you currently place on it. Indicate your level of agreement or disagreement as shown on the top of the next page.*

A   = Agree
SA  = Somewhat Agree
SD  = Somewhat Disagree
D   = Disagree
NA  = Not Applicable

You will be provided instructions for scoring once you have completed your responses.

| A | SA | SD | D | NA | | *Meaningful Material Objects Score* |
|---|----|----|---|----|---|---|
| O | O | O | O | O | 1. | I am satisfied with my current housing situation. |
| O | O | O | O | O | 2. | I am satisfied with the furnishings in my home. |
| O | O | O | O | O | 3. | I am satisfied with my wardrobe. |
| O | O | O | O | O | 4. | I am satisfied with my access to reliable transportation. |
| O | O | O | O | O | 5. | I am satisfied with the electronic devices which provide entertainment or save time and effort. |
| O | O | O | O | O | 6. | I am satisfied with my access to stores where I can find an adequate variety of reasonably priced products which I consider essential to my quality of life. |

Meaningful Material Objects Score  ———————

| A | SA | SD | D | NA | | *Money* |
|---|----|----|---|----|---|---|
| O | O | O | O | O | 1. | I have sufficient money to acquire and maintain those material objects that make my life satisfying. |
| O | O | O | O | O | 2. | My level of income and/or assets is sufficient to secure the respect and perhaps admiration of those people who are important to me. |
| O | O | O | O | O | 3. | I have enough money to engage in the interpersonal activities that interest me. |
| O | O | O | O | O | 4. | Money does not block me from participating in close and revealing interpersonal interactions. |
| O | O | O | O | O | 5. | I can afford to participate in activities that enhance my health and prevent illness. |
| O | O | O | O | O | 6. | I have sufficient money to obtain quality healthcare when I need it. |
| O | O | O | O | O | 7. | My level of compensation is fair and reasonable for the work I do. |
| O | O | O | O | O | 8. | I can afford to participate in a sufficient variety of renewing recreational activities. |
| O | O | O | O | O | 9. | My income and/or assets are sufficient to provide me with an adequate number of options in everyday life. |
| O | O | O | O | O | 10. | My income or assets are sufficiently reliable to make me feel safe. |

Money Score  ———————

*Indicate your level of agreement or disagreement:*

| | |
|---|---|
| A | = Agree |
| SA | = Somewhat Agree |
| SD | = Somewhat Disagree |
| D | = Disagree |
| NA | = Not Applicable |

| A | SA | SD | D | NA | | *Affirmation* |
|---|----|----|---|-----|---|---|
| O | O | O | O | O | 1. | I am satisfied with the affirmation I get from people in my community. |
| O | O | O | O | O | 2. | I am satisfied with the affirmation I get from coworkers. |
| O | O | O | O | O | 3. | I am satisfied with the affirmation I get from my supervisors. |
| O | O | O | O | O | 4. | I am satisfied with the affirmation I get from friends. |
| O | O | O | O | O | 5. | I am satisfied with the affirmation I get from my children. |
| O | O | O | O | O | 6. | I am satisfied with the affirmation I get from my parents. |
| O | O | O | O | O | 7. | I am satisfied with the affirmation I get from my extended family. |
| O | O | O | O | O | 8. | I am satisfied with the affirmation I get from my spouse or romantic partner. |
| O | O | O | O | O | 9. | I am satisfied with the affirmation I receive from my pet. |
| O | O | O | O | O | 10. | I am satisfied with the affirmation I get from God. |

Affirmation Score _____

| A | SA | SD | D | NA | | *Companionship* |
|---|----|----|---|-----|---|---|
| O | O | O | O | O | 1. | I am satisfied with the level of companionship I receive from the people in my community. |
| O | O | O | O | O | 2. | I am satisfied with the level of companionship I receive from coworkers. |
| O | O | O | O | O | 3. | I am satisfied with the level of companionship I receive from my friends. |
| O | O | O | O | O | 4. | I am satisfied with the level of companionship I receive from my children. |
| O | O | O | O | O | 5. | I am satisfied with the level of companionship I receive from my parents. |
| O | O | O | O | O | 6. | I am satisfied with the level of companionship I receive from my spouse or romantic partner. |
| O | O | O | O | O | 7. | I am satisfied with the level of companionship I receive from my extended family. |
| O | O | O | O | O | 8. | I am satisfied with the level of companionship I receive from my pet. |
| O | O | O | O | O | 9. | I am satisfied with the level of companionship I receive through my relationship with God. |

Companionship Score _____

| A | SA | SD | D | NA | | *Intimacy* |
|---|----|----|---|----|---|-----------|
| O | O | O | O | O | 1. | I am satisfied with the intimacy I have with my friends. |
| O | O | O | O | O | 2. | I am satisfied with the intimacy I have with my children. |
| O | O | O | O | O | 3. | I am satisfied with the intimacy I have with my parents. |
| O | O | O | O | O | 4. | I am satisfied with the intimacy I have with my extended family. |
| O | O | O | O | O | 5. | I am satisfied the intimacy I have with my spouse or romantic partner. |
| O | O | O | O | O | 6. | I am satisfied with the intimacy I have within a professional relationship, such as with a pastor, rabbi, or mental health practitioner. |
| O | O | O | O | O | 7. | I am satisfied with the intimacy I have with God. |

Intimacy Score    —————————

*Indicate your level of agreement or disagreement:*

| A | = Agree |
|---|---------|
| SA | = Somewhat Agree |
| SD | = Somewhat Disagree |
| D | = Disagree |
| NA | = Not Applicable |

| A | SA | SD | D | NA | | *Health* |
|---|----|----|---|----|---|---------|
| O | O | O | O | O | 1. | I have a general sense of physical well-being. |
| O | O | O | O | O | 2. | I rarely feel physical pain or discomfort. |
| O | O | O | O | O | 3. | I rarely feel depressed. |
| O | O | O | O | O | 4. | I rarely feel anxious or worried. |
| O | O | O | O | O | 5. | I am confident that I will continue to experience physical and emotional well-being. |

Health Score    —————————

| A | SA | SD | D | NA | | *Rewarding Occupation** |
|---|----|----|---|----|---|---|
| O | O | O | O | O | 1. | I have mastered the skills required to successfully complete the tasks of my occupation. |
| O | O | O | O | O | 2. | I enjoy performing the tasks required by my occupation. |
| O | O | O | O | O | 3. | Completing the tasks required by my occupation gives me a sense of accomplishment. |

Rewarding Occupation Score _____

| A | SA | SD | D | NA | | *Renewing Recreation* |
|---|----|----|---|----|---|---|
| O | O | O | O | O | 1. | I have sufficient opportunity to engage in activities which have the primary purpose of pleasing me in some way. |
| O | O | O | O | O | 2. | The recreational activities I choose send me back to the tasks of living with a sense of being refreshed and renewed. |
| O | O | O | O | O | 3. | I look forward to my recreational activities when I am involved in the tasks of living. |

Rewarding Recreation Score _____

*\* If you are a full-time homemaker or a full-time student, answer the items in this section in terms of the tasks involved in the work of a homemaker or a student.*

A = Agree
SA = Somewhat Agree
SD = Somewhat Disagree
D = Disagree
NA = Not Applicable

| A | SA | SD | D | NA | | *Freedom* |
|---|----|----|----|----|----|-----------|
| O | O | O | O | O | 1. | Any constraints that restrict my actions are reasonable, appropriate, and acceptable. |
| O | O | O | O | O | 2. | I can express my thoughts and feelings without fearing I will be rejected, ridiculed, or punished in some way by people in my community. |
| O | O | O | O | O | 3. | At work, constraints on my actions and the expression of my thoughts and feelings are reasonable, appropriate, and acceptable. |
| O | O | O | O | O | 4. | Among friends, I can express my thoughts and feelings without fear I will jeopardize the relationship in some way. |
| O | O | O | O | O | 5. | With my parents, I can express my thoughts and feelings without fear I will jeopardize the relationship in some way. |
| O | O | O | O | O | 6. | With my spouse or romantic partner, I can express my thoughts and feelings without fear I will jeopardize the relationship in some way. |

Freedom Score_____

| A | SA | SD | D | NA | | *Security* |
|---|----|----|----|----|----|-----------|
| O | O | O | O | O | 1 | In the future I will be able to maintain possession of or access to those material objects which I currently enjoy. |
| O | O | O | O | O | 2 | In the future I will have enough money to maintain a reasonably satisfying quality of life. |
| O | O | O | O | O | 3 | I will be able to maintain those interpersonal relationships which provide affirmation. |
| O | O | O | O | O | 4 | I will be able to maintain those interpersonal relationships which provide companionship. |
| O | O | O | O | O | 5 | I will be able to maintain those interpersonal relationships which provide intimacy. |
| O | O | O | O | O | 6 | I am confident I will continue to have the degree of health and emotional well-being I currently enjoy. |
| O | O | O | O | O | 7 | In the future I will continue to experience at least the degree of occupational satisfaction I currently enjoy. |
| O | O | O | O | O | 8 | In the future I will be able to continue at least the degree of enjoyment that my recreational activities currently provide. |
| O | O | O | O | O | 9 | I am confident future constraints on my actions will be reasonable and appropriate, and I will be able to express my thoughts and feelings with members of my community, workplace, and family as well as with friends and my romantic partner without fear of jeopardizing these relationships as a result. |

Security Score　　_____

## GENERAL INVENTORY OF LIFE
## SATISFACTION SCORING SHEET

Use a calculator to figure out your score on each section of the GILS according to the following procedure:

Count the number of items marked "A" and then multiply that number by 10.
Count the number of items marked "SA" and then multiply that number by 7.5.
Count the number of items marked "SD" and then multiply that number by 2.5.
Count the number of items marked "D" and multiply that number by zero.
Add all of these numbers together and divide that sum by the number of items in the category minus the number of items marked "NA."

Score

*1. MEANINGFUL MATERIAL OBJECTS* ............................... _____

*2. MONEY* ................................................................. _____

*3. AFFIRMATION* ...................................................... _____

*4. COMPANIONSHIP* .................................................. _____

*5. INTIMACY* ............................................................ _____

*6. HEALTH* ............................................................... _____

*7. REWARDING OCCUPATION* ..................................... _____

*8. RENEWING RECREATION* ........................................ _____

*9. FREEDOM* ............................................................ _____

*10. SECURITY* .......................................................... _____

ADD THEM TOGETHER TO COMPUTE YOUR
    GELS* SCORE ...................................................... _____

*\*If one of the value scores is zero because all items were marked NA, a prorated GELS score can be obtained by multiplying the sum of the other value scores by 1.1. If two or more value scores are zero because all items were marked NA, no GELS score can be obtained.*

Plot your scores with respect to each value on the following graph:

*Range of Life Satisfaction Scale*

*Inventory of Life Satisfaction Profile Sheet*

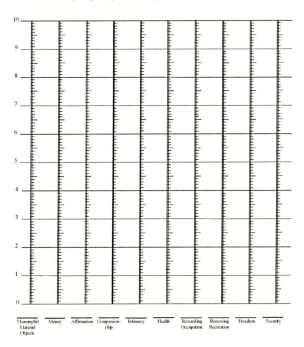

## INTERPRETATION

A score in the *satisfied* range indicates you are generally a happy person. Although there may be some areas in your life in which you are less than fully content, the degree of satisfaction you are currently experiencing means you are enjoying a rich and rewarding quality of life.

A score in the *somewhat satisfied* range indicates you are less happy than you would probably like to be. You have good access to several core values, but you are less than fully satisfied with your access to others. Your quality of life could probably be better than it is today.

A score in the *somewhat dissatisfied* range indicates you are currently unhappy. You have limited access to a number of core values, and you are probably less than satisfied with the degree to which you have been able to obtain and maintain most of the others. Your quality of life could probably be much better than it is today. If you are not already in treatment you could probably benefit from consulting a mental health professional.

A score in the *dissatisfied* range indicates you are currently extremely unhappy. In all likelihood your access to virtually all of the ten core values is limited. In addition to being terribly unhappy, you are probably clinically depressed. Your quality of life could significantly be better than it is right now. If you are not already in treatment you should consult a mental health professional.

# INDEX

affirmation, 36-39, 41, 49, 58, 77, 82, 84, 93, 98, 99, 101, 102, 105, 108, 112, 114-117, 120, 121, 123-126, 128, 160, 163, 177

all-or-nothing reasoning, 97

*American Psychologist*, *xxxv*

anger, 12, 13, 147

anthropologists, xiv, 60, 65, 182

antidepressant medication, xviii, 21

anxiety, xx, 3, 11, 13, 17,154, 177

Argyle, Michael, xxxv

Aristotle, xiii, 153

attitudes, xviii, xx, xxviii, xxxvi, 15, 89, 93, 96,

Beck, Aaron, xxv, xxxvi

behavioral approach, xviii, xix

*Being and Time*, *xxxv*

Bible, 71, 144, 153, 179

biblically based moral principles, 180

biochemical theory, xviii

brain chemistry, xviii, xix, xx, 135

Brandon, Nathaniel, xxv, xxxvii

Broszormenyi-Nagy, I., xxxvi

burnout, 65

Burns, David, xxv, xxxvi

charity, 160

Christians, xxi, 179, 182

circumstances, xix, xx, xxi, xxii, xxiii, xxiv, xxviii, 2, 10, 11, 14, 23, 54, 81, 91, 93, 94, 98, 119, 179, 182, 217

circumstances of birth, 98

cognitive psychologists, xviii, xix

*Cognitive Therapy and Emotional Disorders*, *xxxvi*

commercial relationships, 35, 37, 44, 49, 101

companionship, xix, xxiv, 34, 43–45, 47, 49, 58, 63, 77, 82, 84, 91, 93, 98, 99, 102, 103, 105, 109, 112, 114, 115, 117, 118, 120, 121, 123, 124, 125, 127, 128, 149, 160, 164, 175, 177, 188

Compte, August, 153

conditions of human existence, xxiv, xxv, 173

consequential reasoning, 151, 152

core beliefs, 173, 174, 175

core principles, xxx, 16, 166, 167, 169, 170, 173, 174, 180, 182

core values, xxv, xxvi-xxix, xxxi, 15, 16, 23, 45, 52, 54, 57, 63, 67, 73, 76, 78, 81, 82, 84, 85, 87-89, 91, 94, 96-100, 105-108, 116, 118, 120, 121, 124, 126, 127, 128, 129, 130, 134, 147, 153, 154, 159, 166, 167, 170-173, 179, 183, 185, 188, 207, 215, 237, 239, 241, 249

courts of law, 176

creativity, 177

Creator and Sustainer of the universe, 153, 181, 182

Csikszentmihalyi, Mihaly, xxii, xxxv

deceptive behavior, 128, 129, 130, 137, 141, 148, 162, 165, 174, 179

denial, 136, 137

depression, xviii, xx, 12, 13, 21, 77, 112, 132, 171

disaffirmation, 38

discounting the positive, 96

discrimination, 141, 156

disrespectful behavior, 120, 139, 143-146, 148, 164

Eastern mystics, xxi

emergency services, 176

emotion, xxii, xxiii, 10, 11, 138, 171

emotional reasoning, 150, 151

environmental concerns, 178

envy, 3, 7, 12, 13, 172

Epicureans, xxi

Epicurus, xiii

equity, 115, 161, 162, 169, 170, 171, 178, 180

Erickson, Eric, xxv, xxxvi

ethnicity, 141

excitement, 14, 38

expectations, xvi, xviii, xx, xxviii, xxxvi, 15, 20, 43, 89, 91-93, 96, 102, 241

family relationships, 36

fate, 134

features determined at conception, 141

*Feeling Good: The New Mood Therapy, xxxvi*

FELS, 214, 217, 219, 237, 239

FILS, 206, 207, 217, 223, 224, 239

fire department, 176

Forecasted Estimate of Life Satisfaction, 215, 219, 239

Forecasted Inventory of Life Satisfaction, 206, 223, 225, 237, 238, 239

freedom, xxiv, xxxvi, 69-74, 76, 78, 83, 85, 94, 98, 100, 104, 105, 116, 117, 120-124, 152, 160, 161, 176-178

Freud, Sigmund, xiv, xxv, xxxvi, 144
friendships, 35
GELS, xxvii, xxviii, 23, 86, 88, 90, 91, 94, 214, 219
gender, 141
General Inventory of Life Satisfaction, xxvii, xxx, xxxi, 23, 30, 184, 218, 219, 241
genetic approach, xviii
genetics xix, 135
GILS, xxvii, xxviii, xxxi, 23, 85, 90, 91, 92, 93, 184, 185, 200, 216, 217, 219, 241,
Global Estimate of Life Satisfaction, xxvii, 23, 86, 219
God, xiii, xxi, 38, 45, 50, 102, 103, 135, 144, 145, 153, 179, 180, 181, 182, 183
Great Commandments of Christ, 179
guilt, 8, 13, 143, 145, 148, 172
gurus, xiii
gut reactions, 138, 139, 150
happiness, xiii, xiv-xxiv, xxvii-xxxi, xxxiii, xxxiv, xxxv, xxxvi, 1, 2, 5, 7, 9, 10, 14-17, 20, 22, 23, 25, 26, 28, 29, 33, 34, 36, 38, 39, 45, 47, 51, 55, 58, 62, 63, 67, 69, 73, 78, 81, 82, 85, 86, 89, 93-97, 106, 107, 114, 119, 134, 135, 138, 144,

147, 150, 152, 153, 156, 157, 160, 166, 167, 170, 172-180, 182-185, 214, 217, 218, 222, 223, 241
health, xv, xxi, xxiv, 27, 54, 55-58, 82, 85, 87, 88, 99, 103, 105, 108, 131, 149, 154, 161, 176-178, 183
healthcare institutions, 178
hedonism, 22
heedless behavior, 107, 108, 110, 111, 131, 135, 136, 138, 142, 153, 155, 164
Heidegger, Martin, xxxv
hierarchy of basic needs, xxxv, 84
honesty, 162-167, 169, 170, 171, 179, 180
Horney, Karen, xiv, xxv, xxxvi
*Identity, Youth and Crisis, xxxvi*
ill-considered interpersonal interactions, 131, 137, 140, 148
industry, 2, 158-160, 162, 169-171, 178
interpersonal interactions, xxiv, xxv, 26, 34, 35, 130, 137, 139, 140, 148, 173
*Interpersonal Theory of Psychiatry, The,* xxxvi
intimacy, xix, xxiv, 34, 49, 50-52, 58, 63, 77, 82, 84, 91, 93, 98, 99, 103, 105, 109, 112, 114, 115, 117, 118,

120, 121, 123, 124, 127, 128, 149, 183, 174, 177, 178

*Introductory Lectures on Psychoanalysis, xxxvi*

intuitions, 138, 150

*Invisible Loyalties, Reciprocity, and Intergenerational Family Therapy, xxxvi*

isolation, 50

Israelites, xxi

James, William, xiv, xv, xxxv

jealousy, 12, 13, 172

Jesus, xiii, 71, 140, 145, 181, 182

joy, 3, 6, 7, 14, 44, 55, 77

Jung, Karl, xiv

Kant, Immanuel, 153

King Midas, 29, 30

Kohlburg, Lawrence, xxxvi

larceny, 159

libraries, 178

life hereafter, 153

loneliness, 45, 50

love, xix, 2, 8, 13, 14, 19, 34, 39, 40, 47, 51, 73, 76, 99, 102, 112-114, 122, 130, 139, 162, 171

luck, 56, 160

*Man's Search for Himself, xxxvi*

manufacturing interests, 178

mastery, xix, xxviii, 172, 174

materialism, 22

matrix, 81, 84, 85,

matrix of core values, 81, 82, 84, 106, 215

May, Rollo, 36

Mazlow, Abraham, 35

meaningful material objects, 19, 21-23, 26, 32, 76, 84, 98, 100, 105, 108, 116, 128, 160, 163, 176-178

mental processes, xviii, xvix, xx, xxi, xxviii, 89, 91, 97

Merleau-Ponty, Maurice, xxxv

military, 4, 76, 176, 178

Mill, John Stuart, 153

mining, 178

*Miser, The,* 29, 30

Mohammed, xiii

Molieré, 29, 30

money, xix, xxiv, 3, 8, 20, 25-30, 57, 58, 60, 67, 78, 82, 85, 89, 94, 98-101, 105, 108, 113, 115, 116, 117, 118, 120, 123, 126, 128, 129, 131-133, 137, 155, 158, 159, 160, 163, 167, 173, 176-179

*Moral Stages and Moralization, xxxvi*

Moses, xiii

*Motivation and Personality, xxxv*

Myers, David, xxxv

need, xxiv, xxv, 17, 18, 21, 26, 60, 65, 67, 84, 85, 89, 93, 100, 103-106, 113, 118, 121, 167, 171, 175, 176, 178, 207, 216, 217, 223

negative emotions, 13, 171, 179

*Neuroses and Human Growth,* xxxvi

*New Ideas in Psychology,* xvii, xxxiv

nonproductive behavior, 116-118, 131, 136, 138, 142, 158, 164, 169

norm, 142

norm-based reasoning, 142, 143

*On Becoming a Person,* xxxv

optimism, xxiv, 6, 16, 172, 175

overgeneralization, 97

personality traits, 172

*Phenomenology of Perception,* xxxv

philosophy, xiv, xxi, xxiii, xxxiv, 153

pleasure, 5, 22, 23, 45, 54, 55, 61, 65, 110, 118

police, 35, 60, 108, 123, 128, 148, 151, 176

positive emotions, 13

positive psychology, xix, xxiii, xxiv

positive reinforcement, 62, 147, 148

prayer, 45, 71, 103, 181

precipitating cause, xx

pride, 13, 14, 19, 171

principled reasoning, xxxiv, xxxvii, 151, 152

principles, xv, xvi, xxx, xxxvi, 16, 103, 105, 144, 147, 152, 153, 159, 163, 166, 167, 169-171, 173, 174, 179, 180

priorities, 15, 89, 90, 91, 96, Program for Personal Strategic Planning, 106, 184

*Psychology of Self-Esteem, The,* xxxvii

public education, 178

*Pursuit of Happiness, The,* xxxv

race, 141

religion, xiii, xiv, xxiii, 144, 145, 153, 179, 181

renewing recreation, 66, 67, 85, 90, 104, 115, 117, 154, 178

rewarding occupation, 61-63, 83, 85, 91, 103, 109, 116, 117, 120, 126, 131, 154, 163, 169, 174, 175

rituals, 181

Rogers, Carl, xiv, xxv, xxxv

romantic relationships, xv, 34, 36, 37, 45, 50, 56, 72, 73, 97, 102, 110, 120

sacrifices, 181

Schwartz, Norbert, xxxv

security, xxiv, xxxvi, 4, 28, 47, 76-79, 83, 84, 94, 98-100, 105, 116, 117, 126, 160, 163, 176-178

self-actualization, 85

self-defeating behavior, xxix, xxx, xxxi, 15, 16, 17, 108, 122, 134, 147, 148, 151,

153-156, 162, 166, 167,
205, 206, 221,
self-defeating beliefs, xxx, 15,
156, 162, 164
self-defeating patterns of behavior,
xxix, xxx, 15, 144, 149
self-defeating thought processes,
xviii, 97
self-effacing behavior, 113, 147,
148, 154, 175
self-esteem, xix, xx, xxxvii,
13, 16, 17, 28, 62, 96, 172,
173, 175
selfishness, 157
self-respect, 153-158, 160,
162, 167, 169, 170, 175,
177, 178, 182
Seligman, Martin, xxxv
sensation, 22
set point for happiness, 135
shamans, xiii
sin, 145
Socrates, xiii
Spark, Geraldine, xxxvi
Stoic philosophers, xiii
Strack, Fritz, xxxv
*Subjective Well-being, an
interdisciplinary
perspective, xxxv*
Sullivan, Harry Stack, xiv,
xxv, xxxvi
taxes, 176
Ten Commandments, 179, 180
the pursuit of happiness, xiv,
xxxvi, 23, 28, 67, 69, 82,

107, 119, 150, 167, 170,
175, 222
thought processes, xviii, xxxvi,
15, 96, 97
unfaithful behavior, 127, 128,
132, 139, 161, 169
universal values, xxiii, xxiv,
xxv,
wagering, 160
wellness principles, xvi, 103,
105, 171
witch doctors, xiii

Printed in the United States
52587LVS00002B/220